CAREER
OPPORTUNITIES
in

THE FILM INDUSTRY

SECOND EDITION

CAREER OPPORTUNITIES in

THE FILM INDUSTRY

SECOND EDITION

FRED YAGER
JAN YAGER

Foreword to the Second Edition by DAVID CARRADINE
Actor, Director, and Author

Foreword to the First Edition by PETER GUBER
Founder and Chairman, Mandalay Entertainment

Checkmark Books®

An imprint of Infobase Publishing

Important Note and Disclaimer:

While this book provides general information and opinions on career opportunities in the film industry, since every person is unique, it is not intended to be a substitute for individual career counseling or coaching. It is sold with the understanding that the publisher and authors are not engaged in rendering career, film production, legal, literary, or other professional services. Readers are especially advised to consult the appropriate union or association if they have any questions about the most up-to-date minimum rates or salaries as well as qualifications for specific jobs. Throughout this book, especially in the appendixes, you will find contact information for associations, organizations, schools, and companies. Since this information may change at any time, including even the name of an association, the existence of a company, or the presence of a Web site on the Internet, neither the publisher nor the authors take any responsibility for the accuracy of any listings.

Any corrections to any listings in this book, or suggestions for possible inclusion in the next edition, should be sent to: Fred and Jan Yager, P.O. Box 8038, Stamford, CT 06905-8038 (e-mail: fyager@aol.com or jyager@aol.com).

Career Opportunities in the Film Industry

Copyright © 2009, 2003 by Fred Yager and Jan Yager

Checkmark Books
An imprint of Facts On File, Inc.
132 West 31st Street
New York NY 10001

Library of Congress Cataloging-in-Publication Data

Yager, Fred, 1946–
  Career opportunities in the film industry / Fred Yager, Jan Yager ; foreword
to the second edition by David Carradine ; foreword to the first edition by Peter
Guber. — 2nd ed.
    p. cm.
  Includes bibliographical references and index.
  ISBN-13: 978-0-8160-7352-8 (hbk. : alk. paper)
  ISBN-10: 0-8160-7352-X (hbk. : alk. paper)
  ISBN-13: 978-0-8160-7353-5 (pbk. : alk. paper)
  ISBN-10: 0-8160-7353-8 (pbk.: alk. paper) 1. Motion pictures—Vocational
guidance. I. Yager, Jan, 1948– II. Title.

  PN1995.9.P75Y34 2009
  791.43023—dc22

                               2008040906

Ferguson books are available at special discounts when purchased in bulk quantities for businesses, associations, institutions, or sales promotions. Please call our Special Sales Department in New York at (212) 967-8800 or (800) 322-8755.

You can find Ferguson on the World Wide Web at http://www.fergpubco.com

Series design by Kerry Casey
Cover design by Takeshi Takahashi

Printed in the United States of America

Bang Hermitage 10 9 8 7 6 5 4 3 2 1

This book is printed on acid-free paper.

This book is dedicated to our sons, Scott and Jeffrey, and to those professionals who are part of the dynamic film industry or are aspiring to join it

CONTENTS

FOREWORD TO THE SECOND EDITION

By David Carradine
Actor, Director, and Author

Did I always want to be an actor? No. But I always had the itch to perform. My first gig that I remember was at about eight years old at summer camp. At the campfire show, I sang "Red River Valley" a cappella and recited "Casey at the Bat."

At 10 or so, I wanted to be a cowboy. But my first real ambition was to be a sculptor. Then I realized that would mean living in a garret, working alone in a room with a cold north light with a big piece of rock and maybe a pretty model, and never making any money. So I switched my plan to studying music composition and theory, the idea being to write operas. There was hardly such a thing then as a popular American opera, except for *Porgy and Bess*—an open field, I thought. And I'd be surrounded by singers, dancers, art directors, and musicians. There'd be tuxedos and champagne, and I'd get to meet Leonard Bernstein. So I enrolled at San Francisco State College as a music major. The music department and the drama department were in the same building, and while drifting down the hall, someone asked me to be in a play. The rest, I guess, is history. The main reason for the shift, though, was that my girlfriend was really excited by me as an actor. So I guess you could say the reason I went into acting was to get girls. I think that's why most of us got into it.

After I got out of the army, I went to New York to make it on Broadway. Eventually I accomplished that, but in the meantime, when nothing was happening, I took the offer of a screen test for Universal. My first

job for them was a movie, *Bus Riley's Back in Town*, starring Michael Parks and Ann-Margret. One day's work. Three lines.

I never took acting classes until I'd starred on Broadway and had my own TV series. That was about 15 years into being a professional actor. But I had a lot of mentors. My teachers were my directors. I think the most seminal influence on my acting was a director of a little theater, Robert Ross, one of those unsung geniuses. I met him in Berkeley in about 1957. We hung out together, and he filled me with ideas, some of them very radical. We actually lived together in the same apartment for a while—he, his family, and I. We talked philosophy, economics, politics, music—he played the clarinet and drums—and, of course, acting and revolution. We were living on Milvia Street in Berkeley, right next to the shack where Jack Kerouac wrote *The Dharma Bums*. This was the time of the Berkeley free speech riots. Revolution was in the air we breathed.

Being Part of a Family of Actors and an Acting Heritage

There are at least two sides to that. The first is that that's how I grew up. I have no knowledge of what it's like *not* to have an actor for a father. To me, that was normal life. The other aspect has been that, yes, there is a dynasty there, a tradition that I am bound, perforce, to uphold and nurture. Some think it's a shield I carry. To me, sometimes, it's a cross I have to bear. I've tried to release my kids from that obligation.

Some Career Highlights

It used to be, of course, the *Kung Fu* series, *Bound For Glory*—Hal Ashby's second-best movie—and, I guess, *The Long Riders,* by Walter Hill. Then there are my own projects, my directing gigs: *You and Me*, a lost mini-masterpiece; *Americana*, which has become a cult classic of sorts; and the unfinished *Mata Hari*. But since *Kill Bill*—definitely a highlight—I've found a whole new cornucopia of small films that I actually rate above the big stuff I did back then. None of them is released yet. When they are, I'll be looking at a whole new world. Watch for them: *Big Stan, Homo Erectus, Camille, Chatham* (my personal favorite), and the stuff I'm doing right now in China: television miniseries that are epic in scale. The truth is, though, I don't feel as though I've even scratched the surface yet. I'm still, at the age of 70, just getting rolling.

Advice for Someone Starting Out Today

Keep trying. You can't have a failed career unless you give up. From time to time, I meet actors who were at one time absolute icons who don't work at all anymore. They want to, but nothing is happening for them. I can't understand that. You just have to work harder at it. I went for decades without a studio picture, but I never stopped working. I took jobs where everyone but me was an absolute amateur. Sometimes I worked for nothing. People might think I was lucky to find Tarantino to kickstart a rematch, but actually I stalked the man. I tracked him down at the Toronto Film Festival in '96 and kept at him for five years.

You can't just sit in your pad and wait for the phone to ring. And you can't just say to yourself, "I'm going to make it." You have to have a plan. You have to get a specific idea and worry it to death.

My father told me, don't learn something as a backup. Don't, for instance, get a teaching credential. Acting is such a hard road that if you have something to fall back on, you will, and that will be the end of it. My father also believed that if he could discourage his sons from entering the trade, he should, because if we could be discouraged, we should forget it. You need an overriding passion for the art to survive.

Changes in the Film Industry

The film industry has changed a lot, but in many ways, it's still the same. It would take a book to describe this. The main difference is that moviemakers do not control the process anymore. It's run now by businesspeople. However, because of the stranglehold that the distributors have on the industry, the independent movement has gained incredible momentum. We now see films made in the United States that make me think of Godard, Truffaut, Fellini, Bergman. This is brand new. In the old studio days, theirs was the only game. There's not a lot of money in this movement, but that's not why we became actors, is it?

That things will change is about all I know. It was Jean Cocteau who said that movies will never be an art form until the materials are as accessible as pencils and paper. That has actually happened. Anyone with a camcorder can make a movie and might even get it released.

The other thing is the computer graphics explosion. Though I'm tired of all that stuff in the blockbusters, I have to admit that, now, anything you can imagine can be shown on a movie screen. It could be that in the future, movies will just be everywhere, like DVDs and movies on your cell phone.

The Importance of Talent Doing Publicity

Well, sure, it's important. Movies are not like paintings. To be a painter, all you need is a bare canvas and some paint. And your brother can store your paintings in the back room until you're dead and become famous. Or to be a writer, all you need is a typewriter. But a movie takes a couple of hundred people and millions of dollars. You can't support all that without a paying audience. You won't get the chance to publicize yourself until you become sort of successful. And then, when the studio says to do this talk show or take this tour, you'd better set things aside and do it. Not for the fame or the fortune, but to make sure that someone sees the work you did—you and those 199 other people it took to make the movie.

About David Carradine

Screen legend David Carradine has appeared in more than 100 movies and numerous television shows, including Quentin Tarantino's *Kill Bill: Volume I & II* (2003, 2004), *Bound for Glory* (1976), for which he was nominated for a Golden Globe and was declared best actor by The National Board of Review; and in the TV series *Kung Fu* (1972–75) and *Kung Fu: The Legend Continues* (1993–97), among other roles. Carradine is from a family of actors: his late father, John Carradine (1906–88), who made more than 500 movies, including westerns and horror films such as *The Man Who Shot Liberty Valance* (1962); his three brothers—Keith, Robert, and Bruce—and his nieces Ever Carradine and Martha Plimpton are actors. David Carradine has also directed movies, including *Americana* (1983) and *You and Me* (1975); authored several books, such as *Spirit of Shaolin* (1993), *Endless Highway* (1995), and *The Kill Bill Diary* (2006); and is a singer-songwriter with a number of CDs to his credit.

FOREWORD TO THE FIRST EDITION

By Peter Guber
Founder and Chairman, Mandalay Entertainment Group

People come into the film industry from everywhere. They come from the exhibition business and the distribution business. They come from the investment banking business, the theater business, the electronics business, and the dry cleaning business. I came into the movie business by accident.

In 1968, I took a job offer from Columbia Pictures while I was still a student at New York University's Graduate School of Business. I had no interest in film or the entertainment business. I wanted to teach. But within a year, Columbia was making a film called *Easy Rider*. When I saw the film, I went, "Wow!" This was different than all the other films Columbia was making. It was a radical change in what films could be, and it was very exciting.

I was relatively young, 26 years old, and everybody else was 65. I suddenly realized, hey, wait a minute, there's an opportunity here. This is really interesting. So, I got more interested in the creative process; I got really fascinated by how to exercise storytelling in this environment.

The sight of a flickering image on the screen, watching in a darkened theater as 700 or 800 people laugh or cry at some film that you've made or written, produced, or directed, and seeing your name associated with it, is an aphrodisiac. It's seductive. I think anybody coming into this business recognizes that seeing something you've done on a 60-foot screen has a tremendous effect on you.

But if that's the reason you're doing it, you're going to come up short, because there's so little of that. The question becomes: What's your real motivation for doing this? If your intention is to be involved in the creative, collaborative business of exercising yourself, of learning how to craft material, how to put it together, and how to manage the process through to its end, then the film industry might be right for you. You've got to be doing it because you somehow have a love of storytelling, a love of connecting first with yourself and then with an audience.

You will face interminable "no's" all the time and must somehow get through it. You will be challenged by the orthodoxy of the business, no matter how stupid you think it is, but you will find a new way to do it. Then you will realize the fact that whether the film is successful is important, but it's not the only measure.

We have such hubris about this business we call filmmaking, whether it's movies for theatrical, television, or large-screen format. The reality is that cinema is only just over 100 years old. Any rules we have are subject to change without notice, and that's really the conundrum. Storytelling itself is 25,000 years old. We're wired in a particular way, a narrative way, and to look at everything we do in a narrative way. That's the way we hold information. That's the way we talk to each other. That's the way we emote and motivate ourselves and others.

At the same time, there's a real craft to storytelling, whether it's done by the campfire or by projecting images on the celluloid screen.

People make their way into the film business from lots of schools. I'm associated with UCLA so I have a particular favorite. But whether you attended NYU or USC, it's not just what you learned, it's *how* you learned it. Did you stock up on information with no resonance, or did you learn as a living, breathing emotional experience? Did you peel it apart, or was it laid out in a thing all made for you?

You can't teach people to have art—you can't put in what God left out. But you can assist people to have craft. The craft is not just in how to turn the camera on and off or what scenes to keep in and edit out. It is also how to survive the collaborative interaction we call filmmaking and those intra-psychic elements that occur between observers and participants that often determine the film's success or failure.

Is geography a critical element to job opportunity in the film industry? Yes and no. If you're enormously talented as a screenwriter and can get your screenplay seen by an agent, a studio, or a network, then you can live in Oshkosh. It will not matter where you live. Actors generally have to apply their craft; once they're successful, they too can live anywhere they want, because they're called upon. But when you're just getting started or in entry-level positions, you're constantly networking. You're looking for peer relationships that will grow with you as you all rise up the ranks. As they go up the corporate ladder, the business ladder, studio ladder, the network ladder, they're still your peer group. It's important to learn how to make those relationships, because relationships are more important than transactions. Relationships endure all your life.

It's absolutely critical to be in a place where you're in proximity to those relationships. Physical proximity, where you can talk to them, drink with them, dine with them, walk with them, interact with them. The telephone is not the most perfect instrument to initiate that interaction. So, the answer is to be wherever there is the largest gathering of people involved in the business, not even in your own area, but acting, writing, producing, and all the other aspects. Because the collaborative art of filmmaking is an interdisciplinary skill, you want to mix with as many people as you can to see what's going on. In the beginning part of your career, you want to do that. Reputation is a day-to-day thing. It builds. It's what people see you do. Character is a lifetime thing. It's what you do when no one's looking. You carry your reputation and your character into every meeting.

The word *Hollywood* is an anachronism. Hollywood isn't a geographic reality, although there's a place called Hollywood. It's an international mindset. It's a type of entertainment configuration that could be in New York; in London; it could certainly be in California; and it could be in Silicon Valley. Hollywood is an attitude. So, a film could be made anywhere but have the feel of Hollywood, like *Enemy at the Gates,* made with a French filmmaker, shot in Germany, with two English actors as leads, and with an American composer. It wasn't even edited in the geographic Hollywood, but it's still a Hollywood film. On the other hand, *Amélie* is clearly not a Hollywood film: It's a local French repertoire film, even though it was navigated and moved and exhibited in the United States with good result.

The tools, rules, and guidelines governing the film industry are:

1. You want to be where the action is.
2. Proximity is power. You want to get the power of other people. Be close with them. Associate with them.
3. You have to manage relationships more than transactions, and that takes physical proximity.
4. Ideas live in the ether where all creative people live, and you have to steep yourself in that ether.

On the other hand, when you reach the status of being the center of your own gravity, then your reputation allows you to live where you want to live.

Filmmaking is a collaborative process. It's a process of one by many. I often say if you want to shoot the screenplay, what you really do is stand it up on a shelf and take pictures of it. But nobody's going to come see it. A screenplay is a blueprint for a film. It gives direction as to what is the intention of the vision keeper. Good old-fashioned words on the page form the idea, and then it becomes a very collaborative enterprise. Then the interpretation of that, the execution of that, is also very collaborative. It doesn't mean it's compromised. It means that good ideas can come from lots of people. If you hire and commission people, you have to be prepared to listen to them, to hear them.

You have to know how to recognize that connection, how to translate that connection, how to get other people to collaborate with you in that vision. Not to have someone take over or take away the vision, but to have someone collaborate in that vision. To collaborate in that vision, you have to be able to let go of it in order to let other people have room to hold on to it. It's a hard thing to understand. You can't be proprietary about it, but you have to be the vision keeper and make sure that it's consistent with the original vision, even though the way of executing it and collaborating about the execution can be done in many different ways.

You can't complain about a vision of a movie that didn't get made that you were involved with. If you were that determined, you would have gotten it made that way. So, don't lament the film that didn't happen, especially if it didn't happen because you didn't make it happen or because you allowed something else to happen. It's very interesting. If you're involved with a film, it's your film, even though people—even you—often try to hide from their failures or grasp on to their successes. The reality is that your credentials precede you. The idea that you're somehow immune from failure if you're successful is incorrect. You learn from failure, you know how to get up when something's failed in order to achieve success. If a person hasn't failed along the road, she or he hasn't taken enough chances. Filmmaking is a constant struggle between success and failure.

Whether a film succeeds is often in the laps of the movie gods. Success or failure are millimeters apart and exist together inside every great flop and every great hit. But if you're not active in your own rescue in the process, you'll surely fail. Everyone in the film industry has an objective. What is your objective? If you're the actor, you show up on time, prepare your lines, and do the work. As a producer, you have to define that role, whether you're the writer-producer, producer-producer, director-producer, studio-producer, whatever it is. You're the center of gravity.

You can't be in the business unless you're *in* the business. If you're truly serious about a career in the film industry, get in the business anyway you can. That gives you a chance to have proximity to power, and power is the wellspring from which all happens. Once you get into the business, make relationships and contacts. Get experience and exposure.

If you look at the qualities to be successful in the film industry they are persistence, tenacity, and commitment.

About Peter Guber

For more than 35 years, Peter Guber has been making films and teaching about the film industry. Head of production at Columbia Pictures by the age of 30 and, later, CEO of Sony Pictures Entertainment, Guber founded Mandalay Entertainment in 1995. He is a full professor at the University of California in Los Angeles (UCLA), School of Theatre, Film and Television, where he has taught continually since 1969, and he is founding chairman of the Producers Program. Guber has produced more than 30 films, including such critical and box office hits as *I Know What You Did Last Summer, Batman, Rain Man, The Deep, Midnight Express, Taxi Driver, Flashdance, Donnie Brasco, Enemy at the Gates,* and *The Score.* He is also coauthor, with Peter Bart, editor in chief of *Variety,* of *Shoot Out: Surviving Fame and (Mis) Fortune in Hollywood* (Putnam, 2002), based on the graduate course they co-teach in the Independent Film and Television Producers Program at UCLA.

INDUSTRY OUTLOOK

When most people think of working in the film industry, what probably jumps to mind are these four primary jobs: actor, director, screenwriter, and producer. But if you've ever read the end credits of a movie, then you know that for most films there are scores of other jobs employing hundreds of people, ranging from set builders to electricians, costume designers, and sound engineers. Many of them have less familiar titles, such as "gaffer," "best boy," or "foley artist." Each job is important and plays a significant role in the making of a film. Several people working in behind-the-scene positions, such as the director of photography, editor, composer, costume designer, and, in some cases, even the caterer, may earn more than $100,000 a year. *Career Opportunities in the Film Industry* explains who these people are and what they do and offers detailed information on 84 jobs available to someone who wants to work in this glamorous, creative, exciting, awe-inspiring, and important industry.

Since the first edition of *Career Opportunities in the Film Industry* was published, the digital revolution, combined with a blossoming broadband business on the Internet, has changed the way many movies are shot, edited, distributed, and even viewed.

Due to the low-cost conversion to high-definition production and digital distribution, there are now far more movies being made and shown at festivals (more than 13,000 in 2006) than there were just three years ago, and there has also been an increase in the number of films being released—close to 607 films in 2006, which is an 11 percent increase over the 549 films made in 2005 and an even more dramatic increase over the 467 films released in 2002.

Furthermore, the Internet has opened a whole new world of entering the film industry for potential filmmakers. Studios, talent scouts, and production companies are now looking for the next great director by viewing short films on Web sites such as Youtube.com, Google Video, and iTunes.com.

Netflix and other subscription-based DVD distribution-by-mail services, such as Blockbuster, are changing the way movies earn money, by allowing films that failed at the box office, or never even got distributed in movie theaters, to be discovered by consumers. (As these services become downloadable from the Internet, further distribution changes are occurring.)

Like the music industry, broadband technology has also opened up the Internet to downloadable movies. This is giving consumers more direct control over what they want to see and when they are able to see it. You can now download a movie from iTunes for $1.99. More important, since digital files are so inexpensive to store, any movie made can be converted into a digital file; it is then available forever to anyone who wants to download it. Instead of a movie failing to get released (because of the distribution, marketing, or exhibition costs), *all* movies can be made available online for no cost (to be viewed for free or for a charge for viewing).

Local filmmaking continues to thrive in places like Connecticut, New York City, and Florida because of tax incentives to film companies. This contributes to the continuing decentralization of filmmaking from just a Hollywood, California–based profession. However, Hollywood still dominates the film industry, just as New York City is still central to book publishing.

Another trend is the continued growth of international cofinancing and coproducing of movies. Film festivals, such as the Berlin Film Festival in February and CineMart, the coproduction market of the International Film Festival Rotterdam Film Festival held in The Netherlands each January, offer opportunities for filmmakers, producers, and directors from all the over the world to meet and try to put together an international project. There is funding available for selected filmmakers who have made at least one feature film to attend these festivals to participate in their cofinancing programs.

The number of movies being shot entirely on high-definition video has increased substantially. The last two *Star Wars* movies and *Miami Vice, Apocalypto, Superman Returns, Spy Kids, Sin City,* and *Collateral* were shot completely on high-definition video and converted to film.

In the near future, movie theaters will all be digital and connected either fiber-optically or by broadband so they will no longer have to depend on hard copies of films. Movies are already viewed on giant screens, as well as on cell phones and iPods—trends that will escalate in years ahead.

Another development in trying to woo moviegoers back to the traditional movie theater is the growth of the not-for-profit movie theater, such as the Avon Theatre in suburban Stamford, Connecticut. A subscription-based membership option, in addition to regular customers, enables the Avon to offer educational cultural events beyond just the basic movie screening. For example, Terry George, the director and screenwriter of *Hotel Rwanda*, appeared at the end of the screening of the movie to lead a question-and-answer session with the audience. Interestingly, not long after this movie event, Terry George shot part of his next major feature film in Stamford, Connecticut, using local locations as well as some area residents for extra parts.

In 2008, some movie theaters have turned from selling only popcorn, sodas, and candy to offering high-end restaurant fare as a way to lure back moviegoers.

In the next 10 years, with the expansion of digital cinema and video on demand, the film industry, which started more than 100 years ago, will undergo its greatest transformation since the introduction of sound in the 1920s and color in the late 1930s. Still, making movies will remain a collaborative effort, involving scores and sometimes hundreds of people, depending on the budget and scope of the film being made. Whether it's shot on film or high-definition digital tape, or whether it's shown on a giant Imax screen or the face of a wristwatch, the act of creating the image that ultimately appears will still involve the same basic process. That process is a select group of professionals working in front of and behind the camera, as well as in various stages of preproduction, production, postproduction, and, ultimately, marketing, distribution, and exhibition.

Motion picture production and distribution is a global growth industry. Even during times of economic downturns, going to the movies is seen as a relatively low-cost form of escape (compared to the higher cost of most stage, cabaret, or music shows) that is also a social activity (compared to reading for entertainment, which is usually solitary). Movie box office receipts in the United States for 2006 were $9.5 billion, according to the National Association of Theatre Owners (NATO). The entire motion picture industry, if you include salaries, other fees, and related expenditures, is in the tens of billions of dollars.

In the United States in 2004, there were approximately 368,000 wage and salary jobs in the motion picture production and distribution industry, according to the U.S. government *Occupational Outlook Handbook 2006-07 Edition*. (This is up from the 287,000 jobs in the industry for 2000, as reported in the first edition of this book.) The U.S. Department of Labor, Bureau of Labor Statistics reports that the employment outlook for the film industry as a whole is excellent, with a growth increase over the next decade of 17 percent (compared to 15 percent for all industries combined). Although a majority of the salaried jobs are located in Los Angeles and New York City, there are film industry jobs available throughout the United States and in other countries. In fact, there are job opportunities in the film industry available at any time virtually anywhere in the world. Technology has made it possible for anyone with a digital camera, a computer, and the necessary software to make a feature film. Will this film show up at your local multiplex? Probably not.

But it could wind up on the Internet in streaming video. In fact, two young men shot a short film on digital and offered it to a streaming video Web site. The short, titled *405*, showed a jet landing on top of a car on the 405 freeway. Executives at a studio saw it online, which led to a development deal for the two filmmakers.

Although this book is aimed at the young who are about to embark on their first film industry jobs, it is also for those on their way up in the film industry, as well as anyone who may be considering the film industry as a second or even a third career. Many stars as well as other film industry directors, writers, producers, and other professionals held other jobs either before or while they were beginning a career in the intensely competitive and demanding—but ever glamorous, creative, unpredictable, and exciting—film industry. For example, actor Brian Dennehy was a stockbroker before he became an actor, and Harrison Ford was a carpenter. Screenwriter Alvin Sargent, after giving up on an acting career, went on to sell advertising until the age of 35, when he began writing TV shows. That was followed by his authorship of the Academy Award-winning screenplays for *Ordinary People* and *Julia*, among other screenplays, as noted by Brouwer and Wright in *Working in Hollywood.*

Another misconception is that in order to work in the film industry, you have to be in Los Angeles. While that may be where the great majority of movies are developed and produced, more and more films are being shot on location, as well as in other urban areas with expanding film industries, such as Chicago, Illinois, New York City, Toronto, Canada, and Orlando, Florida. In fact, today all 50 states have at least one film commission for the state, and some states have numerous other film commissions in several cities or regions that post jobs related to the film activities in their community. These jobs range from actors and extras to carpenters, production assistants, camera crews, and other specialists.

But it is also important to be realistic about how competitive the film industry is to break into as well as to stay in, let alone advance. "You must be absolutely relentless," says David Zelon, executive vice president of production at Mandalay Pictures. Zelon continues: "You must know that nobody gives you anything in Hollywood. There's not enough to go around, so if you want something, you have to figure out how to take it for yourself." Furthermore, you need to keep in mind that if you do not have a studio or full-time production company job, you may experience unemployment in between films. Even if you are fortunate enough to go from one movie project to another, you still need to consider whether you have the personality and stamina to constantly look for new work as well as deal with the ever-changing creative and corporate staffs that you will meet on each project.

Some, however, see the unpredictability of the film industry as one of its benefits. It is certainly never dull or boring but is filled with the excitement of being part of the team that creates the next blockbuster, like *Titanic* or *E.T.;* an action adventure classic, like *Star Wars;* the magic of a fantasy epic with moral and political overtones, like *The Wizard of Oz;* or surprise hits, like *My Big Fat Greek Wedding, Four Weddings and a Funeral, The Blair Witch Project, Ghost Rider,* and *300* (which brought in $70 million in ticket sales from Friday to Sunday when it was released in March 2007). A career in film offers gratification and rewards unique to the film industry.

So, if your dream is to work in the "dream factory," or feature film industry, then now is as good a time as any to start to make your dream come true.

ACKNOWLEDGMENTS

First and foremost, we want to thank our editor, James Chambers, editor in chief, Arts & Humanities, at Facts On File, Inc., headquartered in New York City. Jim has been an enthusiastic and concerned editor from the moment we proposed this project for the well-regarded Facts On File, Inc. (Checkmark Books) Career Opportunities series.

Thanks are also due to Sarah Fogarty, project editor at Facts On File, Inc., who worked diligently on the first and second editions of this book. Laurie Katz and Erin Shea are also appreciated for publicity and promotional activities related to this title, as is Mark Amundsen, an in-house editor.

Our deepest thanks to David Carradine for writing the foreword to the second edition of this book. We also want to thank Peter Guber for the foreword to the first edition of this book, as well as Richard Laermer, CEO of RLM Public Relations, and publicist Annie Turn for arranging Jan's meeting and interview with Peter Guber.

The list of people to thank in the research and development of this book is vast and ever-expanding, even as we go to press with the manuscript. Whether or not someone is named in the book, or even in this acknowledgments section, everyone that spoke to us, or sent us a reference or publication, contributed to this project. Thanks to those we interviewed for this book as well as for previous film industry–related research and writing: Alan Alda, Stewart F. Lane, Terry Lawler, Gayle Nachlis, Lisa Charnes, Susan Johnston, Donna DeStefano, Daniel H. Schneider, Esq., Susan Granger, Bill Contardi, Cynthia Wade, Gayle Kirschenbaum, Maxine Kozler, Lane Shefter Bishop, Andrew Bishop, Isil Bagdadi, Orly Adelson, Alexi Mazareas, Aleen Stein, Michael Levine, Peggy Howard Chane, Mirembe Nutt-Birigwa, Milt Shefter, Joy Shefter, Jone Bouman, Jan Caputo, Tonya Obeso, Karen Rose, Carola Myers, Jennifer Ash, Tom Quinn, Gary A. Marsh, Nicole Williams, David Zelon, Jane Covner, Annie Flocco, Deena Kalai, Alita Renée Holly, Cynthia Fuchs Epstein, Alexander Steele, Lynda J. Moore, Marie Gallo Dyak, Marilyn Ness, David Goodman, Francesca Prada, Adam Meyer, Noel E. Jefferson, Melisssa Houghton, Edith Grant, Jerome Courshon, Pauline Steinhorn, Marjorie Kalins, Danielle DiGiacomo; the Producing One-Week Intensive Course that Jan took at New York University the week of July 17, 2006, and her instructor, producer Debbie Elbin, and all the students in the class and the guest speakers; Elizabeth Guider, Jayne Pliner, Gloria Amadeo, Sandra Lord, Ellen Giurieo, Eric Butler, Isabel Shaw, Kristen Crawford, Diana Osberg, Dallas Dorsett, Eli Davidson, Gregory Feldman, Yvette Maas, Etta Devine, Cindera Che, Kat Kramer, Barry Goldberg, Melissa Kent, Julian Myers, Joy Montgomery, Gabriel Diani, Robin Lynch, Alesia Glidewell, Jeffrey R. Gund, Amy Yukich, Mare Costello, Judith Smith, Donna Wisdom, Paula Fins, Joanne McCall, Jason Nadler, Barrett Garese, Judy Kauffman of Storyworks, Charlie Ryan of Soundtrack Music Services, a composer's agent; the Women in Film Hugo Boss Mentor Program master class organized by Women in Film that Jan and Fred attended in Los Angeles, which included illuminating and informative presentations by special effects makeup artist Stan Winston *(Jurassic Park, Aliens),* costume designer Mary Vogt *(Men in Black),* beauty makeup artist Angela Levin *(Scream 3),* and costume designer Gloria Gresham *(The Natural, When Harry Met Sally);* former executive officer of Women in Film Selise E. Eiseman, who moderated that memorable panel, as well as Diane A. Sherer, former associate executive officer of Women in Film; Mae Woods, who graciously organized a get-together of the Los Angeles chapter of Sisters in Crime, an association of mystery writers and enthusiasts, in our honor when we were in Hollywood; the staff and fellow members of New York Women in Film and Television and Los Angeles–based Women in Film; Michael K. Eitelman, director of development at Serendipity Films; Kate Schumaecker, former director of development, Chicagofilms; Dan Victor, president/CEO Boneyard Entertainment; Bonnie Black, president, Bonnie Black Talent & Literary Agency; Allison Shigo, director of development, Revolution Films; Gerard Sellers, location manager; film instructor and David Lynch biographer Martha P. Nochimson; actor James Garrett; Bob Mead; producer Martin Poll; director and producer Gil Cates; Diane Sokolow, president, Sokolow & Company; Adina Kahn; Trina Wyatt, COO and CFO, Tribeca Entertainment; producer Joel Simon; the late Harold Hoffman, executive secretary of the Screen Actors Guild; Richard Brennan of Ocean Blue Entertainment; Lee Levinson; Mary Tierney; Sharon Fisher; Judy Copeland; David Carradine; Marilyn Horowitz;

Arthur Vinci; Elia Schneider; Jose Ramon; Lee and Suzanne Cobb; the staff and fellow members of the Writers Guild of America, East (Fred's a member); Heidi Wall and her Fast Forward seminar (Fred attended); Sherri Klein; publicist Maureen Lutz; Cammie Morgan of Filmline International; the late Carl Sautter; IFP (Independent Feature Project International, of which Fred and Jan are members), American Screenwriters Association, Women's Media Group (Jan's a member); and Andreas Grunberg, Grunberg Film. Actors, directors, producers, and other film industry professionals that Fred or Jan have interviewed over the years, including Steven Spielberg, Tom Hanks, the late James Cagney, the late Christopher Reeve, Jane Fonda, Sigourney Weaver, Glenn Close, the late Art Carney, Henry Fonda, Francis Ford Coppola, Sylvester Stallone, Arnold Schwarzenegger, the late George Burns, the late Lee Strasberg, the late Gwen Verdon, the late Jim Henson, producer Charlie Matthau, the late Walter Matthau, Richard Benjamin, Paula Prentiss, Steve Martin, Walter Hill, Norman Lear, Glenda Jackson, Liv Ullmann, Diane Weiss, the late Sydney Pollack, the late Richard Burton; Dina Merrill, the late Paul Winfield, Rip Torn, Cliff Robertson, Estelle Parsons, and Harrison Ford.

HOW TO USE THIS BOOK

Career Opportunities in the Film Industry is aimed at anyone considering a career in one of the most exciting and rewarding growth industries in the world today as well as these in the film industry who are looking to advance in it. You will learn about 84 different positions, including the high-profile jobs of actor, producer, director, and screenwriter, along with other essential behind-the-scenes positions, such as art director, editor, costume designer, makeup artist, gaffer, sound engineer, animal safety representative, and dozens of others.

For each category, we provide a description of what the job involves, what education or skills are needed, and several suggestions about how to get started in that job. We also provide salary ranges, employment and advancement potential, as well as crossover opportunities from one job category to another.

For example, not everyone entering the film business gets a starring role in a feature film or even an acting job from his or her first audition. But there could be an opening for an extra or a stand-in for one of the principal players. More than a few stars today were discovered filling the less visible or sensational roles. The key is to get into the business, find out where your talents and interests are, and then make your mark as you gain experience and a positive reputation and as you perform well at each new opportunity for advancement that presents itself to you.

It may not always turn out to be what you expected. Famed special effects designer Stan Winston went to Hollywood to become an actor. He could not get a job acting, so he took one as a makeup artist. While he continued to seek out acting roles, he developed a flair for special effects makeup and later model building. While he may have dreamed of being an actor, he is one of the most famous and well-respected special effects artists in the world, having won an Oscar in the special effects category as the creator of the dinosaurs in the *Jurassic Park* movies.

In his interview published in Alexandra Brouwer and Thomas Lee Wright's book *Working in Hollywood,* Robert Easton, one of the top dialect coaches in Hollywood, talks about how he and his wife created a company called The Henry Higgins of Hollywood, Incorporated. He had been a successful character actor, appearing in dozens of movies, but as he became more and more in demand for his dialect coaching, especially on location in other countries, he was forced to choose which of his two careers to focus on, with dialect coach winning out over actor.

Also, keep in mind that the film industry covered in this guide is the feature film business, whether those feature films are shown in movie theaters or on television, as opposed to the television industry, which includes sitcoms, game shows, dramas, news programs, and other employment situations not necessarily connected to the film industry.

What's New in the Second Edition

David Carradine's foreword is new to this second edition. This talented actor, director, and author shares his insights into the film industry, an industry that he grew up in as the son of well-known actor

John Carradine but one he has very much made his own through the numerous movies he has performed in (*Kill Bill: Volumes I & II* and *Bound for Glory*), as well as the ones he has directed, including *You and Me* and *Americana*, and through the *Kung Fu* TV series that he starred in.

Producer and UCLA professor Peter Guber's foreword has been retained from the first edition. It is still relevant to read about how this Hollywood dynamo got his start in the film industry, as well as his advice to those starting out or wanting to excel in their film career.

Each career profile in this second edition was checked and revised as needed. No jobs were deleted for this second edition, but the following five jobs were added:

- Animal Safety Representative (under "The Talent")
- Development Associate (under "Producers, Studio or Independent")
- Executive Assistant (under "Financing, Legal, and Administrative Issues")
- Association Director (under "Education")
- Film Archivist and Preservationist (under Education)

Also new for this second edition are excerpts from more than 30 original in-person or telephone interviews that are included throughout the book. Excerpted interviews with industry professionals such as David Zelon, executive vice president of production at Mandalay Pictures; film critic Susan Granger; executive producer Orly Adelson; Alexi Mazareas, development associate; producer Susan Johnston; director Lane Shefter Bishop; film archivist and preservationist Milt Shefter; music supervisor Maxine Kozler; film instructor and Academy Award–winning director Cynthia Wade; among others, are featured in the appropriate job category. Most of the time, those quotes were added in the position description part of the job category entry, although sometimes additional comments appear elsewhere in the entry, such as in Tips for Entry. (In addition to those excerpted original interviews, e-mail or in-person communications were exchanged with more than forty additional industry professionals, who shared comments about their careers.)

The appendixes, such as the colleges and universities, degree and nondegree film industry programs, professional unions and associations, competitions, fellowships and internships, festivals, commissions, and selected agencies, and film companies, have been reviewed and updated.

The selected bibliography and especially the Web site resources have been updated. There is, of course, a new index and, finally, About the Authors has been updated, as we have added to our credits since the first edition was published, including a dedicated Web site, http://www.fredandjanyager.com, which highlights our coauthored books, screenplays, plays, novels, and other print and film projects.

Sources of Information

The information offered in *Career Opportunities in the Film Industry* is based on a variety of sources, including:

- Interviews with professionals working in the film industry
- Studio tours in Los Angeles and Astoria, New York
- Attendance at film industry lectures and educational seminars in Los Angeles and New York City
- Trade union brochures, pamphlets, and other written or recorded material
- Web sites of agencies, unions, film commissions, colleges and universities offering film programs, professional associations, and others
- Books about the industry and career books such as the U.S. Government's *Occupational Outlook Handbook,* updated regularly
- Articles in industry newspapers, magazines, and professional journals such as *Variety,* the *Hollywood Reporter,* and *New York Screenwriter,* as well as the popular press

The authors also have firsthand experience with the industry, beginning with Fred Yager's attendance at New York University, where he was awarded a certificate in film production, and the four years he worked as an entertainment writer and movie critic for the Associated Press, interviewing more than 200 film industry professionals, especially actors and directors, as well as screening hundreds of films each year. Fred has been a member of the

Writers Guild of America, East, since 1983; several of his screenplays have been optioned, including one by director Walter Hill *(48 Hours)* and another by producer Aaron Russo *(Trading Places).* For two years, Fred was a full-time screenwriter, living in Hollywood for part of that time while he rewrote one of his scripts in an office on a studio's lot.

Jan is coauthor of several screenplays and novels with Fred, including a romantic comedy, *No Time for Love,* and two thrillers, *Untimely Death* and *Just Your Everyday People* (including published novels based on the thrillers). Jan studied acting at the Gene Frankel Theatre Workshop, the State University of New York at Buffalo, and at the American Academy for Dramatic Arts. For seven years, Jan was a freelance theater critic for *Back Stage* newspaper. In addition to acting in, writing, and directing several student films, Jan attended Dov S-S Simens's Hollywood Film Institute weekend course and an intensive one-week producing course at New York University. Jan has also interviewed film actors and screenwriters for books and articles. The Yagers, who live in Fairfield County, Connecticut, near New York City, have a film company with several projects in development and have also traveled to Los Angeles for meetings and interviews over the last two decades. They are also coauthors of *Career Opportunities in the Publishing Industry,* published by Facts On File, Inc. (For more information about the authors of this career guide, go to the About the Authors section in the back of the book.)

How This Book Is Organized

There are many ways that the 84 jobs explored in this book could have been organized. One way might have been dividing the jobs up by the above-the-line jobs (development, story and screenplay, producers unit, director unit, cast unit, travel and living, fringe benefits, and payroll taxes) and below-the-line jobs (everything from set construction, set dressing, camera, lighting, wardrobe, makeup and hair to animals and transportation). However, using above-the-line and below-the-line sections still would have left out such important additional job categories as publicist, editor, composer, postproduction foley artist, and titles registrar.

We organized the 84 job categories into the following four parts in order to make *Career Opportunities in the Film Industry* easier to use:

Part I: Development/Preproduction
Part II: Production (Principal Photography)
Part III: Postproduction
Part IV: Distribution, Publicity and Advertising, and Education

These parts follow the order in which the various categories are hired during the making and distributing of a feature film. They also correspond to how a film's budget is broken down. However, there is some overlap in certain jobs in each of these divisions: The talent agent may be most involved in the preproduction part of the filmmaking process, when the principal actors are being auditioned and selected, but he or she may also stay involved throughout production and in the marketing, sales, and distribution of the film. Similarly, a publicist, although most often concerned during marketing, sales, and distribution of the finished film, may send out a press release to the "trades"—the industry newspapers, *Variety* and the *Hollywood Reporter*—announcing that a particular actor has just been signed to do an upcoming feature film.

Each of these four parts is then divided into subheadings. For example, under Part I, Development/Preproduction, we have the following subheads: The Script, The Talent, Producers, Directors, and Financing and Legal Issues. Under The Script are the following job categories: Screenwriter, Story Editor, Script Reader, and Literary Agent. Under The Talent, you will find Casting Director, Principal Actors, Extras, Talent Agent, Mailroom Clerk, Stunt Coordinator, Stuntperson, Choreographer, Animal Trainer, Animal Safety Representative, and Wrangler. Once again, there may be some overlap in certain categories; for instance, the script reader may be employed by a studio, or by a literary agent, talent agent, or producer who hires a script reader to read unsolicited or solicited screenplays for analysis ("coverage").

Numerous job categories also have alternate titles; those additional titles are listed within each category under "Alternate Title(s)." In the index, a job will be listed by its most common name and any alternate titles to facilitate locating its job category.

We have tried to organize this complex industry in as user-friendly a way as possible, always keeping in mind that you, our reader and film industry job seeker, are most concerned with finding a particular job category where it would most likely be found (with an extensive index at the back of the book providing additional help in locating specific jobs).

The Job Profile

Each job profile gives you basic information about the 84 positions that contribute to the production, marketing, and distribution of a feature film. A profile begins with a Career Profile, a one-line description of the position's major duties, followed by salary range, job outlook, and opportunities for promotion. We also discuss educational requirements, skills, and personality traits best suited for each position. There is a career ladder section that provides a look at a typical career path, showing what various positions can lead to. The job that is being profiled is in the middle of the career ladder, with the job that it usually leads to above it and the job that most likely leads to it below—the highest and lowest "rungs" on the ladder. The rest of the profile is in an expanded narrative format with more detailed information that includes the following:

- Position description, including major responsibilities and duties

- Salary ranges from beginner to veteran
- Employment prospects
- Possibility and suggestions for advancement
- Licensing or certification requirements (if any)
- Unions and associations
- Education or special training
- Experience, skills, or personality traits
- Tips for entry or getting that first job in this job category

The Appendixes

At the back of this book are eight appendixes providing additional resources for the positions profiled in *Career Opportunities in the Film Industry.* Here you will find information on selected colleges and universities offering undergraduate or graduate degrees in film production and/or drama; nondegree programs; professional unions and associations; film festivals; film commissions with state-by-state listings; film studio and production companies, as well as a sample of available fellowships or internships. There is a glossary of film industry terms and a bibliography, including books, industry publications, and Web sites, and, finally, job search sites. An index follows and About the Authors concludes *Career Opportunities in the Film Industry.*

PART I
DEVELOPMENT/ PREPRODUCTION

THE SCRIPT

SCREENWRITER

Duties: Write the screenplay upon which the film is based, whether the story is original or adapted from another source, such as a book, play, or magazine article

Alternate Title(s): Scriptwriter

Salary Range: $0 to $1 million+

Employment Prospects: Good

Advancement Prospects: Fair

Best Geographical Location(s): Although a screenwriter could work anywhere, being located where there is extensive filmmaking activity, such as in Los Angeles/Hollywood, New York City, and other filmmaking centers, may be useful, especially for initial pitch meetings to agents, producers, or directors

Prerequisites:

Education and Training—College or an advanced degree are useful but optional

Experience—Writing background helpful but not essential

CAREER LADDER

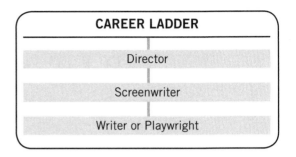

Special Skills and Personality Traits—Ability to create an original story or an adaptation based on other material; creative writing skills with competence at writing dialogue, creating action, and adhering to the specific style and format of screenplays

Special Requirements—Union membership may be required by those studios and production companies that are signatories of the Writers Guild of America (WGA)

Position Description

It used to be said that practically every writer wanted to pen a great novel. Today, writing a screenplay that becomes a hit movie has become a new literary dream.

Movies begin with a script. The Screenwriter writes the script. It is the blueprint for the dialogue and the action that will be spoken by the actors and performed in the feature film.

Screenwriting is very distinct in its style and format. Even the length of a screenplay is specific, depending upon whether the writer is aiming for a typical 90 minute, 120 minute, or longer feature film. Screenwriters create screenplays for feature films in a variety of genres: romantic comedy, action adventure, thrillers, comedy, historical dramas, political dramas, family features, and sci-fi.

There is no mistaking the huge impact one screenplay can have on the millions, even billions, of viewers worldwide who see a movie based on that writer's screenplay. The glamour and excitement of being a writer associated with the film industry is hard to match in any other industry that uses writers, especially since

a successful Screenwriter could command fees upward of a million dollars per script.

The Screenwriter, who is usually behind the scenes and rarely gets the attention of principal actors and actresses or directors (except for those occasional celebrity screenwriters, like William Goldman), were front and center in fall 2007/winter 2008 when their strike dramatically affected the film and TV industries. The key issue was over revenue and residuals to screenwriters from writing that would be distributed through the Internet. Until an agreement was reached, production on new movies was halted, as was the development of new TV series episodes and even most late-night television writing, also covered by the Writers Guild of America contract.

With a loss to the industry estimated in the millions, even billions, the power and importance of the often anonymous Screenwriter was brought home to everyone, within and outside of the film industry. Because actors refused to cross the writers' picket line, even the highly regarded and much-watched Golden Globe Awards, granted by the Hollywood Foreign Press Association, was reduced to just reading aloud the names and credits of the winners rather than the airing of the live televised star-studded red carpet event.

What makes a terrific Screenwriter? Someone who is a creative storyteller with the writing skills to compose memorable dialogue and characters as well as the ability to pace the movie just right.

Every so often, overnight success stories are heard about the unknown writer who sits down, creates a screenplay, and sends it out to an agent "over the transom," only to have it picked up and sold, within days, to a major studio for a million dollars. For most, however, it is a very long and slow process from writing the first screenplay to seeing it put into production, filmed, and released in the theaters. The reality is that more screenplays are sold than actually get made into movies.

Although only a few Screenwriters are household names, compared to how many actors and even directors achieve celebrity status, the Screenwriter, the mastermind of the story, along with the characters and dialogue that are created, are the key beginning elements to every feature film that eventually gets produced.

Screenwriters may create a screenplay completely from scratch or adapt other written material, most often a book or a play, but sometimes from a magazine article. The Screenwriter might buy the right to adapt the material and pay a flat fee to the copyright holder of the original material or he or she may agree to share the future fees or profits on any films that are created by the Screenwriter based on that material.

There are Screenwriters who only write or have only written screenplays; others first wrote newspaper articles, short stories, novels, nonfiction books, or plays, and then learned the craft of screenwriting.

Those unfamiliar with the art and techniques of screenwriting are surprised at how rigorous and demanding a skill it proves to be, especially if they are accomplished fiction or nonfiction writers. Of course, having a fresh and original idea is an important starting point for a Screenwriter, as well as creating memorable characters and engaging dialogue.

There are other distinctions between screenplays and other kinds of writing. First of all, it is well known that screenplays are not just written, they are rewritten, often by a writer or writers other than the original Screenwriter.

Screenwriters, once they sell a screenplay to a signatory of the Writers Guild of America, a union for Screenwriters, and have an employment contract, can join the union. As union members, they are then entitled to certain financial guarantees for each aspect of their work, such as the minimum allowed for creating a treatment for a screenplay (a detailed synopsis of the plot and characters in the screenplay that is usually 20 to 30 pages long), an option for the completed screenplay (a fee paid to give a director, producer, or studio the exclusive right to the screenplay for a period of time in order to get the production of the film underway), and, once the film is actually in production, a purchase price for the screenplay (either a flat fee or a flat fee plus a percentage of the film's budget and/or the film's net or gross profits). There are other important issues that the Writers Guild of America has negotiated on behalf of its Screenwriter members, such as when and how the screenwriting credits will be posted on a screenplay or, if rewriters are called in, how much rewriting needs to be done to the original screenplay before the first author's name is removed or shared with any other Screenwriters.

Screenwriters may be self-employed, selling their screenplays "on spec" once the screenplay is completed. Or they may be hired by an independent film company or a studio to work on a screenplay "under contract" with payment on a per project or a salary basis.

Because of the legal implications of reading unsolicited material that may lead to future accusations of plagiarism, almost all major studios are unwilling to read screenplays by Screenwriters who lack an agent or an entertainment lawyer who is known to that studio. Some independent feature film companies, however, may be willing to read treatments or screenplays if they are queried first—never send a treatment or screenplay unsolicited—and a signed submission agreement is included.

Before a Screenwriter sends a treatment or a completed script to anyone, the material should be protected by establishing the date of authorship. The Writers Guild of America offers this service to members at a reduced fee ($10 per registration) or $22 per registration for nonmembers. The Writers Guild of America, East, Inc., has automated the registration process, and most registrations are now done online. The material is sent as an attached file. A receipt will be sent approximately two weeks later. For more information, go to the Web site of the Writers Guild of America, West: http://www.wga.org. (Please note that registering your original treatment or screenplay with the Writers Guild does not replace or substitute for the protection your material receives if you register with The Library of Congress, the U.S. copyright office. For more information on the cost and procedures for filing a copyright, as well as forms you may download to submit with your copyright claim, go to the government's The Library of Congress Web site: http://www.copyright.gov.)

A Screenwriter who is looking to make a career out of writing screenplays is well-advised to find a literary agent who will submit work on the Screenwriter's behalf as well as keep his or her ears open to any potential writing assignments suitable for his client. In order to even be considered by an agent, however, an aspiring Screenwriter will usually have to write at least one complete screenplay entirely on speculation. It may take a few weeks, months, or even years for a satisfactory screenplay, often known as the "work sample," to be well-written enough to give the Screenwriter a chance at representation and a possible sale. (For a discussion about how to approach a literary agent, see the entry under Literary Agent.)

There are numerous excellent books that a Screenwriter may read, such as Linda Seger's *Creating Unforgettable Characters* or *Making a Good Script Great,* as well as *Story* by Robert McKee or *The Screenwriter's Workbook* by Syd Field. There are also seminars that may be attended, not to mention studying screenwriting at college or in graduate school as part of a degree (or non-degree) program in film or creative writing. The format for writing a screenplay can be learned, and there is software now that enables writers to adhere to the screenplay format as they write. Skills and techniques can be taught. However, the magic of creativity and originality is still very much an individual matter and, alas, a talent and gift that can be nurtured but cannot be taught if the basic proclivity toward screenwriting is missing. Screenwriters need an ear for language and dialogue as well as the ability to write action and to "show—not tell."

Screenwriters also need to keep up on what movies are being made and shown as well as what is in the works. Being called "derivative" is one of the biggest insults you can give a Screenwriter; being called innovative, creative, fresh, and memorable are what most Screenwriters strive for (and for which there are the greatest artistic and financial rewards).

Although you can write from anywhere in the world, especially in the beginning of your screenwriting career, it may be useful to live near a center of filmmaking, such as Hollywood or Manhattan, so that it is easier to "take a meeting" with a studio executive or independent film producer if there is interest in you as a Screenwriter and your screenplay.

For Screenwriters, as for any other kind of writer, you are only as good as your most recent effort. The adage goes that you can't make a great film from a bad

screenplay, but you can make a bad film from a great screenplay. So, a Screenwriter needs to take pride in his or her work and to write the best film he or she can, but, since making a movie is a collaborative effort with forces and creative elements impacting the final product beyond the Screenwriter's control, he or she must also be able to "let go" of that final screenplay as it becomes another entity, a film.

Salaries

Salaries vary widely, from writing "on spec" or for free for nonunion films to receiving $1,000 for an option or several million dollars for a completed, acceptable script (plus such negotiable terms as profit-sharing in the net or gross revenues of the film).

The Writers Guild of America has developed a new program to encourage low-budget filmmakers to become signatories: In general, low-budget is considered a film with a budget of less than $750,000; a high-budget feature film has expenses of more than $5 million. Here are the basic minimums, from the 2004 Basic Agreement, for Screenwriters who are members of the Writers Guild of America: For writing a treatment that is an original story, $24,129: for writing a completed screenplay, including a treatment for a low-budget movie, $53,256, (an option is 10 percent of that minimum); $99,980 for a high budget. An original story treatment for a high budget film is $39,957. Note that these minimums may be raised each year, so check with the Writers Guild of America (http://www.wga.org) or your literary agent for the most recent minimums. Salaried positions on staff are rare for screenwriters, although many work as story editors or directors of development while awaiting their big break.

Employment Prospects

The film industry is a growth business, and since the Screenwriter is fundamental to every film, employment prospects for Screenwriters are good. Screenwriters are basically in two employment groups: freelance Screenwriters, who sell their work and live by those sales, and Screenwriters who have an employment contract with a producer or a studio for a specific movie or time period.

There is little job security for most Screenwriters, unless they write a screenplay for a movie that becomes a big box office hit and it is clearly their authorship of the screenplay that is acknowledged (and thus they get multiple job offers).

Screenwriters need to get their movies made in order to advance, even if they have to find the money to make the movies themselves. Getting a movie made, seeing how the words on paper actually sound coming out of the mouths of actors, will help to elevate the Screenwriter's work from an outline for a movie to the basis of a real movie. That is why some Screenwriters, growing impatient and weary of the frustrations of failing to see their screenplays turned into feature films, are making a short trailer of a film based on their screenplay to show as a work sample.

The Screenwriter who lacks a major movie to his or her credit will want to have another source of income, whether that job is in the film industry or in an unrelated industry. Fortunately, screenwriting is a job that can be done anywhere and anytime, although, at some point, when a movie is being made, if the producer and director want the Screenwriter there for any rewrites that occur during shooting, he or she may have to take time off from another job to be present during those days, weeks, or months of shooting the script.

Advancement Prospects

This is a very competitive part of the business and advancement will only occur if the Screenwriter's screenplays are bought, turned into movies, with his or her credit recognized, and are commercial and creative successes.

There are no guarantees in screenwriting for advancement, but a track record of successful, well-reviewed films will certainly help seal a Screenwriter's future.

Education and Training

Although some Screenwriters are self-taught, a more typical path is to already be a writer, whether of fiction, nonfiction, or drama, and to study at a film school in a degree or nondegree, undergraduate or graduate, capacity. Since the style of screenwriting is so specific, including the number of pages for a film of a certain length as well as the standard formatting of each page, some training is necessary to acquire those skills, even if self-taught or through the use of screenwriting software.

Basic English composition and writing skills are certainly beneficial to anyone aspiring to screenwriting. Depending upon the kinds of screenplays someone chooses to write, different kinds of educational backgrounds might prove helpful. For example, someone who wants to specialize in historical screenplays, or "period pieces," might benefit from studying history, someone looking to write thrillers might benefit from studying or working in criminal justice programs or facilities, and someone interested in writing sci-fi adventures might benefit from studying astronomy, biology, or paleontology.

Experience, Skills, and Personality Traits

Screenwriters need to relish and study movies, so they can understand what makes a movie work or fail. They need to be willing to write and rewrite until they perfect the script, not just for themselves but for the cast that is assembled to speak their words and act out their scenes, once a screenplay is put into production.

The hardest part of screenwriting, getting the screenplay down on paper, is also the part that, for most, has to be done alone. Therefore, a Screenwriter should be comfortable spending hours, days, or weeks alone, although he or she may live and work among others as long as they are able to find some writing "alone" time.

Their personality hopefully enables them to work as part of a team, once their screenplay is completed, taking beneficial suggestions from everyone involved in the film, from their agent, the entertainment lawyer, director, or producer to the actors, stunt coordinators, and publicists. The Screenwriter has created an imaginary world on paper, but these other members of the film "team" are the ones who will tell him or her if that world works or not. Some scenes may be too expensive or dangerous to film; others may slow down the action or confuse the story.

It's a cliché, but for the Screenwriter it is a truism that bears repeating: Screenwriters need to have stick-to-itiveness and a thick skin. There are few overnight successes in the screenwriting business and those examples, though few and far between, still need to be followed up with hit after hit after hit.

Taking pride in a well-written script should be its own reward; a Screenwriter needs to take a very long view of his or her career. Being pleasant to be around is certainly a valuable trait for a Screenwriter, in addition to the obvious one of having good writing skills, since Screenwriters may be involved with a production team on a film for months or years till the film is actually released.

Unions and Associations

Membership in the Writers Guild of America (WGA) is required if a Screenwriter sells a screenplay to a studio or production company that is a signatory of the Writers Guild of America.

Since networking is a key aspect of the film industry, membership in associations increase the chances of knowing more "players" in the industry and may be beneficial. There are associations, such as IFP (Independent Feature Project) or Women in Film, with affiliate chapters in New York, Chicago, Orlando, and numerous other cities and countries including Canada, the Netherlands, England, and France, as well as other related associations, listed in this book's appendixes.

Tips for Entry

1. During middle school, high school, college, or graduate school, get involved in any aspect of film-making or writing available to you, from writing for the school newspaper to writing a play to creating student films with a video or digital camera.
2. Attend seminars that are given by successful Screenwriters and learn how they got started, what books they read, how they trained, and how they got their first break.
3. Discipline yourself to write, and keep writing, until you have a completed spec script that you can show to an agent, producer, or director. If you're short on ideas of your own, option the play or book written by another and buy the right to adapt that material into a screenplay.
4. Enter your completed screenplay in screenwriting contests. Even if you don't win, you will be exposing your writing to others who might help you get started by recommending you to their agent, attorney, producer, or director. You can also submit your completed screenplay to film associations that have readings of works in progress. Not only could you benefit from hearing your words spoken and acted out, someone might read your work, or attend the reading, that could help you get your first break as a Screenwriter.
5. Attend film festivals and network with those in the film industry, from entertainment lawyers and producers to actors and directors.
6. Study screenwriting as part of a degree or non-degree college or graduate school program in writing or film. There are also credit or non-credit summer screenwriting courses available at many colleges and universities including New York University, the University of California, Los Angeles, University of Southern California, and The New School. Online courses are also available.
7. Job postings for writers may be announced through free industry employment Web sites such as http://www.mandy.com, http://www.infolist. com, or http://www.entertainmentcareers.net, as well as through the fee- and subscription-based e-mail newsletter *InkTip*, available for purchase through http://www.inktip.com.

STORY EDITOR

CAREER PROFILE

Duties: Look for original, published, or theatrical material that a company might want to purchase, adapt, and develop into a movie

Alternate Title(s): Associate or Executive Story Editor

Salary Range: $35,000 to $60,000

Employment Prospects: Good

Advancement Prospects: Good

Best Geographical Location(s): Although a Story Editor could work anywhere, being located where there is a lot of moviemaking activity, such as Los Angeles/Hollywood or New York City, may be preferable

Prerequisites:

Education and Training—Although a degree is not required, a college or graduate degree with specialization in film is useful

Experience—Internship; on-the-job training as an assistant to the vice president or director of development

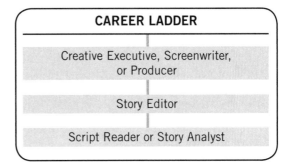

CAREER LADDER

Creative Executive, Screenwriter, or Producer

Story Editor

Script Reader or Story Analyst

Special Skills and Personality Traits—Friendly; team player; able to find out about available properties through reading, networking, and maintaining a clear vision of what movies he or she wants to help acquire and develop; excellent writing skills

Position Description

The Story Editor supervises the script readers or story analysts who work in his or her department or on a freelance basis. They are in charge of all the readers of screenplays who collectively are on the lookout for material for a film company to develop into a movie. That material might be from an original screenplay, a book, a play, or an article that is optioned and developed into a screenplay, or other related material such as true-life stories from the news.

What a Story Editor does may depend upon the size of the company he or she works for. A smaller production company may have just one person who is the Story Editor and reviews screenplays, plays, or books that are sent to the company for consideration. At a larger production company, a Story Editor may not be allowed to cultivate relationships with agents or publishers for direct submissions; that may be the job of the creative executive. At some companies, however, the Story Editor may be performing that function as well.

If the assistant to the vice president or director of development has done all the more entry-level jobs, such as answering the phone, and he or she has been learning the ropes just by being at a production company or working for a literary agent or film studio, the next step is to become a Story Editor.

One of the key tasks of the Story Editor may be to supervise the script readers or story analysts in his or her department. According to Linda Stuart, a story analyst and author of *Getting Your Script through the Hollywood Maze,* in some smaller film companies the Story Editor may also be the story analyst. In a larger company, such as Disney, as many as 18 full-time story analysts may be employed, and Warner Brothers has 14. By contrast, according to Stuart, a smaller production company may rely on freelance story analysts, and the Story Editor may coordinate getting the materials to them and relaying their analyses to the director of development.

Although for many the job of Story Editor is a step on the ladder toward creative executive and, eventually, being head of one's own studio, it could also be a way to read many scripts and see which work and which do not, so that the next step is to become a screenwriter. This is another possible career path for a Story Editor and the one followed by Dan Bronson, who had a Ph.D. from Princeton University and taught English and American literature at Prescott College before getting an internship at Universal Studios. In *Working in*

Hollywood, Bronson describes how that internship led to his job as a story analyst in the story department followed by a job as executive Story Editor at Paramount Pictures. Bronson then became a full-time screenwriter; he adapted the novel *The Last Innocent Man,* starring Ed Harris, among other film writing projects.

Salaries

Salaries vary according to the budget for this position at the independent film company or studio. On average, Story Editors earn $35,000 to $60,000 a year.

Employment Prospects

There are more people reading scripts and writing coverage than there are Story Editors supervising their activities. However, it is a necessary job category in the film industry. Your employment prospects will be improved if you've come up the ranks at a smaller film company as an intern or a script reader or as a freelancer or staff story analyst at a studio. Literary or talent agents may have a Story Editor to supervise script readers, and casting directors may also have a Story Editor if their agency has enough script readers that need to be coordinated.

Advancement Prospects

Going to the next step in the career path ladder, director of development or creative executive, will depend on many factors, including having an opening in the next slot at the company you're at or being able to find a new company to relocate to where you can move up. Making good choices about whom to hire as a script reader, as well as what material or scripts to consider or develop, and networking so that others know about your skills as a Story Editor, will help you to advance.

Education and Training

Majoring in film, theater, communications, or English in college or graduate school, as well as being versed in all the classic and contemporary best movies, may provide a helpful background. Having excellent management skills, the ability to meet deadlines, being able to juggle multiple assignments, and a talent for finding the needle in a haystack—discovering the next big movie—will also help.

Experience, Skills, and Personality Traits

Story Editors should have a pleasant personality that makes others want to be around them. They must be able to work at a fast pace, often for little money. They should be articulate, good at networking, fast readers, humble, efficient, and excellent communicators.

Unions and Associations

Membership associations, such as Women in Film, New York Women in Film and Television, or the American Screenwriters Association, may help you find out about job openings as well as new screenplays or available properties that you could read and bring to your boss for consideration.

Tips for Entry

1. Intern at any independent film company or studio, which might lead to a job in the story department.
2. Find out if someone is leaving a job and ask to be considered as his or her replacement.
3. Keep up with the industry news and follow up if you learn that a company is rapidly expanding and needs someone to manage their story department.
4. Bring an amazing property to a company and let them know you're the one that discovered it.
5. Be willing to make someone's coffee and read scripts, for little or no pay, if necessary, just to get your foot in the door.
6. Accept a secretarial or clerical job at a film company, studio, literary, talent, or casting agency, and volunteer to read and evaluate screenplays, whether or not it is part of your job responsibilities.
7. Check out relevant openings listed at http://www.mandy.com or http://www.entertainmentcareers.net.

SCRIPT READER

CAREER PROFILE

Duties: Read screenplays and provide "coverage," including a summary of the screenplay and a recommendation about whether or not the script should be given further consideration by an independent production company, literary agency, or film studio

Alternate Title(s): Hollywood Reader; Story Analyst

Salary Range: $40 to $60 per script (nonunion); $27.89 to $33.52 per hour (Editors Guild Members)

Employment Prospects: Excellent

Advancement Prospects: Fair

Best Geographical Location(s): For staff jobs, major urban centers, especially Los Angeles/Hollywood and New York City; for freelancers, anywhere in the world

Prerequisites:

Education and Training—Bachelor's degree in English or film could be useful

Experience—Critical reading for book reports throughout school; writing film reviews for high school or college papers; internship during or after college; on-the-job training

Special Skills and Personality Traits—Vast knowledge of film classics and contemporary films; excellent writing skills; able to summarize and explain in a succinct and well-written way; organized; able to meet deadlines and perform under pressure; able to say no without guilt or remorse; hardworking; diligent; articulate; able to be critical

CAREER LADDER

Story Editor, Director of Development, Producer, or Agent

Script Reader

Administrative Assistant

Position Description

From the smallest production company with a staff of two to the largest studio with thousands of employees, the first person to read a screenplay and decide whether or not it goes on to the next step often is the Script Reader. Although many see this job as a stepping stone to becoming a story editor or director of development, some are content to stay Script Readers.

The Script Reader does for the producer, director of development, or literary agent what those busy professionals have no time to do, based on the sheer volume of material sent to them for consideration: They read through submissions and decide which ones are worth pursuing and which ones should be ignored. These Script Readers are not reading unsolicited material, since practically no one will read unsolicited material anymore for a whole host of reasons; they are the first to consider material that has been requested by the literary agent or the director of development.

In her book, *500 Ways to Beat the Hollywood Script Reader,* Jennifer Lerch, who has worked for more than a decade as a Hollywood Reader, including eight years at the William Morris Agency, explains the compelling force behind a Script Reader: "Every script reader in today's Hollywood wants to be the one to bring her boss the next Academy Award winner, the project that will draw top talent, the screen story that will define a generation—the best script around."

Lerch, who has covered nearly 10,000 projects, describes the key function of the Hollywood Reader as writing the document that can sink or swim a screenplay's chances of getting read—the dreaded coverage. She highlights four elements to coverage:

1. A one- to two-sentence summary of the story's *concept.*
2. Several paragraphs or pages that provide a detailed *synopsis* of the screenplay's storyline.
3. A *comments* page discussing the screenplay's pluses and minuses, comparing it to other movies, and with a definite decision about whether or not the company should buy, produce, or cast the screenplay.
4. A *graph* that shows whether the characters, dialogue, story and structure are excellent, good, fair, or poor and whether, ultimately, the Script Reader feels the screenplay falls into one of these three categories: *recommend, consider,* or *pass.*

Obviously, the best way to increase the prospects for advancement is to be the one who recommends not one or two but many screenplays that go the next step and actually do get made and become the big successes of future years. For some busy producers, directors, or literary agents, coverage may not substitute for reading the finished product but coverage that gives a "pass" usually guarantees a property will get rejected, at least at that company.

With so few screenplays that are actually optioned or developed ever becoming movies, let alone successful ones, it is clear why breaking out of the more entry-level slot of Script Reader is more difficult than it might seem.

Salaries

Nonunion readers who often work on a part-time or freelance basis get $40 to $60 per script. Members of the Editors Guild union receive $27.89 to $33.52 per hour minimum, depending on the length of time in the union. Hourly rates are $37.12 to $42.02, depending upon the length of union membership, if a treatment synopsis is required.

Employment Prospects

As long as there are more screenplays, novels, or plays that have to be evaluated for possible new movies than there are decision makers who have time to wade through all the material, there will be a need for Script Readers. Whether the Script Reader works for a literary agent, a small production company, or a major movie studio, Script Readers are the first step in a long and complex process. The story department at a studio has to first go to the union of Script Readers if they need to hire someone. If all the union readers are unavailable, a nonunion Script Reader may be hired. After working for 30 consecutive days, the nonunion Script Reader is eligible for membership in the union.

Advancement Prospects

Although there is always a need for Script Readers as the first line of consideration for new material, there are fewer slots as people wish to go up the ladder. It is probably easier, initially, to move horizontally, from Script Reader to another Script Reader position at a different company, than it is to move up to the next rung, story editor.

Education and Training

Although not a requirement, having a college degree and even a graduate degree in film or film studies may help you land that first job. It is especially useful if the college has an internship program with production companies, which are always looking for new Script Readers because the pay is so low and the turnover is so great. In addition to studying film at film school or in college, having excellent writing skills is a must. Have a work sample ready when you are job hunting so that you are able to show that you know how to write coverage on a screenplay.

Experience, Skills, and Personality Traits

A Script Reader needs to be willing to take directions and commands from her or his superiors as to what screenplays or properties are to be read and as to when the coverage is due back. The ability to adhere to deadlines, often tight, is a must, as is the ability to write clearly, succinctly, and definitively under pressure. The Hollywood Reader has to form an opinion about a screenplay and back up that decision, as well as handle the ramifications of being wrong, saying something should be passed on only to have it picked up by another studio that turns it into a big hit, or suggesting something be bought and developed, only to have it turn out to be one of the biggest failures of the year when it is finally released.

Unions and Associations

The Story Analysts Local 854 merged with Editors Guild Local 700 (http://www.editorsguild.com), part of the International Alliance of Theatrical and Stage Employees (IATSE). It is now called the Motion Picture Editors Guild, IATSE Local 700. Union Script Readers usually work at the major studios. Freelance story analysts need not be in the union, but membership in various film industry professional associations, such as Women in Film and New York Women in Film and Television, may be beneficial.

Tips for Entry

1. Throughout the school years, including as early as middle school and high school, work on your critical skills with every book you read and report on as well as every movie you watch. Learn to compare and contrast new writing to published books.
2. Watch as many classic and contemporary films as possible, so you have a vast knowledge of film to compare any new properties to.
3. Let everyone and anyone know that you're looking for work as a Script Reader and that you're ready to take an internship or an entry-level job whenever it becomes available. Don't be shy about asking anyone and everyone you know who

knows someone in the movie business if they know someone who could use a Script Reader.

4. Develop a wide network of other Script Readers and keep tabs on who is moving up and moving on so you are ready to jump in if a job becomes available.

5. Go to screenplay seminars and film festivals and network for jobs.

6. Think long term. If this is a stepping stone to your film career, focus on the experience you will gain and the knowledge you will develop of what works and does not work as a screenplay.

7. Take a course in story analysis at a local college, such as the course offered by UCLA in the Extension Department, "Story Analysis and Script Development for Film and Television."

8. Go through the *Hollywood Creative Directory,* a regularly updated very comprehensive guide to independent producers and film studios, available through local bookstores or through their Web site, http://www.hcdonline.com. Contact every company listed where you would want to work and ask if they need a Script Reader.

LITERARY AGENT

CAREER PROFILE

Duties: Sell the work of screenwriters; get screenwriters writing assignments; represent screenwriters to producers or film companies; and handle the optioning of novels or other literary materials for possible development as movies

Alternate Title(s): Agent

Salary Range: $15,000 to $200,000+

Employment Prospects: Good

Advancement Prospects: Fair

Best Geographical Location(s): It's preferable to be based near the movers and shakers in the film industry in Los Angeles/Hollywood or New York City, so that in-person meetings are easier, but the Internet, fax, and cell phone makes it possible to work from anywhere as long as there is a willingness to travel for meetings on a regular or as-needed basis

Prerequisites:

Education and Training—Although not a requirement, a college or advanced degree in film or English is helpful; on-the-job training at a film company or literary agency

Experience—Internship; starting as an administrative assistant and working up to assistant to a Lit-

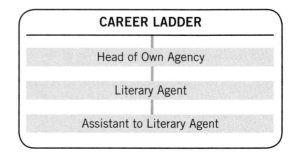

CAREER LADDER

Head of Own Agency

Literary Agent

Assistant to Literary Agent

erary Agent; reading screenplays at a production company is also helpful experience

Special Skills and Personality Traits—Able to deal with people; comfortable juggling multiple projects and personalities; capable of performing well under pressure; able to say no; hardworking; able to develop screenwriting talent and cultivate good working relationships among the various components of the film industry, including the screenwriter, director, producer, casting director, and actors; legal knowledge to negotiate contracts or the ability to delegate that aspect of the contract to a lawyer on staff or on retainer

Special Requirements—Signatory of the Writers Guild of America is helpful

Position Description

There are Literary Agents who only represent screenwriters to independent production companies or the studios. There are also Literary Agents who deal with the film industry and who also represent book authors, publishing companies, or playwrights, but those representations are for the film rights of those properties only, not for additional book deals or stage performance rights.

Sometimes, the Literary Agent who specializes in representing screenwriters is part of a multipurpose literary agency that also has agents for book authors or playwrights. Sometimes, the agent may have an agency devoted just to screenwriters and the film industry. Or, the Literary Agent may be in the literary department of a talent agency, such as William Morris, with the literary department handling the screenwriters and film rights to book properties, and the talent agents representing actors, directors, and producers.

Unlike the book business, where most Literary Agents were once book editors at publishing companies who went off on their own and now represent authors to the publishers, agents who represent screenwriters may have a more eclectic road to this specialty. Bonnie Black started her talent agency in the mid-1990s and then branched out into representing screenwriters. Bonnie, who is president of Bonnie Black Talent & Literary Agency in Valley Village, California, began representing screenwriters when a friend with whom she played bridge, the author of a major hit movie, encouraged her to put in the paperwork with the Writers Guild of America and become an agent. Like many agents who represent both screenwriters and talent, she first tries to package a property with her own clients, but if she is unable to do that, she will go to the casting directors for other possibilities.

Do you have to live in Hollywood to be a Literary Agent? At the beginning stages of pitching a property to the film studios, you could do it all by phone. But once it is time to "take a meeting," as they say in the movie business, you need to be there in person, although you could of course fly in from anywhere for the meetings. "I always go with my client," says Bonnie Black.

There is a growing trend toward personal managers for screenwriters. A personal manager is someone who goes out and gets the work for his or her client. They usually work on a commission basis, like a Literary Agent, of 10 percent, but they are not authorized or trained to negotiate a deal for their client, only to find the deals. A screenwriter, even if he or she hires a personal manager, would still need a Literary Agent or an entertainment attorney or lawyer to negotiate the deal.

A specialized type of Literary Agent in the film industry is one who sells the film rights to books—final manuscripts or published books—nonfiction or fiction, but not screenplays. New York City–based literary agent Bill Contardi wears two hats: as a Literary Agent developing book writers and selling their work to publishers and as an agent who sells the dramatic rights for books to film and TV companies.

As a book agent, he works exclusively with Brandt & Hochman Literary Agents, Inc. As a dramatic rights agent, he works for himself on behalf of other independent agents and occasionally for Brandt & Hochman as well. Contardi has been with Brandt & Hochman for five years, representing a range of fiction and nonfiction that includes Valerie Ann Leff's debut novel, *Better Homes and Husbands*, which was optioned to NBC for development as a TV series. Previously he was a dramatic rights agent at William Morris Agency for 11 years. Prior to William Morris, Contardi was vice president of literary affairs at Warner Bros. and United Artists; in both instances, he was finding books for the studios to develop into features.

Contardi started out in the business as an editor, working for 10 years at various publishing companies. As a dramatic rights agent, Contardi has done book-to-film/TV deals for *The Lovely Bones, Roswell* (the TV series), *Princess Diaries, Earthsea* miniseries, and *Missing* (a Lifetime TV series), among others. He points out how much harder it is to sell the dramatic rights to books these days. Contardi says, "The era of the network TV movie is long gone with a few high-profile exceptions. For the most part, that was a great source of activity in the seventies through the 1990s for dramatic rights. Today there are fewer places to go in television with your less-than-best seller book. And the studios are looking for franchises—big-budget projects that have sequel potential like Indiana Jones, *Pirates of the Carib-*

bean, and Harry Potter and could yield megabucks [in the] box office and lucrative ancillary rights potential."

Contardi feels that all job experiences can be beneficial as long as you are learning. His background has been on all sides of the publishing business—from magazines, when he was just out of college, to paperback editorial, then brokering books to film and television. In his present work as a Literary Agent, Contardi draws on all these varied work experiences. The common denominator has been books and their potential as stories that can be told in all forms of media.

How do you break into the film business as an agent? You can follow Contardi's example, "covering all the bases" as he went from magazines and production to working in editorial at a publishing company to being employed in the literary department of a film company, followed by building a list of authors for a literary agency. But Contardi points out other routes: "You can go from assistant to an agent, seeing it from the ground up, or working as a book editor for a while and then switching over to the other side of the fence and selling books as a literary agent. You can also segue into film. Some literary agents are producers and agents or agents that become producers."

Salaries

From $15,000 to $25,000 (for entry-level jobs) to $200,000 or more. Most agents work on a commission basis, earning 10 percent to 15 percent of their clients' payments. Some may work on a salary basis at certain agencies.

Employment Prospects

Entry-level jobs are easier to get than those higher up the ladder. There is a lot of turnover at literary agencies, because the pay is so low for entry-level positions. Getting in the door as a Literary Agent is challenging, but it is a more accessible position than others in the film industry with more specialized educational, training, or union requirements, such as director. Ads for Literary Agent assistants will often appear in the trade publications or online; family friends or relatives may need a Literary Agent trainee on a part-time, seasonal, or permanent basis. Taking any secretarial or clerical job assisting at an established Literary Agent, with the agreement that you will also be allowed to learn how to evaluate screenplays and work toward an agent's position, is another way into this key job in the movie business. Even more than the publishing business, where there is still a possibility of a book author making submissions without a Literary Agent, screenwriters, especially if they wish to have their screenplays considered by major film studios, need a Literary Agent to represent their work.

Becoming a Literary Agent in the film industry is an exciting, high-powered job with enormous creative and earning potential. However, a Literary Agent's judgment has to be right enough times that his or her projects get made and earn creative acclaim as well as big box office grosses; word of mouth and a proven track record will build a reputation and help to keep getting those A-list screenwriters.

Advancement Prospects

If you make good decisions and the screenwriters you represent are successful, you will advance. If your clients' films don't get made, regardless of whether this is because of bad luck, bad timing, or a studio going belly up, your advancement prospects will be bleak to nil. A Literary Agent's reputation is based on the accomplishments of his or her clients and what money those clients are earning, since often the Literary Agent is paid on a commission basis (10 percent to 15 percent). Some Literary Agents also ask their screenwriter clients to cover certain out-of-pocket expenses, such as long-distance phone calls or overnight delivery services; others absorb those costs as part of the commission.

Education and Training

No formal education or training is required, although most Literary Agents will be college- or graduate-school-educated, with a major in film, film studies, theater, or English. However, any major in college or educational background will do, since the ability to recognize excellent screenwriting talent requires a judgment about screenplays that may be as much instinct as training. A knowledge of great movies, as well as a familiarity with the screenplays upon which those movies were based, is also useful. The selling part of the job, as well as the negotiating and contractual skills and knowledge that a Literary Agent needs, may be gained by studying marketing and contract negotiations and through an on-the-job apprenticeship, an internship, or paid job experiences.

Special Requirements

It is preferable to become a member of the union for screenwriters, the Writers Guild of America (WGA). Go to http://www.wga.org to find out what documentation and supporting materials are required. Signatories of the Writers Guild of America agree to adhere to the minimum payment schedule negotiated by the WGA on behalf of its screenwriter union members. Literary

Agents who are signatories also agree not to charge a reading fee to screenwriters whose work they agree to consider.

Experience, Skills, and Personality Traits

Literary Agents should have good communication skills over the phone, in person, and in writing. Being discreet and tight-lipped about deals and clients will help, as will getting a reputation for sound judgment and shrewdness. Honesty and reliability are other personality traits that will help an Agent go far, as will working hard to get the best possible deal for one's clients. Any experience in the film business that opens up the web of contacts that a Literary Agent needs, from the directors, casting agents, producers, and directors of development to the talent agents and Literary Agents for book authors, will increase the value of a Literary Agent to his or her clients.

Working for a Literary Agent, especially one who handles screenwriters, is excellent on-the-job training, as is working at a film studio or on a film to get a first-hand look at the film business.

Literary Agents need to handle many clients all at once and yet somehow make each client feel as if he or she is the only one being represented. Enjoying travel, for meetings or to film festivals to see the work of current or potential new clients, is also a plus. Being efficient, being able to delegate clerical work, and working well with others are other personality traits that will take a Literary Agent far. Most important of all is, of course, the good judgment about what screenplays will make great movies and which screenwriters have potential that should be cultivated. Relationships have to be fostered with producers, directors, casting directors, talent, independent film companies, and studio executives.

Unions and Associations

Membership in the Society of Authors' Representatives (SAR) is recommended but not necessary.

Tips for Entry

1. Find a screenwriter who is not yet represented by a Literary Agent and whose screenplay you believe has merit. If the screenwriter gives you the right to do so, sell it on his or her behalf. Nothing helps you gain entry to the world of agents than a successful deal, and the bigger, the better.
2. Offer to intern, for no pay if necessary, as the assistant to a Literary Agent or as the assistant to his or her assistant, just to learn the ropes. Offer to read scripts and write reports. (You will find

screenwriter agents listed at the Web site for the Writers Guild of America, www.wga.org)

3. Attend film conferences, film seminars, and screenwriting contest seminars and let Literary Agents know you are looking for a job, as well as tell screenwriters that you want to become a Literary Agent.

4. Take a related course in how to become a Literary Agent at an adult education program. If the teacher has a literary agency, offer to work for him or her as an intern if a paying job is unavailable.

5. Ask everyone you know, from family members to college or graduate school friends, acquaintances, or career counselors, to refer you to a Literary Agent, film company, or studio looking for someone to read and evaluate screenplays or even answer the phone and sort mail.

6. Check out the listings for assistants to literary agents at http://www.entertainmentcareers .net, http://www.mandy.com, and http://www. publishersmarketplace.com.

THE TALENT

CASTING DIRECTOR

CAREER PROFILE

Duties: Break down the script to determine what roles need to be filled; find, audition, and negotiate for the services of actors for a movie

Alternate Title(s): Casting Agent

Salary Range: Varies widely

Employment Prospects: Fair

Advancement Prospects: Fair

Best Geographical Location(s): Los Angeles/Hollywood, or any major urban center where there is a lot of moviemaking activity, such as New York City

Prerequisites:

Education and Training—No educational requirements, although a knowledge of film and acting is useful; most training is on-the-job in the casting department at a studio, production company, or casting agency

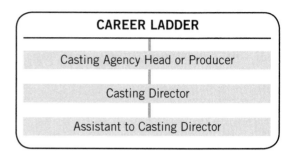

CAREER LADDER

Casting Agency Head or Producer

Casting Director

Assistant to Casting Director

Experience—Several years in lower-level positions, such as administrative assistant, receptionist, or assistant to a Casting Director

Special Skills and Personality Traits—Instinct about acting talent; ability to apply an actor's proven abilities in one role to a new, unknown one; organized; knowledge of Screen Actors Guild (SAG) rules, how to hold auditions, and contracts; excellent networking skills; team player

Position Description

Even when a movie goes into production with some major box office stars attached, there is still a need to find, audition, and select the other principal and supporting actors.

The Casting Director works for the studio, production company, director, or producer. They do not work for talent, in contrast to the literary agent, whose client is the screenwriter, and the talent agent, whose client is the actor. The Casting Director's client is the company making the film.

The Casting Director's first job is to take a script and break it down into scenes, noting all the characters in the screenplay, how many lines of dialogue they speak, and their characteristics. Breaking a script down as thoroughly as possible may make a big difference in casting options, as well as the movie's budget. Knowing that a particular character only says so many lines or is in so many scenes might make it possible to hire an actor who would be unavailable for more extensive scenes and days of shooting.

Janet Hirshenson and Jane Jenkins, who founded The Casting Company in 1981, discuss their careers as Casting Directors with coauthors Alexandra Brouwer and Thomas Lee Wright in *Working in Hollywood.* Jenkins went from acting to casting; having that back-

ground was definitely a plus for her, as she explained: "The advantage I had was that I knew a lot about actors from my prior existence as an actress." By contrast, Hirshenson got into casting through a temporary secretarial job that landed her in the casting offices of Rastar Films, answering phones. She became the Casting Director's assistant and cast her first movie three years later. Noted Hirshenson: "We start off with the leads—determine whether they're 'name' or 'nonname.' If it's name, then we make some lists, we call for availability. If it's nonname, then we bring in pictures."

Although there are lots of business details associated with being a Casting Director, Jenkins, who together with Hirshenson has cast such films as *A Beautiful Mind* and *When Harry Met Sally,* emphasized: "Business aspects aside, most important of all, you've got to learn who the actors are and learn as much as you can about what they are capable of."

Salaries

Since there is no union for Casting Directors, salaries will vary depending on a film's budget and whether a casting agent is a freelance or independent Casting Director, working for a studio casting department. As a Casting Director gets a reputation for excellent choices that help a film's success, he or she will get larger fees.

Well-established Casting Directors may earn much more than six figures a year.

Employment Prospects

Casting is pivotal to every film project, so there will always be a need for entry-level workers employed by a studio or in an independent casting office.

Advancement Prospects

This is a highly specialized skill and talent that is developed over years of on-the-job experience. Since so much of the knowledge is acquired by working from the bottom up, advancement prospects are improved if you take a longer view of your career. Directors or producers will request a specific Casting Director with whom they've worked before.

Education and Training

Studying acting or film, especially casting, may be helpful but is not necessary. Being able to recognize acting talent, being able to understand the director's vision for the character, and being able to find an actor who will best fulfill that vision are skills acquired through on-the-job training. Go to as many plays as possible, and see as many movies as you can, to become knowledgeable about good acting, as well as the acting range of available actors, since you will be drawing from that same pool of available talent for your own casting assignments.

Experience, Skills, and Personality Traits

Doing the casting in student, local, or professional plays or films offers training. The ability to pick the right talent for each part is the key skill for a Casting Director; being able to meet deadlines and work with the film's team, especially the director and producer, are also important. Organizational skills will help the Casting Director keep on top of all the available talent as well as the résumés and head shots that are submitted from all the potential new talent. Networking skills will help the Casting Director know who's doing what, as well as introduce him or her to the talent agents whose clients he or she will be considering for parts.

Unions and Associations

Casting Directors are not part of a union. Membership in the casting association, Casting Society of America (http://www.castingsociety.com), may be useful for networking and learning about potential jobs.

Tips for Entry

1. Begin as an administrative assistant or receptionist to a casting agency or in the casting department at a studio.
2. Cast a student film or a low-budget independent feature film and let those in the industry, including established Casting Directors, see the finished film as an example of your casting skills.
3. Find out about any local activities of film associations, attend film festivals, and sign up for seminars that include Casting Directors, and network for possible job openings.
4. Apply for a for-credit or noncredit internship in the casting department at a production company or studio or working for an independent casting director.
5. Attend any networking functions open to the public organized by the Los Angeles or New York offices of the Casting Society of America. They hold an annual awards ceremony that bestows the Artios Awards for excellence in casting. Visit their Web site, http://www.castingsociety.com, for details on upcoming awards and other educational and networking events that you could attend.

PRINCIPAL ACTOR

CAREER PROFILE

Duties: Play the characters in a film; act out the screenwriter's words and movements; become the vehicle through which the writer and director's vision for the story are communicated to the audience

Alternate Title(s): Thespian; Film Star; Talent

Salary Range: Varies widely

Employment Prospects: Fair

Advancement Prospects: Fair

Best Geographical Location(s): Major filmmaking centers, especially Los Angeles/Hollywood and New York City

Prerequisites:

Education and Training—Formal education is not necessary, but a college or graduate degree, studying acting or film, is helpful; also useful is training in acting for film, as well as related skills, such as dialect, dancing, fencing, or singing

Experience—Working on student or independent films, in theater, in commercials, or on television

Special Skills and Personality Traits—Outgoing; introspective; determined; able to withstand rejection; able to interpret a character; willing to dress up in unique contemporary, historical, or fantasy clothing or makeup

Special Requirements—Union membership may be required

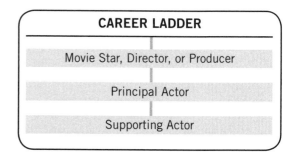

CAREER LADDER

Movie Star, Director, or Producer

Principal Actor

Supporting Actor

Position Description

Being a Principal Actor in a film is the stuff that dreams are made of. Actors have been enchanting audiences for centuries and certainly before movies. Of course some who performed for the stage have attained international reputations and acclaim, but the film industry has catapulted the job of actor to one with global attraction and instant name recognition.

There are as many myths about what it takes to become a successful film star as there are facts. Legions of boys and girls and men and women from throughout the United States and from around the world flock to Hollywood in search of fame and fortune. Few will become the leading stars of the stature of a Greta Garbo or a Laurence Olivier with the wealth of a Will Smith or a Julia Roberts. But there are still jobs for character and supporting actors as well as lesser roles that may provide enough work to earn a living or be the primary wage earner for a family. However, there are simply more people who want to become actors than there are parts for them to play.

Yes, hard work and luck are key factors in determining which actors become famous and bankable "A-list" box office stars. But having enough basic talent, training that capitalizes on that talent, a savvy manager or

talent agent that helps them make the best choices for their career are also important.

As newcomers get positive reviews and begin to make a name for themselves, they are going to be offered parts for certain types. Getting "typecast," as it's called, can be a double-edged sword. On one hand, an actor can begin to build a career around playing a certain character type; John Wayne certainly did. But it could get harder and harder to land those roles if the actor's performance fails to live up to expectations. Also, once an actor is typecast, it becomes more difficult for them to play other types of characters. This isn't always due to acting ability, but often to audience expectation. They identify certain actors with specific characteristics. On the other hand, some actors have succeeded in playing against type. It can be used as a strategy for an actor to make a comeback after their career of playing the same character has waned.

As actors age, they often have to move into a different type or category. This is particularly true for child or teenage actors, such as Roddy McDowall, who worked for years as a child actor and then later as a middle-aged character actor. Since so many movies are made for younger or teen and young adult audiences, there are fewer and fewer leading parts for aging thespians. A willingness to play supporting roles or character parts will help extend an actor's longevity in the movies.

Unfortunately, just as many think that if they can put a sentence down on paper, they should be able to write a screenplay, there are those who think that because they excelled as the lead in the college play, they can be a movie star. Some will be able to, and they will make it; others may not have the talent, the timing, the right support for their career, or even the stamina to take the rejection after rejection that may be necessary before getting that first role or that ideal part that makes one shine.

Many of the leading movie stars today started out on the stage, doing sitcoms on television, or even having supporting or leading roles in movie of the week (MOW) or made-for-TV movies. Still others got much needed experience doing commercials or acting in amateur or regional theater companies.

Joining SAG is an enormous step. According to the Screen Actors Guild Web site (http://www.sag.org), "Performers are eligible to join Screen Actors Guild after working on a SAG film in a principal role, gaining 'Taft-Hartley' status 15 days after the first day of work—or meeting background entry requirements."

Being eligible to join the union is a rite of passage in a film actor's career; it means that the actor will now be compensated under the contracts SAG has negotiated on behalf of their members with SAG signatories, that is, producers who sign a contract or letter of agreement with the union that they will abide by the union's terms. Once an actor joins SAG, he or she is forbidden from working for free or for companies that fail to become signatories. At the SAG Web site, this mandate is referred to as Rule One.

Nonunion members may work for a SAG signatory for 30 days; after that time, they must join the union in order to accept any additional union work in the future. New members pay an initiation fee plus the first semiannual basic dues. Those who are eligible to join are asked to contact the nearest SAG office before scheduling an appointment so they can be notified about the amount of their joining fee. After that, SAG dues are based on a percentage of all earnings under SAG contracts in the prior calendar year. For details on how to qualify for SAG membership, go to their Web site or contact the headquarters in Los Angeles or the affiliated office in New York City (see Appendix IV).

A career as an actor in the movies requires working long hours for weeks or months at a time, often in rough terrain or distant locations. It is possible to have a career as a movie actor from anywhere in the world, if you are willing to travel for auditions and to whatever locations are necessary for the shoot. In practice, especially when starting out, it is much harder outside of Hollywood than if you live there or nearby. The majority of movies are still made in Hollywood and other parts of California. Although it is unlikely that you'll be discovered waitressing in a coffee shop on Sunset Boulevard, it is a lot easier to rush from the all-important day job to an audition if you live in the same city than if you're across the country or in another state.

You can learn how other actors have succeeded by reading their autobiographies or biographies, as well as by attending seminars where they are guest speakers. But every story is unique; you may pick up some suggestions from what worked for others, but ultimately you have to forge your own trail.

Alan Alda is an actor whose career has included starring as Hawkeye in the hit TV series *M*A*S*H*, which had an enormously successful 11-year run; writing, directing, and starring in such movies as *The Four Seasons* (1981); as well as acting in numerous other movies or TV series, such as *The Aviator* (2004), *Resurrecting the Champ* (2007), and *The West Wing* (TV). He's also added best-selling author to his credits with the publication of his two memoirs: *Never Have Your Dog Stuffed* (2005), followed by *Things I Overheard While Talking to Myself* (2007).

More than two decades ago, Alda said to Fred Yager, who was interviewing him for the Associated Press about his just-released movie *The Four Seasons*, "Nothing important has ever been accomplished without chutzpah." Alda went on to say, "You can't be successful [as an actor] without being exposed to criticism," advice he stands by today.

Salaries

Of the almost 120,000 members of the Screen Actors Guild (SAG), the average yearly income for most actors is $5,000, because employment may be intermittent and irregular. At the other end of the spectrum, some stars get $20 million for one film. In 2000, the median annual income was $25,910. As of July 1, 2007, actors who are members of SAG or the American Federation of Television and Radio Artists (AFTRA) with speaking parts must earn from $759 to $2,634 for a 5-day week.

Sometimes, in order to get a low-budget feature film made, actors are willing to work for "scale," the minimum amount of money allowed for a particular part and number of days by the union, and to defer additional income, if and when the film earns a profit. That arrangement is, of course, a gamble on the actor's part, since he or she could be out the millions in salary that he or she could command for another movie if the movie fails to turn a profit. Jack Nicholson took a deferred salary for his performance in *Batman,* as did Tom Hanks for his role in *Forrest Gump.* For both the gamble paid off financially, as they each earned tens of millions of dollars.

Employment Prospects

This is an extremely competitive category. There are simply many more people seeking acting roles in movies than there are roles to go around. There are nearly 120,000 members of the Screen Actors Guild, and only a fraction are employed at any given time. Also, an actor has a series of temporary jobs; once a film is finished, the job is over and the search for employment begins all over again.

Advancement Prospects

If breaking into acting is highly competitive, growing a successful career is even harder. Only a handful of the thousands of actors starting out each year become movie stars. Some, such as Drew Barrymore or Mel Gibson, take control of advancing their careers by becoming producers or directors.

Education and Training

Acting in school, college, or graduate school is helpful but not required. Studying acting at an acting school, in college, or in graduate school may also be beneficial in terms of skills as well as networking. On-the-job training—acting in theater, commercials, television, or film—will be helpful. The variety of roads to success as a film actor are varied and diverse. Walter Matthau (*Grumpy Old Men, The Odd Couple*) studied acting at the Drama School of The New School in New York. Ben Stiller (*Meet the Parents*) dropped out of the University of California to pursue his acting dream. Stockard Channing (*Six Degrees of Separation*) graduated from Radcliffe College. Sylvester Stallone (*Rocky*) wrote the screenplay for *Rocky* and refused to sell it unless he could play the lead. Countless film actors started off performing on the stage. Brian Dennehy started acting off Broadway, became a film actor, and then returned to the stage on Broadway in *Death of a Salesman.* There are also examples of wrestlers-turned-movie-actors, such as Hulk Hogan and The Rock, as well as fashion models or rock stars who become successful actors, including Vanessa Williams and Jon Bon Jovi. Tom Hanks and Tim Allen starred in television sitcoms before becoming movie box office draws.

Even after graduating from acting school or majoring in drama at college, actors may continue to work on their acting techniques by studying with an acting teacher or coach or taking an acting class. Actors may also go for specialized training, depending on the specific parts they are auditioning for or are hired to play, such as learning how to box, practicing karate moves, conducting interviews, or observing in settings similar to the one into which they will be placed. Some actors, if asked to play a real person, may wish to meet that individual, if he or she is still living; others may prefer to study videotapes or audiotapes for physical mannerisms and vocal details. If a screenplay is based on a novel or play, actors may wish to read the original novel or attend a performance of the play to help develop their character.

Fine-tune the actor's instruments—the voice, body, and appearance. Whether you are aspiring to the leading role or a supporting character, you will want to be at your best in your acting skills, knowledge of film as well as of makeup, costume, dance, and speech, with as wide a background in literature and classic and contemporary films as possible.

Special Requirements

Union membership in the Screen Actors Guild (SAG), the union for film actors, may be required.

Experience, Skills, and Personality Traits

The ability to withstand rejection, a good memory, an ear for dialect and dialogue, and the power to understand the world from another's perspective are all important traits for an actor. One most also be at ease performing in front of others or able to do so despite fears or hesitancy. Most actors feel a need to please an audience. The ability to work well with others is essential, especially in taking orders from directors. Of course, there is a lot about acting that includes natural ability, but there is also a great deal that can be learned or fine-tuned, including movement, character interpretation, voice, how to audition, finding an agent or manager, and creating a portfolio of head shots and photographs.

Unions and Associations

Film actors may belong to several unions: Screen Actors Guild (SAG) for film work, American Federation of Television and Radio Artists (AFTRA) for television, and Actors Equity (AEA) for live performances on the stage. Associations such as Women in Film, Academy of Motion Picture Arts and Sciences, or clubs like the Players Club (http://www.theplayersnyc.org) may be helpful for networking about new job opportunities as well as for offering a place to share the common challenges of trying to make it as an actor.

Tips for Entry

1. Get plenty of training, whether at acting school, college, or graduate school, as well as acting experience through school, amateur, regional, or Broadway shows and in student or independent low-budget feature films.

2. Have a positive attitude, and follow up on every legitimate audition or acting lead.

3. Associate with other actors. Make sure casting directors or talent managers have your most recent head shot, credits, and demo video, so they can send you out on auditions.

4. Even if you have the talent, there's still a lot of luck and timing involved in breaking into acting for films. There may be as much time in between parts as there is doing a role, so be ready for those lulls, if they occur. Just keep acting and believing in your dream.

5. Read the trade publications *Variety* and the *Hollywood Reporter* in either the print or online versions (variety.com and hollywoodreporter.com).

6. Attend educational seminars on acting, film festivals, and film conferences.

7. Study with acting teachers who have excellent reputations as well as good connections in the business. They may recommend you to a talent manager or casting director that they know is looking for your type.

EXTRA

CAREER PROFILE

Duties: Appear in a film in the background or in crowd scenes

Alternate Title(s): Background Actors; Walk-ons, N/S (nonspeaking); Supporting Artists; Background Talent

Salary Range: SAG (Screen Actors Guild) rates are $130 to $145 a day

Employment Prospects: Good

Advancement Prospects: Poor

Best Geographical Location(s): Los Angeles/Hollywood, or anywhere there are a lot of movies being filmed, such as New York City, Orlando, and Toronto

Prerequisites:

Educational and Training—Acting training is not necessary but is helpful

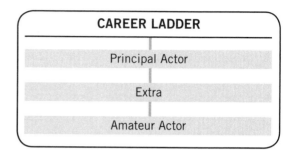

CAREER LADDER

Principal Actor

Extra

Amateur Actor

Experience—On-the-job training from each Extra experience

Special Skills and Personality Traits—Able to work long hours; able to wake up early in the morning, even as early as 4 A.M., for all-day shoots; patience; flexibility; available on short notice

Position Description

Extras or background actors are those union (SAG) or nonunion actors who make up crowd scenes, indoors or outside. In general, an Extra does not have speaking parts; but some may have speaking parts for which they receive higher pay.

Like so many others in filmmaking, the job of Extra appears to be easier than it really is. In addition to the time they might take to get into makeup or a costume, Extras must be available on short notice and willing to wait for hours—or longer—until their scene is shot. An Extra's work is often uncredited and, depending on how the film is cut, the scene that he or she appears in may not even make it into the final movie. Therefore, enjoying the work itself and being part of the process of making a movie, rather than fame, fortune, recognition, or even being part of the final cut of the movie, are some of the requirements of Extra work.

If a production company is a signatory of the Screen Actors Guild, there are guidelines about how many SAG Extras need to be employed before opening the hiring up to non-SAG members. These numbers vary by state; the production company should know what the guidelines are for their specific film.

There is another benefit to being an Extra. If a non-union actor has three jobs as a background performer (Extra) on a SAG film and the films have received waiv-

ers to employ him or her based on a special need, such as he or she has a certain look or speaks a language and the film company could not find a SAG member who could fill that part, those extra work experiences could qualify the actor to join SAG. (For more information on SAG, see the section on Principal Actors, the listing on SAG in Appendix IV, or go to their Web site, www.sag.org.)

Salaries

Most Extras also have another part-time or full-time job, or are students, since the work is so sporadic and short-term. Background actors who are members of the Screen Actors Guild (SAG) are entitled to the union minimums, which are $130 for a general Extra, $140 for someone whose photo is used in a scene or who has special abilities (such as roller skating), and $145 for an Extra who is a stand-in for a principal actor. Few Extras get rich from their experiences, but it is a way to get involved in the world of movies as well as to have the thrill of observing the making of a major feature film.

Employment Prospects

This definitely depends on where you live, since there will be much more work for Extras in Hollywood and New York City than there will be in cities or towns with fewer movies in production. However, even in the smallest community, if a movie is being filmed, there will probably be a need for Extras—and lots of them.

(To find out if a movie is being made in your area, contact your local film commission. See the state-by-state listings in Appendix VII.)

Advancement Prospects

Most Extra parts are nonspeaking, but there is the possibility of moving up to a part with a few speaking words or lines as well as getting known as an Extra with a special ability or distinctive feature that might make you someone who is requested for certain crowd scenes or situations.

Education and Training

Some acting training may be useful, but since Extras are technically often supposed to be just the "people on the street" or "faces in a crowd," no formal training is required.

Experience, Skills, and Personality Traits

Having a flexible schedule, so you can get a job as an Extra on very short notice, is a plus, as is having the patience to sit around for hours at a time waiting until you are needed. Extras have to be comfortable with their largely anonymous role, since they are not listed in the credits of a movie as actors will be. Being cooperative, able to take orders, willing to dress in whatever costume is necessary, and prepared to have any makeup applied or hairdo changes made for your specific part are also requirements.

Unions and Associations

It is not necessary to be in the acting union, the Screen Actors Guild (SAG), to get a job as an Extra. However, under certain circumstances, as noted above, acting in Extra parts could give an actor the credits he or she needs to be able to join SAG.

Tips for Entry

1. Keep track of movies that are being made in your community. Contact the state film commission; they may post that information at their Web site.

2. If you know anyone who is working for a film company or even a student who is shooting a film, let him or her know that you are willing to work as an Extra.

3. Check out what information and services are offered by Hollywood Operating Systems, a company that offers various services to Extras, including finding casting agencies that are looking to hire Extras mostly in Southern California. There is a minimum membership requirement of 3 months to join. For more information, go to http://www.hollywoodos.com.

TALENT AGENT

CAREER PROFILE

Duties: Manage the talent—actors, producers, directors, or musicians—who make movies

Alternate Title(s): Talent Manager

Salary Range: Varies widely

Employment Prospects: Fair

Advancement Prospects: Fair

Best Geographical Location(s): Los Angeles/Hollywood, and New York City are the best locations, followed by any other major urban centers where there is a lot of film activity, such as Chicago and Toronto

Prerequisites:

Education and Training—A college education, with a major in the liberal arts or business, as well as any graduate or specialized education in acting and film will be helpful

Experience—Working for a Talent Agent in a paid or internship position

Special Skills and Personality Traits—Able to thrive under intense pressure; able to handle

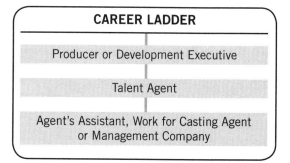

CAREER LADDER

Producer or Development Executive

Talent Agent

Agent's Assistant, Work for Casting Agent or Management Company

numerous clients as well as the multiple creative and business demands of dealing with the talent and their employers, such as film studios or independent production companies, simultaneously; enthusiastic personality; highly productive; able to work long hours; good interpersonal skills; persuasive

Special Requirements—Some states require licensing

Position Description

The power of the Talent Agent reached epic proportions in the 1990s, when the legendary Michael Ovitz was getting his acting clients the biggest salaries in Hollywood history. Talent Agents, in conjunction with literary agents who handle screenwriters, may also "package" movies by putting together the various elements of the film, from actors to director, and then taking the package to a studio. Most actors, as well as directors and producers, rely on their Talent Agent to get them work. It is their job to pitch their clients to the studios, directors, producers, or casting directors, if they hear about a new project that would be right for their client. The Talent Agent's job is not just to get work for his or her clients but to get the right projects. How often has a talented actor, who started out with one or two hit movies, faded into oblivion because the next couple of roles were "wrong" for him or her? Creating and developing a reputation in the film industry is dependent upon making the "right" choices, at least often enough that a body of work evolves that reflects well on the actor, director, or producer and showcases his or her skills in both a creative and commercial way. In addition to securing the work, the Talent Agent will

also negotiate the best deal for his or her client, taking into account such considerations as getting a client a share of merchandising income, a possible share in the profits of a film, and even such luxury demands as a private jet for traveling to and from location. Although the acting or directing unions may set the minimums for their members, Talent Agents can help those in demand get the maximum.

Donna DeStefano runs a talent management company, Siren Song Entertainment, Inc. (http://www.sirensongentertainment.net), based in New York City. She founded the company four years ago; it represents actors, directors, and writers. Although the more traditional career path to becoming a talent manager is to work for a management company or a casting director, starting off as someone's assistant to learn the business, DeStefano broke into the profession in a less direct way. DeStefano, a New Yorker who previously worked as a stockbroker, found that the terrorist attacks of September 11, 2001, caused her to rethink her career and her future goals: "After 9/11, I was staring at, 'What's next?' wanting to evaluate how I wanted to spend the rest of my years. I've always worked with artists. All of my friends were artists. I talked to a lot of people and then

I started with two or three clients. Now we have about a dozen clients."

What DeStefano especially likes about her job, besides helping talent with their careers, is that every day is different, interesting, and exciting. Says DeStefano: "That's the interest in it for me. It's never the same. How you spend the day, every single day, is different. It's that kind of spirit and mindset. It's not going to be a typical day at the office. I have two clients in a play tonight that just runs till the middle of the month so I went to see the matinee yesterday. Afterwards, I called people to tell them how amazing it was, to get people excited and to get people there. I'm just trying to get my clients to be at the top of the minds of the casting directors."

Enthusiastically saying, "I love what I do," DeStefano points out some of the personality traits that may help someone to succeed as a Talent Agent: "You have to be really comfortable with the instability of the job. Stomach for risk, the courage and guts to take a risk and to make a decision. It's a rogue kind of lifestyle. I work with every client differently. You have to be the kind of person who could individualize what needs to be done. It's not the same path twice. You need a real appreciation for the people that you represent, a love for the talent. It would get hard if you're not passionate about it. I've never heard anyone say it's easy. It's constantly complicated."

DeStefano, who works on a commission basis, talks on the phone weekly with her clients and also has individual weekly in-person meetings. She likes to celebrate with her clients when a project comes to fruition. The day after our interview, she took an actress client to lunch to cheer her landing the lead role in a feature-length film.

Salaries

The Talent Agent is paid on a commission basis (usually 10 percent) by the client, but the agent may get a salary from the company he or she works for, unless it is his or her own business. There may be other perks in addition to a salary, such as a company car, an expense account for business lunches, dinners, weekend entertaining, and travel, as well as funds for joining health clubs or associations where the networking to further the careers of their clients may occur. Salaries for Talent Agents range from next to nothing for those just starting out to six or seven figures or more for those who work with major stars.

Employment Prospects

It takes having the right connections as well as clients who are in demand to become established as a Talent Agent. The success of one's clients helps to advance the reputation of a Talent Agent. If a Talent Agent takes a chance on a client and his or her career does not develop in the way the agent had hoped it would, the agent may drop the client and try out new ones. Talent Agents have to meet their overhead, and they cannot do that if their clients are not earning salaries big enough to garner formidable commissions.

Advancement Prospects

Entry-level jobs within a talent agency may be easier to find than advancing to a Talent Agent with his or her own roster of clients. A Talent Agent's advancement is often directly tied to the success of and increasing fees for his or her clients.

Education and Training

A college degree is helpful, including training in business skills, as is a general knowledge of the film industry. However, even more important than education is the ability to work with people, to stand firm in making a deal but to not appear ruthless, to utilize a sense of business, and to show a sensitivity to the creative part of filmmaking. Learning how to negotiate as well as how to network and socialize may be as important as what college or graduate degrees a Talent Agent has achieved.

Special Requirements

Each state has its own licensing requirements. To be franchised by the Screen Actors Guild (SAG) as a Talent Agent, an agent must be licensed if it is a requirement in his or her state.

Experience, Skills, and Personality Traits

Working in an intense, highly competitive environment with multiple demands on your time requires that you be well organized and tough. With dozens or possibly even hundreds of phone calls each day, as well as résumés, pictures, e-mails, and performing DVDs coming into a talent agency on an ongoing basis, it is important to stay methodical as well as current in your client contacts and relationships. A Talent Agent has to know what her or his clients are doing, their availability, and what companies (producers, directors, or casting agents) are looking for. In addition to proficiency in writing, an ability to deal with people, excellent negotiating skills, and an effective phone demeanor are paramount. Talent Agents must also have a good memory, a genuine love of movies and talent, and the ability to make tough decisions about who to sign and who to let go.

Unions and Associations

The Association of Talent Agents (ATA), originally known as the Artists' Managers Guild when founded in 1937, is a nonprofit association of more than 120 agencies engaged in the Talent Agency business. For more information, see their Web site at http://www.agents association.com.

Tips for Entry

1. Get a job in the mailroom or as an administrative assistant at a talent agency.
2. Get your foot in the door at a talent agency by getting a summer internship, apprenticeship, or part-time job.
3. Go to educational seminars offered by the ATA in Los Angeles or New York.
4. Network informally or through associations with directors, producers, actors, and casting agents, and let them know about your interest in becoming a Talent Agent.

MAILROOM CLERK

CAREER PROFILE

Duties: Responsible for all mailroom duties, including sorting and distributing incoming and outgoing mail, managing all express mail service, and running errands

Alternate Title(s): None

Salary Range: $25,000 to $30,000

Employment Prospects: Good

Advancement Prospects: Fair

Best Geographical Location(s): Major urban centers, especially Los Angeles/Hollywood, New York City, and Chicago

Prerequisites:

Educational or Training—A college degree is expected

Experience—No experience is required; part-time or internship experiences throughout high school or college in office environments may be helpful

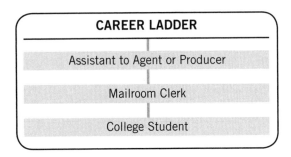

CAREER LADDER

Assistant to Agent or Producer

Mailroom Clerk

College Student

Special Skills and Personality Traits—Computer skills; a pleasant phone manner; ability to work well with people; well organized; enthusiastic; motivated; able to function in a fast-paced work environment

Position Description

A Mailroom Clerk in the film industry is a very different position than a Mailroom Clerk in practically any other industry. In the film industry, legend holds that becoming a Mailroom Clerk may be the rite of passage to becoming a talent or literary agent, executive at a film company, or even a screenwriter. Playwright and screenwriter Neil Simon, for example, was a Mailroom Clerk for Warner Bros.'s East Coast office following his discharge from the United States Army in 1946. The position of Mailroom Clerk includes the obvious tasks of sorting and distributing incoming and outgoing mail, managing express mail service, and performing occasional messenger duties, as well as running errands, handling copying and faxing of documents, and logging DVDs. But what the Mailroom Clerk position affords is truly getting one's foot in the door of the film industry—learning how a company works and who the people are at that company, from the ground floor up.

Salaries

This is an entry-level position. Salaries are determined by the size of the company as well as its geographical location. Some will earn minimum wage, up to $8 to $9 an hour, while others could earn from $25,000 to $30,000 a year. Mailroom Clerk positions at major talent agencies or studios generally receive a full benefits package along with a salary, including healthcare, 401(k) opportunities, and retirement.

Employment Prospects

Every company over a certain size needs a Mailroom Clerk, since dealing with ingoing and outgoing mail and related materials, such as contracts, DVDs, casting photos, résumés, and supporting materials is so much a part of the process of making a movie.

Advancement Prospects

Although all offices over a certain size need a Mailroom Clerk, the opportunities to advance to the next level, mailroom supervisor, and, from there, into a position as a talent or literary agent, script reader, or development executive are limited. The reputation one achieves while performing the Mailroom Clerk duties, the skills that the Mailroom Clerk acquires beyond the regular mailroom duties, and the executives he or she befriends within the company and the industry are factors in a Mailroom Clerk's advancement.

Education and Training

A college degree is expected. Computer skills, such as how to use Microsoft Word or a computer e-mail management program, may be helpful in getting the job initially. Internships or paid jobs throughout the school years or summer breaks that offer opportunities to work with a company's mail, as well as answering the phone and interacting with people in a company setting, will also be useful.

Experience, Skills, and Personality Traits

Although technically no experience is required, prior office or mailroom experience will be useful. Skills related to the duties of the Mailroom Clerk, such as handling outgoing and incoming mail and going on errands, are the obvious ones but it also helps to have an excellent phone manner and to be efficient, hardworking, and pleasant to be around. Knowledge of the various mail services, such as the United States Postal Service, FedEx, and UPS, as well as other overnight options, is useful. Personality traits include being highly motivated, energetic, and committed to a career in the film industry.

Unions and Associations

There are no unions or associations for mailroom clerks.

Tips for Entry

1. Get to know the Mailroom Clerks at the companies you want to work at. Keep track of their career advancement, since they might be encouraged to find their replacement when they are promoted.

2. Read the want ads in the industry trades, such as the *Hollywood Reporter,* as well as online services, such as http://www.entertainmentcareers.net.

3. Network at parties, industry seminars, and trade shows, letting executives or human resource managers at specific companies know that you want to get a job as a Mailroom Clerk.

4. Register with a temporary employment agency and be willing to take any Mailroom Clerk openings, since a temporary replacement job might lead to a permanent slot.

5. To shine above the competition, attend one of the national seminars offered by National Association of Professional Organizers (NAPO) (go to: http://www.napo.net for more information) and also read up on organizing and mailroom procedures.

6. For examples of real-life mailroom-to-major-Hollywood-player stories, read David Rensin's book *The Mailroom: Hollywood History from the Bottom Up* (Ballantine Books, 2003).

STUNT COORDINATOR

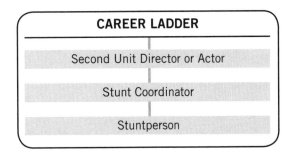

Position Description

The Stunt Coordinator is responsible for all the details related to every stunt in a movie, from the simplest car chase to the most complicated fall or high dive. From the earliest filmmaking days of the stunt-filled comedies of Buster Keaton and Charlie Chaplin, stuntpersons and Stunt Coordinators have been performing in movies. Stuntpersons stand in for principal actors, who may not be capable of such demanding physical actions or who may be unwilling to take the physical risks of getting hurt. Often the financial entity will prohibit a principal actor from performing his or her own stunts, because an injury could cause filming to stop, thereby adding hundreds of thousands or millions of dollars to the budget.

As the types of movies that are popular have changed, so too have the demands on the Stunt Coordinator. For instance, for many decades, the western was dominant in Hollywood, creating the necessity of coordinating the riding of horses. Car chase and car racing movies go in and out of favor. Action movies requiring numerous stunts continue to be among the most popular movies being made today.

Working closely with the director, one of the Stunt Coordinator's most primary concerns is safety. Here, preparation is key. Because stunts are often dangerous to begin with, all necessary precautions have to be taken to ensure that the stuntperson will survive the stunt unharmed.

An experienced Stunt Coordinator will know which stunts are possible and which will have to be replaced by computer-generated digital special effects graphics. Since the Stunt Coordinator hires the stuntpersons on his or her team, he or she will know who is capable of completing each stunt.

Salaries

According to Screen Actors Guild minimums, which increase annually, the weekly rate for Stunt Coordinators is $759 a day or $2,828 per week. More experienced coordinators or those in demand for their special skills can earn higher pay rates.

Employment Prospects

As long as action movies are a mainstay of Hollywood, Stunt Coordinators will be required. However, computer-generated art has been utilized in the last decade for images that previously might have been the responsibility of the Stunt Coordinator.

Advancement Prospects

While Stunt Coordinators may not be as necessary as they used to be due to advances in digital technology, some may make the transition to principal actor or even director. Hal Needham was famous as a Stunt Coordinator before he made his film directorial debut in *Smokey and the Bandit*.

Education and Training

Stunt Coordinators have previously been stuntpersons, so they already have the physical skills that are required to fall without getting hurt and the necessary athletic abilities, including proficiency in such sports as boxing, karate, gymnastics, swimming, and climbing. Training in safety is as important as the preparation for the stunts that they will perform.

Experience, Skills, and Personality Traits

Prior experience as a stunt person is crucial preparation for the job of Stunt Coordinator. In addition to the required athletic skills, a Stunt Coordinator needs to know how to manage a team of stunt professionals, as well as how to work with the director, writer, producer, and talent.

Unions and Associations

There is an invitation-only association for stunt people, with 128 members, known as the Stuntmen's Association of Motion Pictures (http://www.stuntmen.com). Members of the association are required to belong to the Screen Actors Guild (SAG).

Tips for Entry

1. Moving from stunt person to Stunt Coordinator is a usual career progression, so let it be known when you are performing stunts that you would like to become a coordinator.
2. Stay aware of the career plans of the Stunt Coordinators that you are working with. If they move up to second assistant director or leave to become actors, there may be a vacancy.
3. Network with casting directors, writers, producers, and directors, as well as other stuntpersons.

STUNTPERSON

CAREER PROFILE

Duties: Perform the demanding physical stunts or activities that actors cannot or prefer not to do as part of a movie

Alternate Title(s): Stuntman; Stuntwoman; Stunt Double

Salary Range: $5,000 to $70,000; for projects covered by SAG (Screen Actors Guild) $100 to $759 per day, depending on the budget of the movie.

Employment Prospects: Good

Advancement Prospects: Fair

Best Geographical Location(s): Major urban centers where filmmaking occurs, such as Los Angeles/ Hollywood, New York City, Chicago, and Toronto

Prerequisites:

Education and Training—Athletic training; stunt training; safety instruction

Experience—Working in the industry, including TV commercials, TV series, feature films, or documentaries

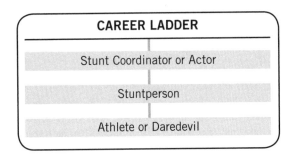

CAREER LADDER

Stunt Coordinator or Actor

Stuntperson

Athlete or Daredevil

Special Skills and Personality Traits—A combination of bravado and caution; the ability to follow the directions of the stunt coordinator and to be part of the filmmaking team

Special Requirements—Union membership may be required

Position Description

Stuntpersons are trained to perform the physical stunts that actors cannot or will not do in a movie. The importance of a Stuntperson to actors is so well established today that a performer may request a particular stunt double as part of contractual arrangements for a new film. Stuntpersons do everything from car chases and horseback riding to karate fighting and jumping off buildings. Stunt performers may specialize in those stunts that they are best at, such as high falls, swimming, horse falls, or karate. Being a Stuntperson, like many jobs that rely on physical stamina and depend upon being in optimum shape, is a career that needs a back-up for future opportunities.

A Stuntperson works for the stunt coordinator, who prepares and choreographs each stunt, making sure all safety precautions are taken and that the illusion that the principal actor is actually performing the stunt is achieved. Keep in mind that this position calls for a high degree of risk and injuries, and fatalities do sometimes occur.

A Stuntperson is a daredevil at heart, and if there is one common trend among action films, it is that stunts have to become more breathtaking each time.

That means whenever a record is set in length of falls, time on fire, or in any number of dangerous stunts, the bar gets raised to appease the audience's insatiable appetite for bigger and better stunts. This job is not for the faint of heart.

During filming, the Stuntperson is dressed and made up to look as much like the principal actor whom he or she is replacing for the stunt shot. For example, if a character has to fall off a roof following a punch, the Stuntperson will be the one falling. Today, with computer-generated digital graphics, an actor's face can actually be digitized over that of a Stuntperson, so that it actually appears as if the principal actor has fallen off the building.

Some actors, primarily male actors, do many of their own stunts, but this usually is allowed only if an insurance policy can be obtained to cover any losses due to delays in shooting caused by a principal actor being injured.

Salaries

Varies from $5,000 to $70,000 a year, with a more typical range of $28,000 to $50,000. Pay is often determined by the experience of the Stuntperson, the nature of the stunt, and the budget of the movie. For projects covered by SAG (Screen Actors Guild), the day rate depends on the budget of the movie: $100 a day for a low-budget film to $268/day, $504/day, or $759/day for a regular-budget film (anything above $2.5 million).

Employment Prospects

Just one of countless examples of movies utilizing dozens of Stuntpersons is the 2002 John Woo movie *Windtalkers*, a World War II movie with lots of action. Stuntpersons are still in demand, even though computer-generated animation is substituted for some stunts. The rising number of films made each year and the continued popularity of the action adventure film genre means that there should be steady opportunities for Stuntpersons.

Advancement Prospects

Qualified Stuntpersons are so specialized that mastering the skills of stunt work leads to good advancement prospects. However, because a Stuntperson's work is very physically demanding, like many jobs that rely almost completely on physical acumen, there are concerns about how long someone would want to continue performing stunt work. Advancing to a stunt coordinator or even an actor are definite career possibilities, as is becoming a second unit director.

Education and Training

To become a Stuntperson, athletic training is useful, including learning such skills as scuba diving, karate, horseback riding, gymnastics, and climbing. Training in how to fall without getting hurt is helpful. College or graduate school education is not a requirement, but it might prove beneficial for pursuing other jobs later.

Special Requirements

Membership in the Screen Actors Guild (SAG) may be required.

Experience, Skills, and Personality Traits

Necessary experience includes having enough familiarity with the required athletic skills so that they can be performed safely in the film. Being as concerned with safety as with the athletic activities is pivotal, as is the ability to work with the stunt coordinator and the other members of the film crew, including the director, producer, writer, casting director, and talent. Some Stunt Doubles may need to look like the actor for whom they are substituting in the film.

Unions and Associations

There is an invitation-only association of Stuntpersons, the Stuntmen's Association of Motion Pictures (http://www.stuntmen.com), that requires membership in SAG as well. For more information, go to the Web site for SAG (http://www.sag.org) or call its headquarters.

Tips for Entry

1. Attend workshops for Stuntpersons and network with the attendees and workshop leaders.
2. Network with casting directors, producers, directors, and writers; let them know that you are available as a Stuntperson.
3. Achieve success in your athletic skills. Let people you meet through athletic events and contests know that you wish to apply your physical abilities to a career as a Stuntperson.

CHOREOGRAPHER

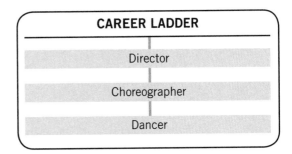

CAREER LADDER

Director

Choreographer

Dancer

Position Description

Choreographers are responsible for creating any dance sequences in a movie, and they can make or break musicals or movies with a dance theme, such as *Chicago, West Side Story, Flashdance, Footloose,* or *Across the Universe*. The Choreographer also scouts and teaches dance "doubles," those dancers who, like stunt doubles, have to perform the dance steps for an actor due to the technical difficulty of the moves; the dance doubles used in *Flashdance* are famous examples of this.

The scope of dance in any particular movie will determine the Choreographer's involvement. Full-blown musicals that require a series of dance numbers usually also require a Choreographer to be brought on during preproduction to work out any complicated dance sequences and shots with the director.

For the film *Flashdance*, Choreographer Jeffrey Hornaday had to create a form of dance that didn't actually exist, except in the mind of the screenwriter. According to the book *Working in Hollywood*, two weeks before principal photography was to begin, Hornaday was brought into the project by director Adrian Lyne, who outlined the emotional framework of the dance scenes and how they fit into the story. It was then up to Hornaday to create the dances to fit the music that had been written prior to the film's shooting.

Salaries

Salaries will vary greatly, depending upon the budget of the film and the reputation of the Choreographer. Choreographers in a movie may earn from $2,000 to $5,000 a week.

Employment Prospects

The success of the movie *Moulin Rouge* in 2001 led to a renewed interest in making movie musicals including the 2002 hit *Chicago* and *Across the Universe* (2007), directed by Julie Taymor and set against a montage of Beatles' songs. Some movies, such as *Flashdance*, have become classic examples of how choreography can be as much a reason for a film's success as the screenplay, talent, or director associated with the project. Employment prospects, though, are not as good as in the days when movie musicals, such as Gene Kelly's *Singin' in the Rain* or *West Side Story*, were much more common. A Choreographer might have to supplement his or her income from working on films by working on related projects, such as music videos, TV specials, and live musicals or revues.

Advancement Prospects

Reputation is as much a key to advancement for the Choreographer as recommendations and word-of-mouth. Being associated with a hit movie that is successful because of its choreography, such as *Moulin Rouge, Chicago, Flashdance* or *Dirty Dancing,* can be a ticket to career security and employment.

Education and Training

Training as a dancer followed by education and training as a Choreographer at a dance school, in college, or graduate school, majoring in dance, is usually required. Studying privately with renowned dancers and Choreographers or doing choreography for music videos or live musicals are other ways to train and gain the necessary education. Learning about film and the filmmaking process will also help the Choreographer who wants to work primarily in film. Training as an actor may also be useful. Teach yourself by watching and studying movies with impressive dance routines, such as *Cabaret,* and figuring out what works and why.

Experience, Skills, and Personality Traits

Working on films as a dancer will provide background experience, as will working as a Choreographer in other creative settings, such as stage musicals or music videos. Choreographers must communicate to other dancers what their vision is for the dance sequences of a movie, so they must be articulate. They also need to have the special skill of creating dance routines, as much a question of innate talent and a knowledge of dance as it is of experience.

Unions and Associations

The Society of Stage Directors and Choreographers is the only union for Choreographers, and it covers all Choreographers, whether they work in film, on stage, or in television.

Tips for Entry

1. Dance in any performing arts opportunities available on television, in the movies, in live stage musicals, or in plays.
2. Assist anyone who is a Choreographer on a film, whether as a paid employee, as an intern, or as an apprentice, to see firsthand how the process works.
3. Choreograph music videos and send cassettes of your work to directors, producers, screenwriters, casting directors, or composers, who might then hire you to choreograph a film.

ANIMAL TRAINER

CAREER PROFILE

Duties: Responsible for teaching and training all types of animals used in movies

Alternate Title(s): Trainer; Head Trainer

Salary Range: $18,000 to $34,000+

Employment Prospects: Fair

Advancement Prospects: Fair

Best Geographical Location(s): Training may be acquired anywhere, but it may be necessary to move to Los Angeles/Hollywood

Prerequisites:

Education and Training—A high school degree is expected; a B.A. degree possibly in zoology; specialized education in training animals for the film industry

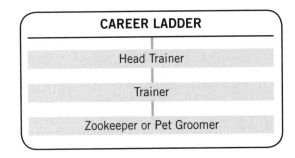

Experience—Working at a zoo, with Animal Trainers, or with a dog or cat groomer

Special Skills and Personality Traits—Patience; hard-working; genuine rapport with animals; ability to use positive reinforcement as a training technique

Position Description

Animal Trainers are a pivotal part of the moviemaking team whenever a live animal is used in a film, from movie stars such as the dog Benji to all-animal casts, as in *Homeward Bound,* to exotic animals. The person in charge of livestock animals, such as horses, burros, sheep, cows, goats, or hogs, on a film is called a wrangler. If a trainer's animal stars in a movie that becomes a blockbuster hit, like "Mike the dog," the star of the movie *Down and Out in Beverly Hills,* trained by Clint Rowe, the trainers and their star animals will be in demand.

Animals are a natural part of many movies, even if they don't play a starring role. They can appear as pets or as police dogs. They can show up as animals in a forest or in a jungle. Each animal you see in a film has a trainer working with it so that it appears on cue, walks in a certain direction, or does whatever the script calls for it to do, from licking its paws to rolling over to sniffing a suitcase to chasing down a bad guy on a street. On occasion, an animal may even have to play dead, and it's up to the trainer to make this happen in a believable way without harming the animal.

Some trainers actually train an animal and become associated with just that one animal. The trainer and that animal are then hired, rather than having an animal work with an unfamiliar trainer. In that case, a trainer would invest the time and money in training an animal

that would then be marketed to the casting directors, directors, producers, and screenwriters in the same way as any new talent starting out in the film industry, such as getting into any and all films—student, independent, or TV—in order to be seen.

Salaries

An established Animal Trainer can earn $28,000 a year, on average. This can range from $18,000 to $34,000, depending on demand. Trainers of celebrity animals may receive larger sums.

Employment Prospects

This is a highly competitive and specialized field, which may require that an Animal Trainer supplements his or her income from the feature film industry with work for television shows, commercials, music videos, and even still photography shoots in addition to feature films.

Advancement Prospects

Training an animal that is the star of a feature film that achieves critical acclaim and is financially successful will definitely help advancement in this highly specialized field.

Education and Training

Animal Trainers in the film industry have a variety of backgrounds. Some attend the unique two and one-half-year course at Moorpark College in Moore Park,

California, known as Exotic Animal Training and Management, while others get a degree in zoology from other colleges or work as a zookeeper. On-the-job training as an Animal Trainer, including volunteer work or in an internship or paid apprenticeship, is another way to gain the education and training for this specialized field.

Experience, Skills, and Personality Traits

Experience working with animals, especially the type of animal that an Animal Trainer plans to specialize in, such as dogs, cats, or exotic animals, is useful, as is having the patient and hardworking personality associated with animal training. Another key aspect of the job is making sure that the rules of the American Humane Association (AHA) are observed while the animals are part of the moviemaking process. It is also useful to understand the filmmaking process, so you can apply it to what will or will not work for a particular animal being used in a film.

Unions and Associations

There is no union for Animal Trainers. They work closely with the American Humane Association.

Tips for Entry

1. Gain the necessary knowledge and experience working with animals and training animals, so that you can apply that knowledge to animals in a film setting.
2. Get a job at a zoo, in a pet shop, or for a company that trains animals for any kind of performance work, such as commercials or still photography, as well as for films.
3. Volunteer to work for an Animal Trainer.

ANIMAL SAFETY REPRESENTATIVE

CAREER PROFILE

Duties: Is present during the shooting of a film to ensure the safety of any and all animals, which includes horses, cats, dogs, birds, fish, reptiles, exotic animals, primates, and insects

Alternate Title(s): Certified Animal Safety Representative

Salary Range: $10 to $15 per hour, entry level to mid-range hourly rate, to $39,000/year for full-time salaried position (when traveling to location, all expenses are paid inclusive of food, lodging, and air-fare, including mileage reimbursement, if driving)

Employment Prospects: Fair

Advancement Prospects: Fair

Best Geographical Location(s): Los Angeles/Holly-wood area or wherever there is a lot of filmmaking such as Boston, Massachusetts, New York City, or Orlando, Florida; if on call, wherever a film is being made

Prerequisites:

Education and Training—Background in taking care of animals including formal education in the field at the undergraduate or graduate level, such as the Exotic Animal Training and Management (EATM) program offered at Moorpark College in California, or working at a zoo, a wildlife center, or in a veterinarian's office

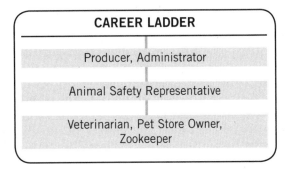

CAREER LADDER

Producer, Administrator

Animal Safety Representative

Veterinarian, Pet Store Owner, Zookeeper

Experience—Working with animals in any capacity including as a veterinarian, a veterinarian's technician, an animal behaviorist, a zoo professional, a state humane officer as well as any film industry-related jobs

Special Skills and Personality Traits—Ability to be assertive with the director, producer, and production team on behalf of the animals used in the filmmaking; patient; observant; attentive to details; love of animals as well as the ability to get along with people; comfortable with change and uncertainty about when or where the next job will happen

Special Requirements—Certification is available through the Animal Humane Association's Film & TV Unit training program including one week of classroom training followed by a supervised apprenticeship working in the field

Position Description

The film industry set up a formal program for monitoring the use of animals in filmmaking beginning in 1925 when the American Humane Association, a national association that has been protecting children and animals from abuse or mistreatment since 1877, created a committee to explore suspected abuse of animal actors.

The catalyst to a more concerted approach to the problem occurred in 1939 during the filming of *Jesse James* when a horse and rider plunged over a 70-foot cliff. Although the rider survived, the animal, which had broken its back during the fall, died. The following year, the Hollywood office of the American Humane Association was granted the authority to monitor movie production that used animal actors.

Animal Safety Representatives are the trained professionals who go into the field, to observe what goes on

at a film set in terms of the safety of the animal actors involved. They make sure that if there is a scene that uses a live animal, including horses, dogs, cats, exotic animals, reptiles, primates, birds, and even insects, there is no mistreatment or abuse of the animal actors during shooting. By following the American Humane Association's *Guidelines for the Safe Use of Animals in Filmed Media* and having an American Humane Certified Animal Safety Representative on set, the film will be able to earn and to display the coveted end-credit disclaimer "No Animals Were Harmed." The public finds that credit reassuring, especially if the film has had a lot of scenes involving horses, dogs, cats, or primates acting in ways that might have been perceived as painful or abusive without that credit being displayed.

Jan Caputo, who was president of the Utah Wildlife Rehabilitation Center, has been working for the Film

& TV Unit of the Animal Humane Association as a certified Animal Safety Representative for the last 16 years. Based in Oregon, she spends most of her time on location on film sets, including those of such popular films as *The Horse Whisperer* and *The Mask of Zorro*. She is an on-call rep who has been selected to be on the set of each of the Harry Potter movies over the last five years, spending most of that time on location in Great Britain.

Tonya Obesa recently returned from the Hawaiian rain forests, where for the previous month she had been working on a movie as the certified Animal Safety Representative. "I always loved animals," says Obesa. "Growing up, I knew I wanted to do something with animals. When I was in college, my counselor found this program at Moorpark that is one of the only ones in the world to offer a specialized degree in exotic animal training and management with an opportunity for an incredible experience. I did dog training for a while. Then I worked for a studio company for about a year. I met an Animal Humane representative on the set of a movie called *Black Sheep*. The American Humane rep that day did a fantastic job helping us out with production and the animals, and that inspired me to use my background and experience and apply it to the unique work that American Humane Safety Reps do."

Salaries

From a starting range of $15 per hour or $39,000 per year for a newer animal safety representative, the salary may increase based on seniority or any specialized expertise and experience. When traveling for a job, all expenses will be paid, including food, lodging, and transportation, such as airfare or reimbursement for gas, if driving. Salary may be higher for international placements.

Employment Prospects

Employment prospects are fair for this unusual work. Each year the American Humane Association looks to continue to increase its ability to cover more films, television shows, commercials, and other forms of filmed genres. However, nonprofit ventures may rely on grants and donations to support this work, and as funds become available, they may make efforts to expand their ability to cover as many productions as possible.

Advancement Prospects

These are also only fair because Animal Safety Representative is such a specialized career. Two key means of advancement would be to become an administrator of Animal Safety Representatives, who work in an office,

or to become a producer supervising all the details of the making of a film, not only those aspects concerning the care of animal actors.

Educational and Training

Taking the Exotic Animal and Training Management (EATM) program at Moorpark College, including any animal science courses, is useful, as is having an advanced degree in animal behavioral sciences. Having experience with equines (horses) is very helpful, including knowing how to ride and take general care of horses. Other useful training is working as an animal trainer, at an animal shelter, or as a zookeeper. If you want to work for the American Humane Association's Film & TV Unit, you will be required to participate in its training program and become certified. After your résumé is considered at the Film & TV Unit, an interview will be set up with the director and the production manager of the program. If the applicant is chosen for the training program, she or he will go through a one-week classroom course that covers the *Guidelines for the Safe Use of Animals in Filmed Media*, an 82-page booklet detailing with all the specific rules that need to be followed, in general and for specific species, as well as training in how to write comprehensive reports when on a set observing as well as role-playing typical situations that might arise and how they would be dealt with. After this one-week training, some attendees will be chosen to become a safety representative apprentice and, upon gaining firsthand experience, earn the certified status.

Experience, Skills, and Personality Traits

Animal experience, especially knowledge of equines, is very useful. Knowing when to be firm but tactful with the producer or director is important. Being flexible is a personality trait that is important for an Animal Safety Representative. For example, Obesa went to the set of the film *Evan Almighty,* starring Steve Carell, where more than 100 species of animals had to be monitored. Says Tonya: "It was supposed to be for three weeks, and my time there kept getting extended. By the time I came back, I had stayed for three months." Enjoying travel and being away from home, as well as having to move on to other locations or jobs after a very brief time of, perhaps, only a day, weeks, or months is another necessity for the job. Obesa, whose father was in the U.S. Air Force, says, "I was born in Guam, and we moved every two or three years till my Dad retired." Picking up and moving on is a part of the job that Obesa is comfortable with.

Being at ease around all kinds of animals is an important skill for this job, as is being bright, being attentive to detail on the set, and learning the very specific general guidelines that the American Humane Association enforces, including the specific guidelines listed by species.

Enjoying travel as well as being comfortable in a wide range of environments, including rain forests, mountains, deserts, and wilderness, is another trait for this job. Additional skills that this job requires are conflict resolution and problem solving, adaptability, coping with stress, flexibility in scheduling, and being resourceful.

Unions and Associations

Joining the American Humane Association would be useful if this is a job that interests you.

Tips for Entry

1. Get experience working with and taking care of animals, especially horses.

2. Take any kind of job offering an internship in the film industry, especially at a production company, that requires that you go on location and shoots. This will enable you to understand what the industry is like, especially how a movie is made.

3. Send your résumé to the American Humane Association's Film & TV Unit in Sherman Oaks, California, and express your interest in becoming a certified Animal Safety Representative.

WRANGLER

CAREER PROFILE

Duties: Choose and take care of horses and other live-stock, such as sheep, cows, or mules, used in making a movie

Alternate Title(s): None

Salary Range: $30/hour for a feature

Employment Prospects: Poor

Advancement Prospects: Poor

Best Geographical Location(s): Los Angeles/Holly-wood

Prerequisites:

Education and Training—Knowledge in the selection, care, feeding, and riding of horses and other animals

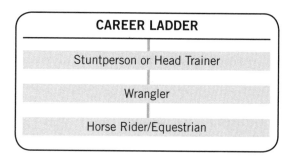

CAREER LADDER

Stuntperson or Head Trainer

Wrangler

Horse Rider/Equestrian

Experience—On-the-job experience working on a ranch and riding horses or with particular animals

Special Skills and Personality Traits—Ability to work with people as well as animals; patience; able to help the actors, as well as the animals

Position Description

Wranglers are most often associated with westerns, but of course any movie that has a horse or other livestock, such as *3:10 to Yuma,* starring Russell Crowe, or Robert Redford's *The Horse Whisperer,* will need a Wrangler. There are even Wranglers for insects and spiders (see the credits for *Arachnophobia,* which had spider wranglers). Horse Wranglers have a knowledge of the selection, care, feeding, and riding of horses, and are also able to train horses to perform in a movie and to fit the right horse to a specific actor if he or she is going to ride in a movie. Unlike stunt doubles, who are members of the Screen Actors Guild (SAG), Wranglers are not seen on camera nor do they perform stunts.

As the caretaker for the film's livestock, the Wrangler needs to know the American Society for the Prevention of Cruelty to Animals (ASPCA) rules so that those rules are respected in the making of the film, including the proper care for the animals.

Wranglers are often used like cowboys on a ranch to keep a herd in control, even, as in *Arachnophobia,* to keep a herd of spiders from escaping and terrorizing the film set. On the film *Indiana Jones and the Temple of Doom,* as well as on other Indiana Jones movies, director Steven Spielberg had a snake Wrangler on hand for those scenes that required a large number of snakes.

Salaries

On union movies, salaries for Wranglers average from $30/hour to $25/hour, depending on whether it is a high- or low-budget feature. Other factors are seniority and their expertise. Specialty Wranglers, such as spider, insect, or snake wranglers, may earn more depending on the specialty.

Employment Prospects

As the number of westerns rises or falls, so do the employment prospects for the horse wrangler. Today, with few western movies, prospects are poor compared to the heyday of the western when John Wayne was a megastar and there might have been literally hundreds of movies that used horses and livestock. In *Working in Hollywood,* Wrangler Rudy Ugland, who worked on such well-known movies as *How the West Was Won* and *The Sicilian,* pointed out that, between 1960 and 1990, the number of Wranglers working in Hollywood shrank from around 300 to just 30. As for spider and snake wranglers, there has never been a large call for them.

Advancement Prospects

Advancement for a Wrangler is poor, since fewer and fewer westerns are being made and there are not many other movies that need their services.

Education and Training

Wranglers need to know everything about livestock, including how to breed horses as well as how to train them. They must also provide the equipment that is necessary to shoot the livestock scenes, such as wagons. Wranglers handling other species, such as spiders and snakes, have to have a working knowledge of them as well.

Experience, Skills, and Personality Traits

Since they will be teaching an actor how to ride a horse, as well as how to mount and dismount, Wranglers need patience to work with both the animals and the talent. They must also understand the film's ultimate visual presentation, as working closely with the director in the selection of the livestock for a film is another skill required of a Wrangler.

Unions and Associations

After working 30 days, a Wrangler is eligible for membership in Local 399 of the Teamsters Union (http://www.hollywoodteamsters.org), which has more than 4,800 members in Los Angeles, California. Besides Wranglers, Local 399 also represents animal trainers, autoservice personnel, casting directors, chief drivers, couriers, dispatchers, drivers, location managers, mechanics, and warehousemen.

Tips for Entry

1. Spend time riding horses or working on a horse farm in California and mingle with filmmakers or screenwriters who are shooting a western.
2. Work for or volunteer as an assistant to a Wrangler with a reputation for working on movies.
3. Have a horse that you own and train. Show your horse in California, so that your reputation as a horse trainer becomes known in the film community.

PRODUCERS (STUDIO OR INDEPENDENT)

HEAD OF PRODUCTION

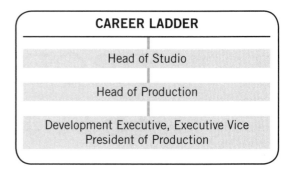

Position Description

For anyone seeking a career in the film industry, the title *Head of Production* is the top of the ladder. While a producer or director makes one or two films a year, the Head of Production can be responsible for 10 to 20 movies a year, depending on how many films the studio or financing entity can afford.

The Head of Production works for the company financing the movie, usually a studio or major production company. As Head of Production, you report to the head of the studio or production company. Your job is to decide which film to make; to determine how much you're willing to spend to make it; to hire the talent, which includes writers, directors, producers, and actors; and then to oversee the preproduction, production, and postproduction phases, as well as the marketing and distribution processes. The Head of Production will have a team of creative executives, director or directors of development, story editors, script readers and others to help in these duties.

In his book, *You're Only as Good as Your Next One,* Mike Medavoy, who has been Head of Production for United Artists, Orion, TriStar, and Phoenix Pictures, says a key aspect of being Head of Production is being able to choose the right talent for the right movie. That means matching the best writer with the best script, finding the

best director to bring it to the screen, and casting the best actors to play the parts.

According to Medavoy, it all starts with the story, which may come from a spec script, a book, a play, a magazine article, or an idea. He says that once the story is selected, the most important factor in whether or not it gets made into a movie is the script. He has four criteria for selecting a compelling script: Does he care about the characters? Does it strike an emotional chord? Is it thematically interesting? Is it unique?

Often, the script will determine the budget. The Head of Production has to decide how much to spend on a particular movie in order to make a profit. Managing this "risk/reward" process determines the overall success or failure of a Head of Production—do the films one greenlights make money or lose money? This doesn't mean that every movie made by a studio or production company has to make money for the Head of Production to keep his or her job. In fact, that never happens. But out of the 10 to 15 movies a Head of Production greenlights every year, the total profits should be larger than the total losses. A Head of Production might be able to survive one or possibly two losing years, but that is usually the limit. This is why turnover in this position is so rapid.

Therefore, a Head of Production may greenlight one or two $100 million dollar budgets, hoping to make

$200 or $300 million in return from worldwide sales, and then balance these large risks with medium- to smaller-budget films that are not expected to make as much as a large commercial picture, but might instead garner critical acclaim or awards.

As screenwriter William Goldman said, "In Hollywood, nobody knows nothing." Therefore, greenlighting any movie is a huge risk. A good Head of Production will hedge and balance this risk in the best possible way by selecting a diverse slate of films that will appeal to a wide range of audiences. He or she may approve two or three "event" big-budget films for Christmas and summer releases and then fill out the schedule with less expensive but hopefully profitable films to be released throughout the year.

Once the script is approved, there are still a number of other decisions that have to be made before a project receives a greenlight or the go-ahead, for production. These include approval of a producer, the director, principal cast members, and the budget. It is up to the Head of Production and her or his team to select the right people for each of these jobs. In order to do this, one must have strong relationships with talented directors, actors, writers, and producers.

How involved the Head of Production becomes in a movie varies from film to film. Often, you give the producer and director enough freedom to make the movie you want them to make. However, if a film is going too far over budget, you or a member of your team may have to step in to either fix the problem to get the budget back in line or to approve more funds to complete a more expensive film.

Once a film is complete, the Head of Production works with the marketing team to make sure an effective marketing campaign is launched to give the film a proper send off. More expensive movies have larger advertising and print budgets, because they have to generate more ticket sales to return a profit. Millions of dollars will be spent on television advertising for these blockbusters, while a smaller, low-budget, character-driven drama may not have any television spots until it begins to generate word-of-mouth Oscar potential.

David Zelon, executive vice president of production at Mandalay Pictures, shares his educational background and work experiences that led him to his current job, which he truly enjoys: "I majored in education at the University of Pennsylvania because both my parents were teachers. But what I really majored in was producing. I started my producing career there. I built a gym in my fraternity house for a powerlifting event. That's where I learned the form and function

of being a producer. The first year we brought in temporary bleachers; by the second year, we had close to a thousand. [After graduation] I packed my bags and moved to Los Angeles. I continued producing the sport of bodybuilding where I met Arnold Schwarzenegger. That was in 1979 and 1980. From 1981 to 1984, I produced the Los Angeles Marathon. During that period I met Peter Guber, who was producing a record album. I pitched him and sold him on a movie of the week about steroids from a book I found called *Death in the Locker Room*, which we made with TNT. It was called *Finish Line* and starred James and Josh Brolin as father and son. It dealt with steroids and sports and aired in 1988."

"In 1992, I accepted a job and transferred to film at Columbia Pictures. I worked at Columbia from 1992 to 1996. Then, in 1996, I went to work for Guber at Mandalay Pictures, where I've been ever since. I have overseen 41 films, which gave me the experience and knowledge I needed when I produced *Into the Blue* and *Never Back Down*."

Salaries

Salaries vary widely for heads of production. They generally begin somewhere in the six-figure range and jump to seven and eight, depending on the success of a studio or production company. Salaries are usually a combination of a base salary, bonuses, stock, and stock options. The bonus can be several times the base salary, especially if the studio has a particularly good year financially. While the Head of Production normally does not receive a percentage of each film, he or she is well compensated for selecting a successful slate of films.

Employment Prospects

There are a limited number of positions in this category, which means employment prospects are not good. On the other hand, turnover is fairly rapid, since a Head of Production has one or two years to prove her or his worth.

Advancement Prospects

Prospects for advancement from Head of Production to studio boss are even harder than becoming Head of Production in the first place. The field of possibilities is tiny, and the competition is fierce.

Education and Training

A broad liberal arts or business degree is probably more important than a degree from film school. As Head of Production, you really don't have to know how to make a movie, but you do have to know what movies to make.

Experience, Skills, and Personality Traits

To be an effective Head of Production, you not only have to love movies, but you must also be committed to the process of making them. In terms of skills, you need an eye for talent, the ability to cast the best actor in the right part, and the ability to forge strong relationships with directors and writers whose visions you admire. One must also know how much to spend on a movie in order to make the money back and turn a profit. You have to be a leader. Most important, you have to be decisive and be a risk taker.

Unions and Associations

As part of the management team, there is no union for Heads of Production. However, people in this position may join many associations, such as the Academy of Motion Picture Arts and Sciences and Women in Film, and become active in a variety of charities sponsored by Hollywood.

Tips for Entry

1. Get experience as a producer working on individual films.
2. Gain producing experience by producing any type of live action event, play, or music event or video.
3. Rise up through the ranks of a talent agency, where you can make contacts and connect with talent.
4. Work your way up through the studio, from director of development to creative executive and so on.
5. Build a solid reputation within the film industry as someone who understands the business from both a financial and an artistic perspective.

EXECUTIVE PRODUCER

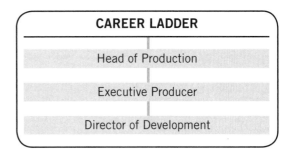

Special Skills and Personality Traits—Able to see problems in production, especially cost overruns; have a thick skin; able to manage strong egos; know what an audience wants to see; passionate for movies

Position Description

The title of Executive Producer is ambiguous within the industry; it can sometimes be given as a perk to someone, such as a powerful agent, who helped get a project made. Sometimes, it is used as currency in exchange for a lower fee paid to a writer, actor, or a director, and other times it is used to attract financing by having a well-known name attached as "Executive Producer" just to add luster to the credits.

Unfortunately, over the years, the title of Executive Producer has come to mean different things to different people working on different films. Usually, it refers to one of two types of people: those who play a role in the film's financing, such as a major investor or a recognizable name that will attract investors; or those who work for the financing entity, such as a studio or production company, and have acted as the "Executive in Charge of Production" on the film.

The title of Executive Producer is sometimes a credit given to a major investor in a film or to a recognizable name within the industry used to raise funding who will likely have no involvement in the actual production of the film. His or her sole purpose is to assist in financing the movie, directly or indirectly. However, if the Executive Producer credit is for someone who is the executive in charge of production for the studio financ-

ing the picture, that person plays a more active role in monitoring the film's production.

Unlike a producer, the Executive Producer, or Executive in Charge of Production, may work on six or seven films all at the same time. An Executive Producer normally will not be on the set every day, and he or she tries to anticipate problems before they get out of hand. Therefore, the Executive Producer will closely monitor day-to-day activities and keep track of whether the film is on schedule and on budget. This is achieved by reviewing production reports, and the Executive Producer only gets involved if he or she finds a problem such as cost overruns. At that point, the Executive Producer would have to confer with the producer and director to see what can be done to get back on track. This might result in eliminating or changing later scenes in order to trim costs.

Orly Adelson is Executive Producer of the production company that bears her name. Born in Israel, she served in the Israeli army, earning the rank of lieutenant. After her army duty, she earned a degree in sociology and musicology from Hebrew University and, at the same time, a degree in music and dance from Jerusalem's Academy of Music and Dance. But she was destined to relocate to America once she met producer Andrew Adelson at a party in Israel, where he had traveled on behalf of the movie *The Postman Always Rings Twice,* and the two fell in love and married.

How many projects does Adelson work on each year? "I would say anywhere from 20 to 30," she replies. "Remember that we can juggle 20, but they can happen five years from now. They're staggered. So I would say that we produce anywhere from four to six movies a year." Since Adelson began producing in 1990, she has produced more than 35 movies and TV series, including *Playmakers,* a 2003 ESPN serial sports drama that won an AFI (American Film Institute) award, and *To Love, Honor and Betray,* a 1999 TV movie starring James Brolin.

Where does Adelson get the energy, work ethic, and drive that enables her to keep developing and producing film or TV project after project? She explains: "I come from a family of lawyers and doctors. In my upbringing, [there was] the sense of duty and responsibility. It was a very important part of growing up, and it carried on into our lives or my life. You do the best you can. If you didn't do the best you could do, then why do it? When there are tedious, long hours, a lot of notes, a lot of editing, we enjoy the moment. We sit and we do notes, and we're enjoying it. It's not a chore. Within my office, we challenge each other. The pursuit itself is where we put our energy into the minute something is done. At that point, it's done. Okay? What's the new challenge?"

She belongs to Women in Film, the Los Angeles–based chapter of the 10,000-member international Women in Film association. Has being a member of the association helped her career? Adelson replies: "For me, it wasn't about helping my career. It was about helping other people's careers. My concern was, 'How do I give back?'"

What are her three pieces of advice to someone starting out in the film industry?

1. Pursue your dream. Don't let anyone stop you.
2. Work as hard as you have to to make it come true.
3. Enjoy the process because if you don't enjoy the process, you won't be able to get to your dreams.

Adelson cautions that there is no one way to achieve your dream. She says, "Everyone has to find their way. That's another thing about this business. Each one has a different journey. There is no one way to achieve it. So the fact that I was interested in various things, I'm sure it helped me in coming to a set. I know about music. I know about people coming from dance and the business side for me, it worked out. But other people can go

to film school and they can get the same thing, or they study literature and get other things."

Stewart F. Lane's road to becoming Executive Producer on the 2007 movie *Brooklyn Rules,* starring Alex Baldwin, Scott Caan, and Freddie Prinze, Jr., as with so many described in this book, was an outgrowth of his other careers. Lane began as a stage actor, but he switched to theatrical production after working for, and then partnering with, the Broadway Nederlander Organization. Lane is a Tony award–winning Broadway producer of such hits as *Fiddler on the Roof, Legally Blonde, Thoroughly Modern Millie,* and *Whose Life Is It Anyway?* Author of three books, including the recent *Let's Put On a Show!,* Lane shares his experiences as Executive Producer on a film, including the new movie *The Berkley Connection,* by Marshall Brickman: "The story line for *Brooklyn Rules* was familiar, but the characters were so engaging that I wept by the end. Having recognizable names was also a good selling point for the theatrical release and the DVD market. *The Berkley Connection* had a wonderful freshness about it and allowed me the opportunity to work with Marshall."

Salaries

Salaries vary widely for Executive Producers and in many cases there are no salaries per se—getting the title is the payoff. Often, an Executive Producer shares in the profits of the film, especially if he or she is a major investor. If the Executive Producer is the Executive in Charge of Production from a studio or production company, then his or her salary will probably be in the six figures, plus a bonus tied to performance of the film.

Employment Prospects

There is no clear career path to becoming an Executive Producer. If someone puts up the money for a movie, he or she might get the Executive Producer title. If someone actually performs the function of overseeing that a film stays on budget, this could earn someone a reputation for being useful to have associated with a film project.

Advancement Prospects

The only advancement prospects involve those Executive Producers who are legitimate Executives in Charge of Production, and in that case, they may be trying to become heads of production or even actual producers. If a film does well, an Executive Producer benefits from being associated with a "winner" and his or her standing will rise within the industry. If an Executive Producer helps make a low-budget film that makes a lot of money, this could help him or her when he or she tries to raise money for a more expensive film.

Education and Training

Executive Producers may have a bachelor's degree or higher degree, have attended film school, and may have extensive training within the film industry at all management levels.

Experience, Skills, and Personality Traits

Since it is so hard to determine what an Executive Producer does on a particular film, it is almost impossible to list skills, personality, and experiences. They range from being concerned with keeping the film on budget and on time to not performing any functions at all, just being a name attached to a project. An Executive Producer who is an Executive in Charge of Production must know how much everything costs on an hourly and daily basis, so if filming falls behind schedule even slightly, he or she can make adjustments to the schedule to help get the production back on track.

But the Executive Producer, who is actually running the company and supervising the production of the film, needs to be a hard worker, energetic, able to put in long hours for a stretch of time, able to lead a team and to supervise and delegate.

Unions and Association

There is no union for Executive Producers. Membership in industry associations, such as the Academy of Motion Picture Arts and Sciences, Women in Film, National Academy of Television Arts and Sciences (NATAS), might be useful for networking and gaining admission to local or national educational events or awards shows.

Tips for Entry

1. Be a successful creative executive at a studio.
2. Have access to funds needed to make a movie.
3. Have authority over the key elements needed to make the movie, such as the director, talent, screenwriter, producer, or casting director.

DEVELOPMENT EXECUTIVE

Duties: At a studio, the Development Executive oversees properties brought in by producers in various states of development. At a production company, a director of development reads scripts, meets with writers and producers and looks for properties the company would want to finance. He or she might also oversee films in production and would carry the title of production executive.

Alternate Title(s): Director of Development; Creative Executive

Salary Range: $50,000 to $100,000+

Employment Prospects: Fair

Advancement Prospects: Poor

Best Geographical Location(s): Los Angeles/Hollywood, New York City

Prerequisites:

Education and Training—Bachelor's or advanced degree in film is recommended but not required

---

CAREER LADDER

Head of Production

↑

Development Executive

↑

Story Editor or Acquisitions Executive

Experience—Extensive experience in script reading, developing, and producing

Special Skills and Personality Traits—Able to tell if a script works; know production inside and out, so you can tell if a project is falling behind; highly organized; have an eye for talent; recognize quality when attempting to acquire a property; have a working knowledge of rights, licensing, and business administration

---

Position Description

A Development Executive—also known as a creative executive or production executive—basically oversees the development and production of a number of projects being financed by a studio or production company. It's the Development Executive's job to make sure everyone else is doing their jobs and that the movie the studio or production company agreed to finance is the movie being developed or produced.

Development and creative executives read scripts and meet with writers and producers to get the script in shape for production. Production executives make sure the director is completing shooting on schedule and on budget. A production executive will also research and determine if the producer's budget matches the true cost of making the film. Once the real budget is determined, the studio will decide if it wants to finance the film.

It is common for a Development Executive and a production executive to oversee several films at the same time all in various stages of development and production.

A third type of executive is the acquisitions executive. This is someone who looks for projects to acquire that may have already been produced or partially produced or just developed and packaged.

Salaries

Salaries vary widely for development, creative, and production executives. There is no union minimum, but studios pay competitive salaries to attract talented executives. A six figure salary is common. Salaries at production companies tend to be as much as half of that, depending on the size of the company.

Employment Prospects

This is a fairly large category, which means employment prospects are probably better than many. It is still very competitive, however.

Advancement Prospects

Prospects for advancement to head of production are extremely limited, due to the small number of openings.

Education and Training

A bachelor's degree in film school, in the liberal arts, or in business is recommended.

Experience, Skills, and Personality Traits

A Development Executive should be skilled in all areas of filmmaking, from the writing and rewriting of the script to the production and postproduction phases of creating the movie. He or she should possess an eye for detail as well as a keen eye for talent. A Development Executive must have the skills to know if a film can actually be made for a particular budget. He or she needs to have a feel for good stories. Development Executives have to be strong willed and able to handle strong egos, especially when it pertains to directors who may be going over budget and need to be reigned in. A Development Director must also have a thick skin because if a picture fails, it is often he or she whom the studio blames and punishes by either a demotion, firing, or criticism.

Unions and Associations

There is no union for Development Executives. They may belong to a number of industry associations, such as the Academy of Motion Picture Arts and Sciences and Women in Film.

Tips for Entry

1. Take a job as a script reader to develop a sense of story.
2. Take any studio or production company job to get in the door.
3. Work in business affairs.
4. Make contacts at film school.
5. Cover the film industry as an entertainment writer and get to know executives.

DEVELOPMENT ASSOCIATE

Duties: Assists the development executive or producer in finding and developing screenplays or material from other sources, such as books, plays, or real-life stories, that will be developed into a film

Alternate Title(s): Development Assistant

Salary Range: $25,000 to $35,000

Employment Prospects: Good

Advancement Prospects: Fair

Best Geographical Location(s): Los Angeles/Hollywood and New York City

Prerequisites:

Education and Training—Bachelor's degree is expected; advanced degree or courses in film could be useful; any film-related job experience

Experience—Reading and evaluating screenplays; working in an office in a variety of administrative and clerical capacities

Special Skills and Personality Traits—Computer and Internet savvy; self-starter but also able to work in a team setting; able to say no to a potential project in a firm but pleasant way; good eye for what makes an excellent film

Position Description

Development Associate or assistant is an entry-level position that enables someone to read and evaluate finished screenplays, treatments, idea pitches, or other materials, such as books, plays, or real-life stories, for acquisition by a production company. This position requires reading and writing comments about screenplays and other materials, as well as performing administrative functions, such as answering and placing phone calls, as the assistant to the development executive. Depending on the size of the production company, this position may combine administrative and development duties, such as in a smaller office with only a few key executives as opposed to a larger company, where only development-related duties are performed by the Development Associate. In a smaller office, the Development Associate or assistant may also be juggling the role of executive or administrative assistant to the development executive, who may also be the president of the company as well as a producer.

Alexi Mazareas is a 23-year-old graduate of Harvard University who majored in film studies and English. His first job after graduating was a full-time position as a Development Associate working for Orly Adelson Productions, a Los Angeles–based production company founded in 1995 that produces movies for television,

TV series, and feature films. Alexi credits his ability to quickly land a Development Associate position with a company, searching for screenplays or properties to produce as well as being an assistant to Orly Adelson, the president of the company, to the two internships he had at other film companies during his college years. Says Mazareas: "I had two great internships. The first one was for the Mark Gordon Company. They did *Saving Private Ryan*. They're doing *Grey's Anatomy* and *Private Practice* now. It was my first time in the business, and I was doing a lot of script coverage. It was a very busy company. The second internship was for The Bedford Falls Company." Bedford Falls is a partnership of director Ed Zwick, who directed *Legends of the Fall* and *Glory*, and Marshal Herskovitz, who is president of the Producers Guild. Says Mazareas: "When I was there in the summer of 2005, they were in preproduction on *Blood Diamond*, so I got to see how that [film] was all put together."

Mazareas got his internships by sending out a lot of inquiry letters. "I didn't know anyone in the [film] business," he explains. "My family is from Boston. My dad's a business consultant, and my mom runs a youth center north of Boston." He sent out 15 letters initially. His plan was to send out another batch of letters if he didn't hear back from anyone. But he got answers from several companies, he flew out for interviews over his spring break from college, and he got a job over the summer vacation.

Caring about what he does and where he works is key to Mazareas, who wants to eventually run his own production company that produces his own screenplays. (He already has five completed spec screenplays.) He credits his grandfather, who came to America from Greece when his father was five, with his commitment to doing work that he loves. As Mazareas explains: "Like my grandfather used to say, you sleep a third of your life and you work a third of your life, so if you're not happy at work, that's two-thirds of your life that's wasted."

His advice to those starting out in film? "You can't be afraid to fail," he says with conviction. "If you love Oliver Stone's company, send them a letter and see if they're hiring. You have to be thick-skinned in this business. Orly [Adelson] has a quote that you may have to knock on a few doors before you find one that opens for you. That's very true. You have to be confident in yourself and be persistent. It's the same thing with scripts. We get scripts that we like that we pass on and it doesn't mean they're bad scripts. You can't get discouraged. Unlike any other business, there are passes, and people move around quickly."

Salaries

Salaries depend on the size of the company, with a starting salary range of $25,000 to $35,000 per year.

Employment Prospects

There are good employment prospects for this job because it is a key job category in every production company, even the smallest ones. Since it is usually an entry-level position, with most Development Associates moving on within a few years to other positions within the company or at another company if there are no openings at the current company, there are usually job openings for this position.

Advancement Prospects

It is harder to advance in this position, especially at the same production company if it has a small staff, because the next highest position, Development Executive, may be occupied by only one person who remains in that job. Advancement will also be based on making recommendations for screenplays or other materials to be made into a film, or passed over, and as those decisions are acted upon, the judgment of the Development Associate will be up for scrutiny in a very competitive industry. Make one or more excellent suggestions, and your career may be launched. Recommend passing over a property that goes on to win the Academy Award, or enthusiastically promote a film that turns out to be a dud, and it may be much harder to advance in this job than it was to get your foot in the door.

Education and Training

A college degree is expected but may not be required. An advanced degree in film or film courses may be useful as well. Taking courses in writing and criticism may also prove helpful in developing the critical skills that enable someone to have a sharp eye for a fresh plot and memorable dialogue. Attending current movies as well as watching classics on DVD will help to broaden someone's knowledge of film. Reading the first draft and shooting scripts of admirable films, or those that did not do well at the box office, may also help to enhance the skills that are so pivotal to the Development Associate.

Experience, Skills, and Personality Traits

Working in the film industry in any capacity will be helpful, as will gaining experience reading and writing literary critiques, including film, book, or theater reviews, for a school or trade newspaper. Writing screenplays may be helpful in gaining an understanding of the process involved.

Excellent writing skills are expected, as are the abilities to read quickly and write insightful and clear coverage about each screenplay or property considered. The Development Associate also has to be able to interact with a range of individuals, from screenwriters and their agents to the development executive to the producer. Being able to find and acquire submissions from agents with talented new or established screenwriters is key. Building a reputation as someone with good judgment and having the ability to recognize a screenplay or property before the competition will increase the likelihood of success in this highly competitive job and industry.

Unions and Associations

Development Associates who are also screenwriters may belong to the Writers Guild of America East or West writers union, not for their development job, but in their capacity as a writer.

Unlike the position of script supervisor, which may require membership in the IATSE union, there is no union for Development Associates. Belonging to an association with members from the film industry may be useful as a way of finding out about screenwriters with treatments or screenplays available for sale, such as any of the chapters of the Women in Film association.

Tips for Entry

1. During college, or even afterward, if a paid or unpaid position is available, become an intern in the development department. Work hard to shine as an employee and in the coverage that you write and let them know that you are available for a full-time job after graduating. If they do not have an upcoming opening, ask for a referral or recommendation to colleagues and friends at other production companies that might have work.

2. Offer to critique a screenplay under consideration at a production company as a demonstration of your critical skills and writing ability. If possible, suggest an available property that you think is ideal for the company of your choice.

3. Search the listings for openings for this job at the major online job search sites, including http://www.entertainmentcareers.net and http://www.mandy.com.

4. Write letters to producers, directors, development executives, or heads of production at production companies that you admire and ask for a job. Write a dynamic cover letter explaining why you admire and want to work for that particular company and enclose your résumé. Be prepared to send a sample of your coverage, if requested. As often as possible, continue the job search process over the phone and, ideally, in person, even if this means taking a long trip to the company.

5. Network with fellow students, family members, friends, acquaintances, alumni, and ask everyone and anyone if they know someone who owns, runs, or works for a film company. Let them know you are interested in getting a job as a Development Associate.

PRODUCER

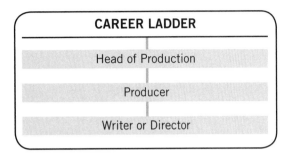

Position Description

When they hand out the Academy Award for best picture, it is bestowed upon the Producer. It is the Producer who makes the picture happen. Of course, every movie needs to be based on a screenplay, but, without the Producer, that screenplay would just be 120 or so pages of type.

A Producer gathers together all the elements of a movie, such as a story or material, the writer or writers, a director, the actors, and the production and editing team. He or she then makes sure they have whatever they need to complete the moviemaking process.

Whether a movie has a budget of $100 million or $500,000, someone has to produce it, even if, as with a low-budget film, the director or screenwriter is also the Producer. Someone has to deal with all the details related to the film. The Producer oversees the whole process, from preproduction through production to postproduction and distribution. The Producer makes the movie happen by putting all the elements together—the screenplay (screenwriter) plus the director, the actors, and the financing, whether independently or by going to a film studio.

There are many categories of Producer. For a small or "no" budget film, there may only be one Producer. On a film with a bigger budget, such as a multimillion dollar studio film, there may be several Producers. The work may be handled by many people, from the entry level production assistants (PA) all the way up to the executive producer.

The first task for a Producer is to find and develop the story, often referred to as the material or property, that will ultimately be made into a movie. This can be in the form of a spec script (a screenplay completed on speculation), a novel or nonfiction book, a magazine article or short story, a treatment, or even an idea or pitch. Even if the story comes in the form of a spec script, in nearly every case, a certain amount of rewriting will be done in order to get the material in shape to attract a director or principal actor. The Producer options the material and then hires either the original writer or another writer to rewrite, reshape, and polish the script before submitting it to a studio or other financing entity.

Since the script is usually the most important ingredient in getting financing, this development process can be costly, time-consuming, and difficult, depending on how many rewrites are required. Each time a principal creative talent is hired, such as a director or main actor, he or she has an opinion regarding script changes, as does the studio or financing entity.

The Producer has to oversee this delicate process of revision to make sure the reason he or she wanted to make the movie in the first place isn't lost in all the rewriting. However, it's a common adage that you can make a bad movie out of a good script, but you can't make a good movie out of a bad script. Therefore, it is imperative for the Producer to get the script the best it can be before production begins.

If the Producer does not have a studio deal or access to funding, he or she will have to arrange financing for making the film. This will often take longer than the actual production process, depending on the Producer's track record or the material that he or she is trying to get financed. Some scripts are easier to raise money for than others, and many require a commitment from a star actor or director before funding becomes available.

For example, it took Producer Wendy Finerman nine years to get financing for *Forrest Gump,* and she was the wife of a former head of production for Columbia Pictures, Mark Canton. The film turned out to be a blockbuster and Academy Award winner. It should be noted that Finerman was one of three people to receive Producer credit on the film. Still, the movie's unusual premise did not have obvious commercial appeal, so getting the money to make it was challenging. In fact, it wasn't until the major movie star Tom Hanks committed to play the lead that funding was approved.

After hiring the best writer or writers to create the best script, the next person the Producer hires is usually the director. The key is to match the right director to the right script and budget. There are a variety of factors that go into this decision: For example, do you want a director who knows comedy, or drama, or suspense? Are you more interested in character development and getting strong performances from actors, or does being able to shoot a good action sequence matter the most?

Next on the Producer's list of priorities comes casting. As in the *Forrest Gump* scenario, you may need to attach a bankable star to the project in order to get financing. But if that is not the case, then selecting the best actor for the principal roles becomes one of the most important decisions affecting the success or failure of the movie. There are three levels to the casting process: first, the principal lead actors; followed by featured supporting roles; and then the small parts, bit players, and extras.

Casting the lead roles will often determine or be determined by the film's budget. If you cast a star such as Tom Hanks, Sandra Bullock, or Tom Cruise, then the film's budget must be high enough to accommodate their multimillion-dollar salaries.

After casting, the next important element is selecting the production staff who will assist in supervising the day-to-day production of the movie. These positions include the production manager, the assistant director, the accountant, the script supervisor, and, in some cases, the technical advisor. This group is respon-sible for keeping costs under control; making sure that the director, cinematographer, sound mixer, and crew chiefs have what they need to complete each shot; and that there is continuity from shot to shot and scene to scene regarding wardrobe, camera placements, lighting, and other moviemaking details.

Work for this group begins during the preproduction phase, when proper planning will play a key factor in whether a production will run smoothly. The first person hired on the production team is the production manager, who does a complete script breakdown to prepare a shooting schedule, from which a production budget is finalized for approval with the studio or financing entity. During production, the production manager is responsible for making sure the director has what he or she needs to complete each day's shoot. The production manager will work closely with the assistant director, who is responsible for managing the day-to-day activities on the set in order to keep everything on schedule. The assistant director works for both the director and the Producer. He or she supervises the actors' call sheets and makes sure the right actors are on the set when they're needed.

When the film enters the production phase, the Producer usually takes a back seat to the director, making sure he or she has whatever is needed to shoot the film. If a principal actor begins giving the director trouble, it is up to the Producer to step in and resolve such disputes. If a particular shot becomes necessary but may delay the schedule or push the film over budget, the Producer will have to go to the financing entity to request approval to spend more money. If they can't, the Producer and director will have to come up with another solution.

Once principal photography is complete, the film goes into postproduction, which includes editing, adding of any special optical and sound effects, and attaching the music scoring. The Producer's role here is to make sure the postproduction crews have everything they need to complete their work. They monitor this process as closely as they monitor production.

Following postproduction, the Producer works with the marketing and publicity teams to sell the completed picture. They often hold test screenings to determine audience reaction, and, if necessary, reshoot or reedit the film to correct those scenes or parts that don't work.

At some point, the Producer has to give up control of the movie and turn it over to a distributor, who, for a percentage of the profits, pays for prints and advertising and books the film into theaters. Even then a Producer's work is not really done, because there will be versions of the film produced for television, for airlines, for foreign language markets, and for DVD and videotape markets. DVDs allow Producers to release all those "deleted scenes" that get taken out of the theatrical release, usually after the film is tested.

A Producer's work on a film is never really complete, because during release you have to track box office receipts, which ultimately pay the Producer's salary. So as long as the movie is playing somewhere, the Producer is making money from it.

Susan Johnston, president of Select Services Films, Inc., is a Producer based in California. When asked how she became a Producer, Johnston replies, "I started out as an actress and was an acting major, dance minor at Rhode Island College. I acted on stage and in featured roles in films such as *True Lies and School Ties.*" She also worked at the Providence and Rhode Island Film Commissions, where she was part of a team that built the infrastructure for filmmaking in the area, including instituting filming permits, location availability, a tax credit, and negotiating terms that filmmakers still use to this day. Susan is proud of those team-building years that honed the skills that she currently uses in her capacity as a Producer.

"When I moved to Los Angeles," Johnston continued, "I took every job that was available. I was a snake wrangler, dolly grip, best boy electric, craft services, wardrobe, assistant camera, you name it. Then I took the Hollywood Film Institute two-day filmmaking course taught by Dov S-S Simens. Quentin Tarantino made his first film after taking his class, so I figured I could too! That was the impetus for my first film. I learned how to go to people who could invest in a film, how to make a film and get it out on the festival circuit. Then I became associate producer on two shorts, then producer on *Room 32,* which became an award-winning 35mm short with worldwide distribution. Right now, I'm the producer on feature-length films such as *Dreams Awake,* starring Erin Gray and Gary Graham, which is now in postproduction, and *Road to Tombstone,* which is getting ready for preproduction. When I bring money to projects, I'll be working myself into executive producer. The producing came out of the acting and a need to get compelling and inspiring stories on the screen."

Peggy Howard Chane, Producer and director at CPC Entertainment, has been in the film industry since college; she majored in film and TV production at the University of Wisconsin. After graduating, Chane moved to New York, where she worked on TV movies-of-the-week, followed by several years in Washington, D.C., where she produced documentaries. Then Chane returned to New York, followed by a move to Los Angeles, where she worked on numerous TV movies and series. That eventually led to starting her own film company, CPC Entertainment, and her return to New York. With *In the Eyes of a Stranger,* a TV movie starring Justine Bateman, to her credit, Chane's company has three movies currently in development —*River to Greyrock, Passing Through,* and *Full Crop of Early.* Chane shares what she has learned during her film industry career that others might find useful:

"If you can write a good script, you can do everything else you want. [That's] my advice to people starting out. Writing is where the power is in the industry. If people like your script, they'll help you and let you find your way. I'm a very good editor and I'm very good at reading a script and figuring out where the problem areas are. I write wonderful treatments, but I'm not a scriptwriter."

What are the traits that have helped Chane in her career as an independent producer that she thinks others also need to have? Says Chane: "You've got to be persistent, spelled in all capital letters. You absolutely have to be determined. *Glamorous* is not a word I would use for this business. There is nothing glamorous about it. [But] It's fun. Every day is different. You have to hone a lot of different skills. The dollars-and-cents thing as well as the creative part. It's fun to use both skills. It's invigorating. It's a people activity. You've got to be with people."

Chane advises anyone who wants to succeed in the film industry not to be afraid of cold calls: "At every phase of the business, there's nothing wrong with cold calls. The worst thing anybody can say is no. You shouldn't be in this business if you have low self-esteem. It's never going to happen for you."

Salaries

Salaries vary widely for Producers and depend on several factors, including whether the Producer has a studio deal. The Producer's fee is usually determined by the film's budget, plus a percentage of the profits. According to the U.S. Department of Labor, the hourly rate for producers in the motion picture industry is $34.01. A film Producer's earnings on any one picture, which might run a year or more, could range from less than a thousand to tens of millions.

Employment Prospects

Since basically anyone can become a Producer, employment prospects are infinite. That doesn't mean it is easy to become a movie Producer. In fact, it is a very demanding, detail-oriented job, since so much is involved in just getting one movie made. Still, the film industry is considered a growth industry, so the need for Producers will only increase as the need for product continues.

Advancement Prospects

Prospects for advancement into the ranks of Producer is fair. Often, writers or directors seeking more control over their work become Producers. But this only occurs after they have proven to those putting up the money that they can fulfill the commitment it takes to produce a film.

Education and Training

A broad liberal arts or business degree couldn't hurt, nor could a degree from a film school. A Producer should be knowledgeable about all aspects of filmmaking, from screenwriting to directing and acting, as well as about the more technical elements of cinematography, production and sound design, and editing.

Experience, Skills, and Personality Traits

Get as much experience as possible in all aspects of filmmaking before attempting to take on this monumental role. Many movie Producers come from television or the theater or began as writers, directors, or agents before taking on the role of Producer.

A Producer has to be many things to many people. First and foremost, she or he has to have a passion for movies, an eye for a good story, and be able to lead a team of creative collaborators through a long and often laborious birthing process. He or she has to be a business person, a psychologist, a parent, a diplomat, a fixer, and a person who finishes what he or she starts, no matter what.

Unions and Associations

There are no unions for Producers, but membership in the nonprofit Producers Guild of America may be useful for networking and skills-building through educational seminars.

Tips for Entry

1. Become a writer or director.
2. Become an associate or line producer.
3. Work your way up the ranks from production assistant.
4. Take a job in television, in theater, at a talent agency, at a casting agency, or anywhere in the film industry to get your foot in the door.
5. Take an undergraduate, graduate, or noncredit course in producing at a film school, such as UCLA or New York University. Let your teacher or professor know that you're interested in producing professionally.
6. Attend events and educational programs sponsored by the Producers Guild of America.
7. Attend a producing program, such as the ones offered at the University of Southern California; the University of California, Los Angeles; New York University; Columbia University; Chapman University; Columbia College Chicago; the University of Arizona, and the American Film Institute.

LINE PRODUCER

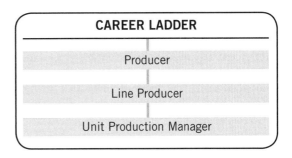

going to cost just by looking at words on a page, such as a scene in a script; able to make quick, creative decisions; flexible; a good mediator; able to say no decisively; most important, know how to assemble the best crew available for a particular film

Position Description

In filmmaking, the terms "above the line" and "below the line" refer to a line in the movie's budget separating certain expenses. "Above the line" expenses refer to the script and rights to the story, if applicable, the producer's unit, the director's unit and the talent (actors and extras). "Below the line" costs cover all other aspects of production, post production and other expenses.

So if one thinks in terms of "above and below the line," the Line Producer is the "line" personified. He or she stands between the group representing the producer, director, writer, and actors and the rest of the production and postproduction crews. The Line Producer is the day-to-day producer of the film, reporting directly to the producer.

The Line Producer is the producer's eyes and ears on the set. He or she is given the role of "fixer" whenever problems occur. The Line Producer makes sure everything is running smoothly during production. He or she is one of the few people who will offer creative input to the director. It is this ability to speak about creative issues with the director that separates the Line Producer from a unit production manager (UPM).

Often, it is the Line Producer who hires the UPM. While the UPM's job also begins in preproduction, it is the Line Producer who attends budget meetings

with studio executives and answers questions about what can and can't be done.

On low-budget films, the Line Producer and UPM are often the same person; in the movie's credits, he or she may be listed as coproducer. A Line Producer has to know everything a UPM knows, which is virtually everything one needs to know to physically produce a movie.

Salaries

The Line Producer's salary may vary widely depending on the film's budget and the location of the project. He or she will earn at least as much as the UPM and usually more, estimated between $3,000 and $5,000 a week.

Employment Prospects

Employment prospects for Line Producers are good, since most studio films have one.

Advancement Prospects

Prospects for advancement from Line Producer to producer are fair, although many producers are not former Line Producers. Being a Line Producer is one of many career paths that can lead to producing.

Education and Training

Besides film school, the best training for a Line Producer is to be a unit production manager. That way you will have worked your way up the production ranks and will know film production inside and out.

Experience, Skills, and Personality Traits

Work as an UPM is the best experience a Line Producer can have. As a UPM you are responsible for most of the same things a Line Producer is responsible for, but without the power. Line Producers need to be creative and quick thinkers. They should be able to mediate disputes, handle strong egos, and fix any problem that arises during production.

Unions and Associations

There is no union for Line Producers, although many belong to the Directors Guild as a unit production manager or are members of the Producers Guild of America.

Tips for Entry

1. After working as a UPM, you will get to know many producers; if they like your work, they'll perhaps hire you as a Line Producer.
2. Take a Line Producer/UPM job on low-budget films.
3. Attend film festivals.
4. Use your college or film school contacts. Network.
5. Check production lists in *Variety* and the *Hollywood Reporter.*
6. Check out the job postings at http://www.indeed.com, http://www.media-match.com, http://www.mandy.com, http://www.infolist.com, or http://www.entertainmentcareers.net.

UNIT PRODUCTION MANAGER

CAREER PROFILE

Duties: Manage all the administrative, financial, and technical elements of a film's production

Alternate Title(s): Production Manager; UPM

Salary Range: $4,313 weekly for a local film; $6,040 weekly for a distant location

Employment Prospects: Good

Advancement Prospects: Good

Best Geographical Location(s): Los Angeles/Hollywood, New York City

Prerequisites:

  Education and Training—Film school, bachelor's, or advanced degree is optional

  Experience—Work in as many positions on a production as possible

  Special Skills and Personality Traits—Able to get things done; able to tell how much something is

CAREER LADDER

Producer or Director

Unit Production Manager

Production Coordinator or First Assistant Director

going to cost just by looking at words on a page, such as a scene in a script; capable of making quick creative and financial decisions; flexible; a good mediator; able to say no decisively; aptitude for assembling the best possible crew for a particular film

Position Description

Although the Unit Production Manager (UPM) is a position covered by the Directors Guild of America, a production manager works for the producer in a role similar to that performed by the assistant director for the director. Sometimes, the UPM and first assistant director are the same person. Other times, the UPM is also the line producer, depending on the film's budget.

The UPM's duties include preparing the production breakdown, setting the shooting schedule, hiring the crew, and making initial contacts for locations. He or she is also responsible for any changes in the budget or schedule. A UPM, seen as the liaison between the producer and crew, oversees all activities of the crew.

The UPM is the hands-on producer and is involved in all aspects of the film's physical production, beginning with preproduction and continuing through production. It seldom carries into postproduction, however, and usually ends when principal photography wraps. Hired by the producer, the UPM hires the crew, prepares a production schedule, and deals with the location manager and scouts. The UPM basically serves as the eyes and ears of the producer during all aspects of production.

The UPM's job begins in preproduction by doing a script breakdown that will determine a production schedule to fit the producer's budget. That means select-

ing locations, production designers, and other members of the production crew involved in the physical creation of the sets.

During production, the UPM arrives on the set early to make sure the director has everything she or he needs for the day's schedule. She or he gets an update from the first or second assistant director. If a cast member failed to show up or a set isn't ready, the UPM will have to decide how to deal with it. This could affect the budget, and he or she will have to grant approval for an increase in expenditure. If she or he can't get the extra money, she or he will have to come up with another solution, usually changing the schedule to accommodate what can be shot that day.

A daily routine for the UPM is dealing with what the director wants and what the producer is willing to give, all the while trying to keep everything as close to budget as possible.

The UPM's job is usually complete when the director finishes, or "wraps," principal photography. There is seldom anything for a UPM to do during postproduction. However, if, after the first assembly, the producer wants the director to reshoot some scenes or change the ending, then the UPM will be called back to help carry out those production demands.

On low-budget films, the UPM will also act as line producer.

Salaries

The Directors Guild of America (DGA) has established minimums for the UPM position on a union film: $4,313 weekly for a local film; $6,040 weekly for a distant location (based on the contract expiring June 30, 2009; check the Directors Guild of America Web site for the new rates beyond that date). On a nonunion film, if there is a UPM, salaries depend on the budget and on whatever the UPM is able to work out with the producer or film financier.

Employment Prospects

Employment prospects for Unit Production Manager are good, since every studio film has one. To work on a studio film, you have to be a member of the Directors Guild of America.

Advancement Prospects

Prospects for advancement from Unit Production Manager to line producer are good. Often, the UPM is the line producer on smaller budget films. Studios are always looking for good UPMs to hire as line producers as more and more line producers become producers themselves.

Education and Training

Besides film school, the best training for a Unit Production Manager is on-the-job training and the DGA training program. After 400 days as a DGA trainee, you become a second assistant director, where you can begin to make a name for yourself. Once you prove yourself as a second assistant director, you will be given an opportunity to become a first assistant director and then a UPM.

Experience, Skills, and Personality Traits

Not all UPMs had experience as a DGA trainee, but it doesn't hurt. Many came up the ranks after working several other production positions on a film. UPMs need strong administrative and accounting skills. They should be well organized, decisive, creative, and able to mediate any disputes that arise between the director and producer.

Unions and Associations

Membership in the Directors Guild of America (DGA) (http://www.dga.org) is not only beneficial but also required if a UPM is hired to work on a studio or union film.

Tips for Entry

1. The Directors Guild of America training program is probably the best entry into becoming a UPM.
2. Take any entry-level job on a production set to begin to gain knowledge about how a movie is produced.
3. Go to film school.
4. Take any entry-level job at a studio or at a film production company to begin gaining experience. One good place to begin is in the budget department.

PRODUCTION COORDINATOR

Duties: Run the production office and coordinate activities between the office and the set

Alternate Title(s): Production Office Coordinator

Salary Range: $30,000 to $75,000, depending on experience and the size and location of the film company

Employment Prospects: Good

Advancement Prospects: Good

Best Geographical Location(s): Los Angeles/Hollywood, New York City

Prerequisites:

Education and Training—An undergraduate college or graduate degree is not required but is helpful, especially a film school background

Experience—Any experience on a film shoot; experience running an office, whether or not it's in the film industry; experience with cable or TV companies, music video or commercial production com-

panies, or business or documentary film production offices

Special Skills and Personality Traits—Strong organizational skills; detail oriented; time management skills; filing and paperwork management skills; good communication skills, especially on the phone; high tolerance for stress; able to get along with a wide variety of personality types

Special Requirements—Union membership may be required

Position Description

The Production Coordinator is basically the production office manager. Duties include administrative responsibilities, such as making sure that all the papers are filed, assisting in the script breakdown, coordinating travel arrangements, and assisting the unit production manager in all administrative areas of production. Working directly for the UPM, the Production Coordinator runs the production office, supervises all paperwork, and performs administrative duties, from answering the phones to coordinating shipping and deliveries to making call sheets.

The Production Coordinator is hired by the UPM during preproduction to help coordinate the script breakdown process by informing anyone involved in production about scheduling and scheduling changes. Primary duties during preproduction involve setting up and staffing the production office, which could include actually leasing a space and then furnishing it as an office.

During production, the Production Coordinator handles all of the paperwork, such as the production reports, call sheets, and camera reports and arranges the schedule for dailies, which are when the director,

producer, and cinematographer view the footage shot that day.

Salaries

Salaries range from $30,000 to $75,000 a year, depending on experience, the size and location of the company, and one's standing in the film industry. The average weekly salary is $1,500.

Employment Prospects

A Production Coordinator is needed on most studio and independent films, so employment prospects are good. The Production Coordinator performs an essential function, assisting the unit production manager by being a go-between for the UPM and the crew members.

Advancement Prospects

Prospects for advancement to unit production manager or line producer are good as long as you develop an excellent reputation and sufficient experience working on well-regarded films. The Directors Guild of America (DGA) union has a DGA training program that is the way for a Production Coordinator to become a UPM. The sequence is to work as a DGA trainee, then to become a first assistant director, and finally to become a UPM.

Education and Training

Advanced degrees are not required, but a degree in English, in communications, or from film school is recommended. Work as an assistant Production Coordinator or take any job available in a production crew to learn firsthand as much about the business of filmmaking as possible.

Special Requirements

Membership in the International Alliance of Theatrical Stage Employees (IATSE) is required in order to work on a studio or union film.

Experience, Skills, and Personality Traits

Working as a Production Coordinator requires strong organizational skills and the ability to retain as many details as possible. The best way to learn the job is by doing it as an assistant Production Coordinator. Mainly, this is an administrative position that involves a lot of details and stress. Paperwork can become overwhelming, and people are often screaming for one thing or another or demanding action or information. It's often up to the Production Coordinator to calmly handle whatever crisis comes up. Excellent phone skills and a pleasant telephone manner are also a plus.

Unions and Associations

The International Alliance of Theatrical Stage Employees (IATSE) offers members networking opportunities and other benefits.

Tips for Entry

1. Take any paid or unpaid job or internship in film production.
2. Get hired as an assistant Production Coordinator or an assistant to a Production Coordinator.
3. Work on low-budget or student, nonunion films.
4. Enter the Directors Guild of America (DGA) union training program as a DGA trainee.

PRODUCTION ASSISTANT

Duties: Support and assist in all areas, from preproduction to production and even in postproduction

Alternate Title(s): PA

Salary Range: $0 for nonpaying or internship positions to $75 to $200 per day or $500 per week

Employment Prospects: Good

Advancement Prospects: Fair

Best Geographical Location(s): Los Angeles/Hollywood, New York City

Prerequisites:

Education and Training—High school diploma usually required; college or film school is helpful

Experience—Work as a Production Assistant on student films or low-budget films; work-related experience at film school

Special Skills and Personality Traits—Hard worker; able to put in long hours; punctual; able to follow directions and take orders; humble; easy to get along with; dependable

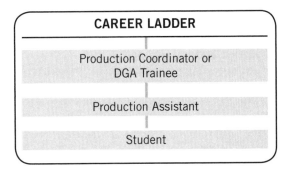

CAREER LADDER

Production Coordinator or DGA Trainee

Production Assistant

Student

Position Description

The position of Production Assistant (PA) is one of the best entry-level jobs in the film industry. Although a PA may do a lot of errands for everyone connected with the movie and may work long hours for very little pay, a PA works in all areas of film production, gaining valuable experience that will help him or her to choose a career path within the film industry. This is where you learn everything they didn't teach you in film school—the reality of filmmaking. PAs often assist executives, such as producers, directors, line producers, and production managers, who can help in their careers as they move up the ladder.

A Production Assistant's typical day depends on what aspect of the film the PA is working on. If the PA is assigned to the production office, chances are he or she will be answering phones, making copies of scripts, running errands, or basically doing whatever everyone else in the production office needs done but doesn't want to do. On location, a PA may be asked to direct traffic or unload and pack boxes. PAs assigned to work on the set usually help the assistant directors control the set. For example, a PA may be assigned to keep people out of the shot or help to maintain quiet on the set.

Being a Production Assistant is one way of getting into the Directors Guild of America (DGA) training program, but it may take a while. One must have accu-

mulated 600 workdays, including 300 shooting days, before a PA can request a note from the production manager to be considered for membership in the union. By then, a PA will have decided whether he or she has had enough of production work or whether he or she wants to go on doing it at a higher level.

Salaries

Salaries for PAs vary, depending on whether it's a union or nonunion film. On a union film in New York or Los Angeles, PAs make around $75 to $200 a day or $500 a week. On some low-budget or no budget films, they may not get anything other than the experience of working on a movie.

Employment Prospects

The employment prospects for becoming a PA are good, because there is a lot of turnover in this entry-level position. Even though it is highly competitive, being eager to learn, doing a lot of hard work no one else wants to do, being available whenever needed, and showing gratitude for the opportunity to work at all will take a PA far toward landing that first job or moving ahead.

Advancement Prospects

You can only get an entry-level position once; for the second position, you are expected to have a reputation for excellence and learned skills that you can bring to the new job. Advancing to the next rung after you've been a PA is determined by your personal career goals as well as being in the right place at the right time when a position opens up.

Education and Training

No formal training is required. Bachelor's, associate's or film school degrees are not required but could be useful. There is a wide range of courses, skills, or jobs that could be useful preparing for a PA job, such as still, film, or video photography; carpentry; metalworking; film; computer; fashion or costume design; theater; acting; directing; sign painting; hairdressing; makeup; clerical or office work; time management; the ability to drive a car or a van; music appreciation; catering; or film/video production.

Experience, Skills, and Personality Traits

To gain experience and the required basic skills, work as a PA on student or nonunion films, make your own movies on video, or work as a PA in television or the theater. Skills should include the ability to work hard for long hours, to follow directions, to be on time, and to do just about anything requested of you. A PA should be friendly, dependable, honest, punctual, and humble.

It is also important to realize that at some smaller film companies, there is nowhere to go but out once a PA has mastered the introductory skills and been there for a few months or a year or two. That is because the only other job is the one of head of the company, and the salaried employee or owner of the company who has that position is not about to give it up to the bright

and eager PA. If you get a position in a company like that, it is best to know when it is the right time to move on rather than getting frustrated by the self-limiting career options or, even worse, making the boss feel threatened that you want his or her job, so he or she then asks you to leave earlier than necessary.

Unions and Associations

There are no unions for Production Assistants, but membership in a film-related association, like Women in Film, may be helpful for networking.

Tips for Entry

1. Work as a PA on any nonunion or student film.
2. Get a list of production companies in your area, and apply for a job as a paid or unpaid PA, just to get your foot in the door.
3. Use your high school, college, or film school contacts to land a PA job.
4. Find out from the local film commission if there are any films shooting in your area who are looking to hire local residents as PAs. Even if the job experience is short-term, it will add to your film-related experiences and might lead to another job later.
5. If you live in an area where there is little film-making, consider moving to New York City, Los Angeles/Hollywood, Orlando, Chicago, or Toronto, where there is much more filmmaking activity and, along with that activity, an increased need for PAs.
6. Check the listings on the Internet, in local newspapers, or in trade publications for available Production Assistant positions.

DIRECTORS

DIRECTOR

CAREER PROFILE

Duties: Responsible for all cast and crew members, especially for directing actors and for taking the screenplay from words on a page to cinematic images that represent the Director's vision for the film

Alternate Title(s): None

Salary Range: Varies widely depending upon whether it is a union or nonunion film, as well as whether it is a low- or high-budget picture.

Employment Prospects: Excellent

Advancement Prospects: Good

Best Geographical Location(s): Los Angeles/Hollywood, New York City

Prerequisites:

Education and Training—Bachelor's or advanced degree optional

Experience—Film school background helpful but not essential

CAREER LADDER

Producer or Studio Head

Director

Screenwriter, First Assistant Director, or Unit Production Manager

Special Skills and Personality Traits—Strong leadership ability; visual creativity; a decision maker; keen judge of talent; able to collaborate; excellent interpersonal skills

Special Requirements—Union membership may be required

Position Description

While a writer creates the screenplay, it is ultimately the Director's vision that appears on the screen. In that sense, some consider the Director the film's true author, which is why many screenwriters aspire to also become Directors. There is an opening credit that reads "A (Director's name) film" or "A film by (Director's name)," since everything you see or hear was created under the direction of that person. It is the Director's dream we see on the screen, but to make that dream real, the Director has to collaborate with dozens of people, from cast members to casting directors, from cinematographers to editors, from screenwriters to set designers. Directors even get involved in decisions about sound, music, costume designer, and special effects.

A Director's job involves a lot more than yelling "action" at the beginning of a scene and "cut" at the end. His or her job is a series of endless decisions that ultimately impact everything that ends up on the screen, since she or he is often the only one who has the vision of what the final film will look like. The Director works closely with the screenwriter, production designer, director of photography or cinematographer, cast, casting director in selection of actors, sound department, editor, and composer.

He or she begins his or her job in preproduction by working with the writer on the script to make it as good as possible. But the script is only the blue print, the starting point. The Director has to transform the words on the page to sound and images on the screen.

Woody Allen used to joke that "the projectionist has the final cut." But, normally, it is the Director who is responsible to the producer and the financing studio to complete the film she or he set out to make. If she or he doesn't complete the film, then the final cut can be taken away from her or him, and the picture can be reedited, scenes reshot, or, if the film is deemed unreleasable, it can remain on the shelf forever.

If you ever attend film industry gatherings that include actors, writers, and cinematographers, sooner or later you're going to overhear someone say, "But I really want to direct." The words have become such a Hollywood cliché that you will find them stenciled on T-shirts worn by people in Los Angeles.

Most Directors came from another profession. Many were either writers, actors, or cinematographers. Some were tape editors or art directors. Occasionally, a prodigy will appear straight out of film school, such as George Lucas or Steven Spielberg. Even Francis Ford Coppola started as a screenwriter before he was given a chance to direct by prolific producer Roger Corman.

There are numerous excellent books that a Director can read, but the only real way a Director is going to learn his or her craft is by directing. Some useful books include *Shot by Shot* by Steven Katz; *Cinematic Motion, A Workshop for Staging Scenes* by Steven Katz; and *The Film Director* by Richard Bare. But it is still necessary to be on the set and see firsthand what works and what doesn't, what you have to do to get a shot or an effect, and how to get the performance you're looking for from a reluctant or hesitant actor.

"I did theater first," says Lane Shefter Bishop, who was born in New York but raised in California. Bishop majored in literature at the University of California at Santa Barbara. She continues: "I came to the realization after college that I could continue in theater and go to New York, or switch to film and stay here."

Bishop decided to remain in California and pursue film, including attending USC (University of Southern California) film school. She has never regretted her decision. "I fell in love with film," Bishop says. "I really enjoyed sitting in the editing room and adjusting performance, nuances as small as a frame. In theater, you lose control. It's different every time. But with film, it will be exactly the way you want it and it will be the exact same way, every time it screens."

She is part of a film industry family. Her father, Milt Shefter, is a film archivist. Her mother, Joy Shefter, did food styling for television before becoming head of food and beverage at Paramount Studios. Her brother is a lawyer, but he also is a professional actor. Her husband is a producer of both live action and animation, who is also currently producing a Web-based reality TV show.

In her 15 years as a film and television director, Bishop is most proud of her 2004 film, *The Day Laborers*, which was an official selection of six film festivals, including the prestigious Milan Film Festival. "There are not a lot of women directors in the industry," says Bishop who is a member of the Directors Guild of America. "Supporting myself as a director was tough sometimes. In between jobs, I used to temp at Disney, Dreamworks, and CAA via agencies that specialize in entertainment industry temps. Disney was a great place to be a temp. Many of the people I worked with 14 years ago at Disney I reconnected with over the last year, since I became the executive vice president of motion pictures and television at TwinStar Entertainment."

Aside from the 16 active projects she is working on at Twinstar, Bishop also has three completed screenplays that she hopes to get produced, but she does not want to direct her own work. "I think 'written and directed by' is the kiss of death," says Bishop. "There are so few people who do that well, like Kenneth Branagh. If you try to write and direct your own material, you don't have enough perspective from one to do the other. You're too close to it to write and then direct it. You really need some perspective."

Gayle Kirschenbaum is a New York–based director, producer, and writer whose earlier training was as an artist and an art school graduate. "I made a transfer into the industry at 32 years old and was awarded my first documentary with no background in film or video, and won an Emmy for it," she explains. Kirschenbaum continues: "I tell everyone your skills are transferable. I knew no one in Hollywood when I moved there and talked my way into an interview with an EP [executive producer] at a PBS affiliate after months of attempts. He was so busy during the meeting—people were in his office nonstop—and I was sitting in front of his wall of Emmys. I had nothing to show him and left thinking, 'How am I going to get an opportunity? What am I going to do?' I was never a writer. I was very insecure about my writing but I came up with an idea for a series and wrote up a two-page treatment and left it at the guardhouse because I couldn't get back on to the lot. He read it and hired me based on that. I had no idea how to make a documentary but came from being an artist and graphic designer who had created multimedia shows which were multiprojector slide shows. I transfer all my skills over, my people skills, visual skills, and skills with making images and using music well."

Kirschenbaum continues: "I spent 13 years in L.A. making documentaries, producing reality TV crime shows, game shows, and talk shows." Over those years, Kirschenbaum did take several film courses. She explains: "When I first moved to L.A., I was put in a directing lab at the Directors Guild with Frances Parker at her master workshop. I studied also with Paul Gray, Ron Richards, and Lilyan Chauvin. In New York, I studied with Arnold Eagle and Ralph Rosenbloom." She was also in a writing class, which she highly recommends doing. "It had simple weekly exercises that got your juices flowing. It's good to write, just write, not necessarily a screenplay, which could be overwhelming, but short pieces, essays, first person, articles, short stories, whatever you want to get out, just get it out."

Kirschenbaum eventually returned to New York City. She says: "I couldn't get used to L.A. and wanted to get back to New York. I returned to New York and hit the streets thinking I had a knack for getting press, but I didn't have a finished movie. The long and short of it, I ended up making this movie with my dog, *A Dog's Life: A Dogamentary*, which, in 2005, was broadcast on

HBO/Cinemax and is out on DVD in wide release. My second film, *My Nose*, a short, is playing the festival circuit now. Both of these personal films thrust me in front of the camera, and I love being there. My next film is going to be a feature film, a romantic comedy. I love telling stories that deal with universal themes and are poignant and humorous."

Salaries

Salaries vary widely, from very little for low and no budget independent films to six to seven figures for $200 million dollar studio epics. If you are a member of the Directors Guild of America (DGA) (see http://www.dga.org), then there are minimums that you will be paid. Because contracts are negotiated periodically, for the most up-to-date information and newest rates, it is best to check the Web site of the DGA (http://www.dga.org). In 2008, for a high-budget union film, the weekly salary for a director was $15,108. The low-budget union film weekly salary for a director, up to June 30, 2011, was $11,331. (Check with the DGA for weekly salary minimums for low-budget films, because they have four low-budget levels, based on the budget for the low-budget film.) Other considerations that are part of the DGA minimum pertain to the number of weeks to prepare as well as the guaranteed shooting period and cutting allowance. This refers to the minimum amount of time allowed for preproduction, production or principal photography and then postproduction or editing. The DGA minimum actually guarantees a Director will be given a minimum number of weeks to accomplish each phase of production.

Employment Prospects

The film industry is a growth business, and since the Director is key to every film, employment prospects for Directors are excellent. Feature-film Directors are basically in two employment groups: union and nonunion. To work on a studio film, you have to be a member of the Directors Guild of America—in the union.

Job security for Directors usually depends on how well their last film performed. There is a belief that one good hit will cover a Director through three or maybe even four flops. Like most positions in films, once the film is complete, the Director is out of a job and has to seek work on another project. The Director is usually hired either by the studio or the producer who owns the property being developed. It is often the first position filled and one of the few that remains through all three phases of a movie: preproduction, production, and postproduction.

Advancement Prospects

Prospects for advancement in the Director ranks are very much determined by each Director's track record. If you direct movies that become financial or critical hits, then your prospects for advancement are enhanced. If your movies fail for whatever reason, then it will be that much harder to get the next job directing, which is one of the reasons most Directors have their next job lined up before the film they're working on even comes out.

Education and Training

There are hundreds of college and university film programs as well as studio training programs designed to help the would-be Director land his or her first job. There are short film workshops where many Directors first learn their craft. The Directors Guild of America has an excellent training program. Another route to directing feature films is to get experience directing music videos, commercials, or documentaries and then move to features.

Experience, Skills, and Personality Traits

The key to directing is knowing what you are doing, which means you have to be experienced in virtually all aspects of filmmaking, from acting and writing to cinematography and lighting to editing and sound. Frankly, the only way to learn how to be a Director is to be one. "Master the craft before attempting the art," wrote Richard Bare in his textbook *The Film Director*. In these days of digital cameras, anyone can rent or buy a digital camera and then use it to direct and shoot a short video.

As for personality traits, a Director has to be comfortable being in charge because she or he is the guide to everything. He or she needs to be self-confident, able to make clear decisions, and to possess a vision for each movie. Another essential characteristic is being able to recognize talent, especially acting and writing talent, because filmmaking is a collaborative medium; in order for the Director to get his or her vision on the screen, he or she has to depend on the talents of other people, including the costume designer, makeup artist or special effects artist, and the director of photography (cinematographer).

Director Taylor Hackford (*Officer and a Gentleman*), in his interview quoted in *Working in Hollywood*, advises anyone interested in pursuing a career in directing to gain as much life experience as possible: "I think it's better to develop a wealth of experience and talent and have something to say before you pick up that camera and try to say it."

Unions and Associations

Membership in the Directors Guild of America (DGA) is required for studio or union films.

Tips for Entry

1. During the school years—middle school, high school, college, and graduate school—get involved in any aspect of filmmaking available to you, such as creating student films with a video or digital camera.
2. Make short films or music videos.
3. Attend seminars that are given by successful Directors and listen to how they got started, what books they read, how they trained, and how they got their first break.
4. Discipline yourself to write, shoot, and keep shooting until you have a completed film or short film you can show to an agent, producer, or studio. If you're short on ideas of your own, option a play or book written by another and buy the right to adapt that material into a film.
5. Enter your completed film in film festivals. Even if you don't win, you will be exposing your directing ability to others who might help you get started by recommending you to their agent, attorney, producer, or Director.
6. Pursue any internship or apprenticeship opportunities available to Directors.

FIRST ASSISTANT DIRECTOR

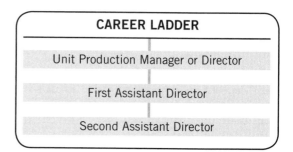

Position Description

Whereas the director yells, "Action!," the First Assistant Director will be the one yelling "Quiet on the set."

The First Assistant Director (1st AD) is the director's right hand, whose main job is to keep everything moving forward to help the director realize his or her vision. The 1st AD is also responsible for the production board, which is an up-to-the-minute shooting schedule. He or she may also fill the role of production manager on low-budget films. The 1st AD is usually hired during preproduction to do a script breakdown and to prepare and coordinate everything that happens on the shoot. In a script breakdown, the 1st AD produces a shooting script with each shot numbered, a cast and crew sheet for each day of shooting, and a sheet with various information broken down for set designers, props, special lighting requirements, costumes, and any details necessary to make sure the director gets the shot she or he wants. The 1st AD will also note which actors and extras are in each scene.

After breaking down each scene, the 1st AD will put the script back together with the aim toward creating the most efficient shooting schedule. That means scenes are seldom shot in the order they appear in the script. If there are a number of shots in the same location, to save time and money and to help with the final film's continuity, the 1st AD will schedule them together no matter where they come in the film. A similar formula is followed when it comes to actors, especially stars whose schedules are often busy. Schedules, however, are never inflexible, because bad weather could force a delay in exterior location shots. It's up to the 1st AD to prepare a realistic shooting schedule that takes into consideration the number of script pages the director is supposed to shoot in a day. This will depend on each director: A good 1st AD will know her or his boss's style. For example, Clint Eastwood, when directing, is known for his rapid shooting schedules and for shooting as few takes as possible, while other directors may require more time to get the shot they want.

During production, the 1st AD does whatever the director needs him or her to do. This could involve managing a large group of extras or making sure the art department has built the correct set. A 1st AD is also responsible for ensuring that the effects department has the right equipment and that the set is ready for shooting.

Salaries

On union films, minimum salaries are set by the Directors Guild of America (DGA). They cover a wide range, depending on several considerations, including whether the employment is at a studio or distant location. For example, the minimum weekly salary at a studio is $4,100; the minimum weekly salary at a distant location is $5,734. Daily minimum rates are $1,025 at a studio and $1,434 at a distant location. (Check with DGA for most up-to-date salaries because a new contract with revised rates is negotiated periodically.) On a nonunion film, a 1st AD's salary depends on the film's budget.

Employment Prospects

Employment prospects for 1st Assistant Directors are good for studio films. Every studio film has one. To work on a studio film you have to be a member of the Directors Guild of America.

Job security for 1st ADs usually depends on how well they got along with their last director and how effectively they performed their job on that film. If a 1st AD has problems on the set, word gets around quickly. Competition is tough, and you have to perform well and be a team player that others, especially the director, want to be around, in order to stay in the business.

Advancement Prospects

The career ladder for 1st Assistant Directors offers two paths for advancement, either to Director or Unit Production Manager (UPM). Advancement prospects for a 1st Assistant Director to become a Unit Production Manager (UPM) are good. However, this choice also indicates a shift in career paths from directing to producing.

Prospects for advancement from 1st Assistant Director to director are poor. A good 1st Assistant Director is hard to find, so once someone establishes him- or herself as a good 1st AD, it's hard to break out of that category. In many cases, in order to move up to director, you have to make your own opportunities, by either writing or optioning a script. It may mean making a short film that shows your skills as a director.

Education and Training

Besides film school, the best training for a 1st AD is the DGA training program. After 400 days as a DGA trainee,

you become a second assistant director (2nd AD), where you begin to make a name for yourself. Once you prove yourself as a 2nd AD, you will be given an opportunity to become a 1st AD.

Experience, Skills, and Personality Traits

Experience as a DGA trainee and then as a 2nd Assistant Director is the standard. It helps if you are able to think quickly, handle large crowds, be well organized, lead your employees, and have a strong working knowledge of film production. Basically, the same experience, skills, and personality that go into making a good director apply to becoming an excellent 1st Assistant Director.

Unions and Associations

Membership in the Directors Guild of America (DGA) is beneficial—and necessary for work on studio and union films.

Tips for Entry

1. Take all the steps necessary to becoming a 2nd AD, since that is the natural progression to 1st AD.
2. The Directors Guild of America training program is probably the best entry into becoming a First Assistant Director.
3. Take any entry-level job on a production set to begin to gain knowledge about how a movie is shot and produced.
4. Meet as many people in the film industry as possible. Let them know what you want to do.
5. During middle school, high school, college, and graduate school, get involved in any aspect of filmmaking available to you, such as creating student films with a video or digital camera.
6. Go to film school.

SECOND ASSISTANT DIRECTOR

Duties: Work for the first assistant director; prepare and distribute the daily paperwork, such as shooting schedules, cast and crew calls, and the production report

Alternate Title(s): 2nd AD; Key 2nd Assistant Director

Salary Range: $687 to $960 daily; $2,748 to $3,840 weekly (check with the Directors Guild of America/DGA for the most up-to-date salaries because a new contract with revised rates is negotiated periodically)

Employment Prospects: Good

Advancement Prospects: Good

Best Geographical Location(s): Los Angeles/Hollywood, New York City

Prerequisites:

Education and Training—Film degree or advanced degree optional but useful

CAREER LADDER

First Assistant Director

Second Assistant Director

DGA Trainee, Film school graduate

Experience—Directors Guild of America (DGA) training program; film school background helpful but not essential

Special Skills and Personality Traits—Able to manage and motivate large groups of people; leadership skills; well organized; visual creativity; overall knowledge of all aspects of filmmaking

Special Requirements—Union membership may be required

Position Description

The Second Assistant Director is there to support the first assistant director. His or her primary responsibility is to carry out various functions of the 1st AD and to get the extras on the set ready for the 1st AD during shooting. They also distribute and maintain the "call sheets," which are records of the day's shooting schedule. The 2nd AD makes notes on the call sheets as to whether they are on schedule or whether there were any problems during the shoot with cast, crew, or equipment. This is used as the basis for a final production report. A 2nd AD is among the first people to arrive on the set and among the last to leave. They also help out in blocking the movements of the extras, while issuing, collecting, and accounting for the extras' pay vouchers. A 2nd AD is also responsible for making sure the cast and crew is in the right place at the right time, maintaining a daily shooting log.

On a typical day, a 2nd Assistant Director arrives before sunrise, and there are only a few other people on the set. The night before he or she gave out call sheets to cast and crew who are supposed to show up today, so he or she has to be there early to make sure hair, makeup and wardrobe are set up and ready before the actors arrive. When the actors arrive, he or she tells them where to go, who gets made up first, who can go eat,

and who needs to be where, when. The extras usually arrive after the actors, since they do their own makeup and hair, followed by the crew. All this time, the 2nd AD keeps track of who's ready, so that if a particular actor is needed for a rehearsal or shot, the 2nd AD will know where the actor is and if he or she is made up and in wardrobe, or not. Like the 1st AD, the 2nd AD's job is to help move things along. When the 1st AD arrives, the 2nd AD reports on who's ready and who's not. Once the actors and crew are ready for a rehearsal or a shot, the 2nd AD prepares, or blocks, the background with extras. Moving extras around is a key part of a 2nd AD's job. There is a certain amount of creativity involved here in that if the background doesn't look right, it will affect the image on the screen. It's up to the 2nd AD to make the background work for the director and the 1st AD. If the scene calls for excitement in the background, people should not be standing around doing nothing—the 2nd AD has to give them directions to get the right effect.

The 2nd AD keeps track of meal breaks and whether a particular actor who is only contracted for a short time will finish her or his work without going into overtime. A 2nd AD has to know the various contracts and keep up with lots of paperwork. The 2nd AD tracks the hours the cast and crew worked, the amount of film shot, the amount of sound recorded, and any injuries, illnesses, or special needs.

During the day, the 2nd AD will often be a liaison between the production manager and the director. For example, the director will tell the 1st AD if she or he needs special lighting for a night shot, which is scheduled for the following day. Since the 1st AD is required on the set at all times, she or he will send the 2nd AD to the production manager with a request for the extra crew members needed to get the special shot. The production manager will either approve the added expenditure or reject it, depending on where the production is in the schedule. If it's already behind schedule and over budget, the director may have to rethink the shot so that she or he won't have to hire more crew.

At the end of the day, the 2nd AD receives the day's shooting schedule of scenes shot and how long each shot was supposed to take and compares it to what actually happened. The 2nd AD is the reality checker. They keep a log of what really happened that day, so if a film went behind or ahead of schedule, the director and producer would know it. This is called the production report, and it is used to keep track of everything that happens during production.

Besides filling in the production, the 2nd AD is responsible for handing out the call sheets for the next day. That means making sure each cast and crew member has a copy of the next day's schedule before they leave for the day.

Salaries

Earnings range widely, with minimums on union films set by the Directors Guild of America (DGA): weekly minimum for a studio location, $2,748; weekly minimum for distant location, $3,840; daily minimum for a studio location, $687; daily minimum for a distant location, $960. (Check with the Directors Guild of America/DGA for the most up-to-date salaries because a new contract with revised rates is negotiated periodically.) A nonunion film rarely has a 2nd AD.

Employment Prospects

Employment prospects for 2nd Assistant Directors are good for studio films. Nearly every studio film has one. To work on a studio film, you have to be a member of the Directors Guild of America.

Job security for 2nd ADs depends on how well the production is moving along. If they are part of an efficient production that came in on time and on budget,

they have a better chance of getting another job than if they were part of a production team that seemed to be unorganized, wasted money, or failed to keep track of the production schedule. If a 2nd AD fails to perform his or her function well, word spreads.

Advancement Prospects

Prospects for advancement from 2nd Assistant Director to 1st assistant director are good. As 1st ADs move on to directing or production manager positions, they leave openings for 2nd ADs. Get to know as many 1st ADs or directors as possible, so that when an opening occurs, they will call on you.

Education and Training

The best training for a 2nd AD is the DGA training program. After 400 days as a DGA trainee, you become a 2nd AD. Film school is also helpful, as is any management training or prior work on film productions.

Experience, Skills, and Personality Traits

Experience as a DGA trainee is the standard. You have to put in 400 days as a trainee before qualifying for a 2nd AD position. It is important to have strong organizational and time management skills, because keeping things organized and moving on time on the set is the most important aspect of the 2nd AD's job. Being able to work with people, motivate them, and direct them, in the case of extras, is also important. You should be patient, energetic, calm under pressure, able to take orders, observant, strong willed, and thick-skinned.

Unions and Associations

Membership in the Directors Guild of America (DGA) is beneficial. Membership in the DGA is required if a 2nd AD is hired to work on a studio or union film.

Tips for Entry

1. Take any entry-level job on a production set to get involved. You will still have to apply for and be accepted into the DGA training program, though.
2. Network. Meet as many film industry people as possible.
3. Get involved in any aspect of filmmaking available to you, such as creating student films with a video or digital camera.
4. Go to film school.
5. Attend seminars and film festivals.

SCRIPT SUPERVISOR

CAREER PROFILE

Duties: Maintain continuity while the film is being shot by keeping track of the different takes, timing the takes, and making notes for the director as an aid for when she or he edits the film.

Alternate Title(s): Continuity Coordinator

Salary Range: $1,800 to $2,400 per week; $25 to $40 an hour for daily union employees depending on their experience and size of the budget

Employment Prospects: Good

Advancement Prospects: Good

Best Geographical Location(s): Los Angeles/Hollywood, New York City

Prerequisites:

    Education and Training—High school education is required

    Experience—To join the union, you must work 30 days on a set and complete an introductory script supervisor course

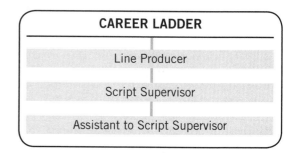

CAREER LADDER

Line Producer

Script Supervisor

Assistant to Script Supervisor

Special Skills and Personality Traits—Strong verbal skills; fluency in written and spoken English; organized; detail oriented

Special Requirements—Union membership may be required

Position Description

The Script Supervisor is the director's extra set of eyes. He or she keeps track of everything being shot—verifying actors' lines, maintaining detailed records of each take, and transcribing, all action, positions, camera angles, additional progressions, and any deviations from the script. The Script Supervisor notes lenses used, timing, f-stops, and focus changes, such as zooms, and keeps continuity of wardrobe, makeup, art work, and virtually everything seen or heard on the screen.

Have you ever noticed a "blooper" in a movie? Chances are it involves a problem with continuity. An actor is wearing a hat as she enters a door, but it is missing in the next shot, which is an interior shot of her standing in the doorway. It's a pretty good guess that these two shots were filmed days apart. It is up to the Script Supervisor to make sure that the hat is in both shots. This may seem like an easy thing to do, but when you consider everything a Script Supervisor is responsible for, it becomes clear how mistakes can occur. In fact, if you look hard enough, you may find an error or two in continuity in most movies, because it is virtually impossible for one person to keep track of everything. But that is what a Script Supervisor has to do. Even if there's an assistant Script Supervisor, which there often

is on big budget studio films, continuity errors slip through. Most of the time, even the audience doesn't catch them, because they are so hard to notice.

Still, without a Script Supervisor tracking continuity, the film would probably be a mess. Therefore, this is one of the most important jobs on a film set. In fact, it is so important that unions now require a Script Supervisor to be on the set whenever the director is on the set.

The title *Script Supervisor* does not reflect the job this person is hired to do. The person doing this job used to be called the "continuity girl," due to the fact that most Script Supervisors were women and also usually the director's secretary. Their primary concern was making sure that there was continuity between shots. This is still their first priority but now they have many others as well.

Since it is nearly impossible for the Script Supervisor to write down everything, they rely on still photographs, taken with a digital camera.

On a typical day on the set, the Script Supervisor carries a thick binder, known as the continuity book, filled with notes on wardrobe, hair and makeup, props, lighting, camera angles, and what lines the actors are speaking. If scene number 55 is being shot that day, the job of the Script Supervisor is to make sure scene

55 matches scene 54, which might have been shot two weeks ago. For example, in scene 54, actor "A" is about to enter a building. As he does, he removes his hat, a brown fedora. The Script Supervisor notes where he is in this movement. Is the hat already off or still on his head as we see actor "A" in scene 55 from the inside of the building in the door way, hat in hand.

The Script Supervisor will keep track of every element of every shot and then stay through the dailies at the end of the day, to make sure nothing was missed.

Salaries

On union films, minimum salaries are set by the International Alliance of Theatrical Stage Employees (IATSE). For those members of the union for script supervisors, IATSE Local 871, there are guidelines for payment: a range of $25 to $40/hour—depending upon how much experience the Script Supervisor has and whether or not the project concerned is a big-budget studio movie—to $1,800 to $2,400 per week. For non-union films, pay range may vary widely.

Employment Prospects

Since the role of Script Supervisor is so important, prospects for employment in this category are good. Every studio film has to have a Script Supervisor and every nonstudio film should have one to protect the film's continuity and in turn its credibility. Too many errors in this area could render a film not fit for release.

Advancement Prospects

The prospects for advancement from assistant script supervisor to Script Supervisor are good. Unfortunately, the ability for a Script Supervisor to advance to unit production manager is not so easy. A separate union is involved. Script Supervisors belong to IATSE, while unit production managers belong to the Directors Guild.

Education and Training

A high school diploma is required, as are strong verbal skills and fluency in written and spoken English.

Special Requirements

To work as a Script Supervisor on a movie that is a studio or union film, membership in the International Alliance of Theatrical Stage Employees (IATSE) is required.

Experience, Skills, and Personality Traits

IATSE has a training program for Script Supervisors. Useful personality traits include attention to detail, observant, strong communication, and thick-skinned. Working knowledge of lenses, camera angles, film production, photography, and shorthand is helpful.

Unions and Associations

Membership in IATSE is beneficial. Membership in IATSE is required if a Script Supervisor is hired to work on a studio or union film.

Tips for Entry

1. The IATSE training program is probably the best entry into a Script Supervisor position.
2. Take any entry-level job and work up to assistant Script Supervisor. Get hired as a Script Supervisor's intern or assistant.
3. Administrative assistant jobs at a film company sometimes lead to a Script Supervisor position.
4. Find out more information at the Web site for IATSE Local 871, the union for Script Supervisors (http://www.ialocal871.org).

DGA TRAINEE

CAREER PROFILE

Duties: Assist the second assistant director
Alternate Title(s): None
Salary Range: $628 to $772 per week
Employment Prospects: Good
Advancement Prospects: Good
Best Geographical Location(s): Los Angeles/Hollywood, New York City
Prerequisites:

    Education and Training—A college or advanced degree in film is helpful but not required

    Experience—Not required for acceptance into the training program

    Special Skills and Personality Traits—Patient; hard worker; able to absorb a lot of information quickly;

CAREER LADDER

Second Assistant Director

DGA Trainee

Production Assistant, Film school Graduate

quick thinker; able to work as part of a team; able to take orders (as well as, when appropriate, to give orders); humble and pleasant to be around

Position Description

Established in 1965 by the Directors Guild of America and the Alliance of Motion Picture and Television Producers, the DGA training program is designed to train future second assistant directors. This is a highly competitive training program that is just one possible way to get into the extremely hard to break into Directors Guild of America. There are two training programs, one on the West Coast, in Los Angeles (http://www.trainingplan.org), and one on the East Coast, in New York City (http://www.dgatrainingprogram.org). Each year, more than 1,400 people apply to both programs; only 25 to 30 are accepted in Los Angeles (out of 1,000 applicants), and only six in New York City (out of 400 applicants). The accepted trainees in Los Angeles are expected to work 400 days of on-the-job training and to attend about 36 seminars. Those in the New York-based program are required to fulfill 350 days of on-the-job training and attend seminars and special assignments in the two-year program. Other requirements include living either in Los Angeles or New York City, having access to a car, and possessing a driver's license. You will be assigned to a variety of productions from features films to episodic television. The program focuses on duties of a director and assistant director as well as on administrative, managerial, and interpersonal skills.

At the end of the training, trainees are then eligible to join the Directors Guild of America as a 2nd AD.

Salaries

The DGA sets the minimum weekly salary for the DGA trainees. As of 2008, the weekly salary for DGA trainees ranges from $628/week in the first quarter to $772/week in the fourth quarter, plus the possibility of overtime.

Employment Prospects

The employment prospects for those who complete the DGA training program are excellent, because the program is so highly regarded and it almost guarantees getting a job at the second assistant director level. There are also phenomenal on-the-job training and networking experiences available to those in the DGA trainee program. However, placement in the program is extremely competitive, with a less than 3 percent acceptance rate.

Advancement Prospects

Once a DGA Trainee has completed the training, advancing from second assistant director may be harder than getting that initial job as a 2nd AD. However, those who are fortunate to have been part of the DGA trainee experience will certainly have potential job referrals from their fellow trainees as well as the DGA membership to draw upon as they move to new jobs or try to move up the ranks.

Education and Training

A requirement is an associate of arts or film degree from an accredited two-year college, a degree from an accredited four-year college or university, or, in lieu of a degree, two years of paid employment. Those who successfully complete the program receive a certificate.

Experience, Skills, and Personality Traits

Applicants must be 21 years of age or older and have the legal right to work in the United States. Get as much experience working on nonunion films or television or on union films as a PA. Be detail oriented, well organized, and creative.

Unions and Associations

Upon completing the internship, it is necessary to join the DGA at the second assistant director level in order to be considered for those jobs on union films.

Tips for Entry

1. Apply through the DGA. Go to the Web sites for the Los Angeles (http://www.trainingplan. org) and New York City (http://www.dgatraining program.org) programs and read over the information, keeping track of the deadlines for applying. Note too when the testing and the in-person interviews occur.
2. Work as a production assistant on any union film to get experience.

FINANCING, LEGAL, AND ADMINISTRATIVE ISSUES

AUDITOR

Duties: Keep track of all production costs; make sure the production stays within its budget

Alternate Title(s): Production Accountant

Salary Range: $80,000 to $120,000

Employment Prospects: Good

Advancement Prospects: Fair

Best Geographical Location(s): Los Angeles/Hollywood, New York City

Prerequisites:

Education and Training—A master's of business administration (MBA) is preferred, with a film minor

Experience—A combination of accounting and film experience is beneficial, including working on a low-budget independent film

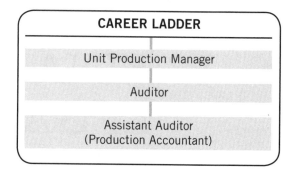

CAREER LADDER

Unit Production Manager

Auditor

Assistant Auditor
(Production Accountant)

Special Skills and Personality Traits—Being good with numbers; strong accounting ability; able to work under pressure

Special Requirements—State license required; certification as a certified public accountant (CPA) is also required

Position Description

The Auditor has the daunting task of keeping track of every penny spent during the making of the film, beginning in preproduction, moving through principal photography, and continuing to the end of postproduction. Often, the Auditor will work with the production manager in preparing a preliminary budget. The Auditor is responsible for managing all expenses as well as all sources of payments during production. He or she must give the production manager and, if a studio is involved, the studio executive in charge, an accurate financial accounting. The goal is to keep all spending within the budget of the film.

The job begins in preproduction, with the preparation of an initial production budget. This budget is used to determine the cost of actually making the movie. The Auditor will make a chart of accounts, listing all departments involved in the production, crew costs, equipment, catering, and other expenses. To do this, the Auditor first reads the script and its breakdown. He or she prepares an above-the-line and below-the-line budget, taking into consideration as many elements as possible. The more elements in place, the easier it is to prepare a budget. Often, the Auditor will have to prepare a very early preliminary budget before a director or producer is even attached.

Once a budget has been agreed upon, it is up to the Auditor to keep costs in line. That means accounting for

every expense and having invoices to go with each expenditure. If a director is taking too long to set up shots or seems to be falling behind the schedule, the Auditor will alert the production manager and studio, and action will be taken. Scenes may have to be cut, and in extreme cases, the director replaced.

During production, the Auditor and production manager approve any changes that affect the costs. It's up to the Auditor to keep accurate daily financial records and to report any overspending or underspending.

An Auditor isn't required on the set everyday. Normally, a biweekly visit is sufficient unless problems arise. Then, the Auditor may be called upon to watch everything more closely.

In postproduction, the Auditor keeps track of the editing process as well as any special effects spending. This part of the process can become quite costly and out of control, if not maintained.

Salaries

Auditors may earn $80,000 to $120,000 a year, depending on their experience, the budget of the films they work on, and whether they are on staff at a studio or large production company. Weekly average earnings for Auditors are $2,200.

Employment Prospects

Employment prospects for Auditors are good, since every studio film needs to have one. Once an Auditor develops a positive reputation for having the combined specialized skills of being both an Auditor and familiar with working on films, more opportunities will open up.

Advancement Prospects

Prospects for advancement are only fair, since Auditors rarely advance out of that category. However, an Auditor with a film school background could aspire to become a unit production manager (UPM). Others have gone on to become producers.

Education and Training

A graduate degree from a business school (MBA) is helpful, as are additional courses in film or a minor or major in film at the undergraduate level. Auditors must also have proper training in accounting and have passed the test to qualify as a CPA.

Special Requirements

Professional certification or state licensure for certified public accountant (CPA) is usually required for an Auditor.

Experience, Skills, and Personality Traits

The best way to get experience as an Auditor is to work as an assistant Auditor; this job lets you learn the way a film is budgeted and see how money is spent.

A background in accounting is helpful, as are good interpersonal skills and excellent negotiating skills. The Auditor will probably have to negotiate with the rest of the production team about whether they can afford to shoot a take or whether they need to cut a scene out completely in order to stay within budget.

Unions and Associations

Auditors are nonunion, but there are numerous professional associations for accountants, such as the CPA Network, Association of Practicing CPAs, and the Society of Financial Examiners, to name a few. Auditors may also join film associations, such as Women in Film, which may also be helpful for educational and networking purposes.

Tips for Entry

1. Move up the ranks from a job as an accountant to that of an assistant Auditor.
2. Work on low-budget independent films that stay within budget. Develop a reputation for doing excellent work as an Auditor and for being personable and easy to work with.
3. Keep track of films going into production that may need an Auditor, attend film conferences and seminars, and network within the filmmaking community.

ENTERTAINMENT LAWYER

CAREER PROFILE

Duties: Handle a variety of legal issues for clients, including contract review, negotiation, intellectual property protection, and preparation of investment packages, such as private placement offerings for independent producers

Alternate Title(s): Entertainment Attorney

Salary Range: Varies widely

Employment Prospects: Good

Advancement Prospects: Good

Best Geographical Location(s): Los Angeles/Hollywood, New York City

Prerequisites:

Education and Training—College and law degrees

Experience—Working in the entertainment industry, such as for the business affairs department of a studio, television agency, or production company

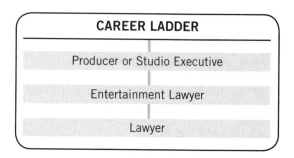

CAREER LADDER

Producer or Studio Executive

Entertainment Lawyer

Lawyer

Special Skills and Personality Traits—A working knowledge of film production, distribution and financing; understanding of the egos involved in the business; diplomatic; aware of the politics involved in the film industry; honest; a high degree of integrity; able to handle a great deal of stress

Special Requirements—State license required

Position Description

An Entertainment Lawyer specializes in legal issues pertaining to the entertainment industry. This may cover a wide spectrum of situations, from contract review and negotiation to preparing private placement offerings designed to raise money to make films. It is the Entertainment Lawyer who actually understands the words in the contract that an agent negotiated on behalf of a screenwriter, producer, or director.

In many cases, the Entertainment Lawyer is the person who makes sure that the contract accurately reflects the deal her or his client has approved. It is the Lawyer's job to protect the client's interests and to ensure that the language used in the contract is acceptable. For example, an agent may have negotiated a terrific deal for a writer but failed to see that in the contract's convoluted wording the writer had given up all rights to the work whether the film was made or not. The Lawyer might revise the wording to reflect a reversion of rights back to the writer after a certain period of time.

Some Entertainment Attorneys only represent writers, directors, actors, and talent, while others represent studios, producers, or production companies. Others specialize in union disputes, tax law, and lawsuits. An Entertainment Attorney who represents a producer or studio may be involved in a number of areas, such as acquiring rights to a book or play, handling contracts with talent and location releases, and negotiating product placements to raise money.

Salaries

Salaries vary, depending on an Entertainment Lawyer's standing within the industry. A well-connected, talented Entertainment Attorney earns six to seven figures a year. Hourly rates range from $200 to $700.

Employment Prospects

It is difficult to break into entertainment law, since it is such a specialized area. However, increasingly complex deals create a steady demand for their services.

Advancement Prospects

Developing a good reputation, and word of mouth, will help an Entertainment Lawyer to advance, as satisfied clients or companies that are represented recommend the lawyer. Advancement within a firm is possible, as is beginning a firm of one's own.

Education and Training

Besides having a law degree, it might help to take courses in film school or business school.

Special Requirements

Entertainment Lawyers must pass the state bar exam to be licensed to practice law.

Experience, Skills, and Personality Traits

Those interested in this job should work in the entertainment industry for an agency, a studio, a union, or a production company to get a working knowledge of the business.

Be ready to work hard, long hours. You should love movies and have a passion for the people who make them, since they are going to be your clients. Be honest and have integrity. Learn to decipher the most densely worded contracts.

Unions and Association

Membership in local and national bar associations is required.

Tips for Entry

1. Get experience at a law firm geared to entertainment law.
2. Go to film school before or after getting a law degree.
3. Attend film festivals and seminars, letting directors and actors know that you're available for legal advice.
4. Work in the legal department of a film studio or independent production company.

TITLES REGISTRAR

CAREER PROFILE

Duties: Protect a film's title by registering it with the Motion Picture Association of America (MPAA) in an effort to lock up usage

Alternative Title(s): None

Salary Range: $45,000 to $60,000

Employment Prospects: Fair

Advancement Prospects: Fair

Best Geographical Location(s): Los Angeles/Hollywood, New York City

Prerequisites:

　Education and Training—Law degree or paralegal training

　Experience—Working in the legal department for a studio or production company

Special Skills and Personality Traits—A working knowledge of copyright and trademark law, as well as laws governing title registration and arbitration; integrity; an eye for detail

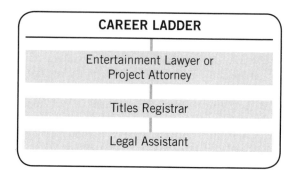

CAREER LADDER

Entertainment Lawyer or Project Attorney

Titles Registrar

Legal Assistant

Position Description

The Titles Registrar works in the legal department of a studio, for a production company, or for an entertainment lawyer. While this position is normally filled by a paralegal, its significance is considerable in that title protection has become a key element in the continued financial success or failure of a film project. It is the Titles Registrar's job to make sure a title is registered and to deal with any and all issues that may ensue, such as titles protestation, even though registering a title with the MPAA does not offer legal protection.

While you can't copyright a title, you can register one with the Motion Picture Association of America (MPAA). This does not offer total protection against an independent producer using a title that may have been registered with the MPAA. But it does offer a limited guarantee that another signatory of the MPAA will not use the title if you've registered it first and intend to use it within a reasonable period of time.

A Titles Registrar gets titles from a variety of sources within the studio or production company. They come from development executives, producers, or other attorneys. Normally, they are titles to films that are in development.

The Titles Registrar fills out the paperwork with the MPAA and then waits for possible protests from other companies who may have similar titles in development.

When that happens, the title is frozen until the issue is negotiated or taken to arbitration.

Often, a company will sell rights to a title if one company is closer to completing production. In any event, companies prefer to negotiate a settlement, since arbitration may take too long and hinder a film's start date.

Salaries

Salaries vary, depending on whether the Titles Registrar is an attorney or a paralegal. Most are paralegals working within the legal departments of studios, production companies, or for entertainment attorneys. They earn an average of $45,000 to $60,000 a year.

Employment Prospects

All studios and most major production companies have someone to register titles. However, there are only a relatively small number of openings, so employment prospects for a Titles Registrar are only fair.

Advancement Prospects

The position of Titles Registrar usually leads to other work within the business and legal affairs departments. For those who continue as paralegals, advancement is limited to areas not requiring a law degree, such as publicity or possibly an entry-level development position. Titles Registrars may also move up by assuming other duties, such as handling credits as well as titles, or working on contract and casting administration.

Education and Training

Training as a paralegal or a law degree is required. Work in a legal affairs office as a clerk or intern while attending law school to gain an understanding of the complex nature of this work. Clerking in a legal affairs office is also helpful.

Experience, Skills, and Personality Traits

You should work in the legal department for a studio or production company. Be honest and have integrity.

Unions and Associations

This is a nonunion position. Film industry associations such as Women in Film may be helpful for networking.

Tips for Entry

1. Get experience in a legal department of a studio or production company.
2. Take a job as a clerk or paralegal for a studio or film company.
3. Attend law school and specialize in entertainment issues.

FILM COMMISSIONER

Duties: Facilitate filmmaking in a region or state by offering information on possible locations, crews, film festivals, state incentives, permission to film, and weather or transportation data

Alternate Title(s): None

Salary Range: $50,000 to $100,000

Employment Prospects: Good

Advancement Prospects: Good

Best Geographical Location(s): Wherever there is a local, regional, or state film commission, or wherever there is a need to form one

Prerequisites:

Education and Training—College degree in film or business is helpful but not required

Experience—Any business experience in sales or management

Special Skills and Personality Traits—Advertising and promotional skills; detail oriented; able to

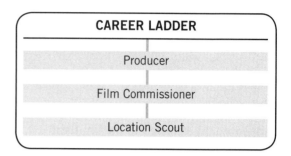

delegate; comfortable with deadline pressure and budgetary concerns; willingness to network within the film industry to promote a territory as a film location; knowledge of the various technical and labor union aspects of filmmaking; understanding of the challenges and benefits of filming in a community or state

Position Description

Film Commissioners take care of all the details in trying to interest filmmakers in shooting a film in their territory. They facilitate the making of a film by centralizing the paperwork that has to be filed to begin filming, grant whatever permissions are needed, and provide knowledge of labor union regulations, as well as information about local crews or talent that may be available. They advertise and promote their territory within the film industry.

Making a movie could mean millions of dollars in revenue to a community or state, so the stakes are high in interesting a movie company, especially a major studio, in shooting a film, sometimes for as long as a year, in a particular area. If the film is a critical and financial success, it will also reflect well on the region where it was filmed, which will usually receive recognition in the end credits when the film is shown and might eventually receive a boost in tourism.

Salaries

Earnings for Film Commissioners are set by an individual city or state. Salaries ranges from $50,000 to $100,000, depending on the needs of the territory, its resources, and its commitment to attracting filmmakers.

Employment Prospects

Certain areas, such as California, have dozens of Film Commissioners for numerous communities and regions, whereas other areas may have just one state Film Commissioner. Depending on geography and whether or not filmmaking is a growth industry in that area, employment prospects may be hopeful or bleak.

Advancement Prospects

Unless a new film commission is initiated, advancement will usually mean working up through the ranks to the one top position. Depending upon how many employees there are at a film commission, as well as the prosperity of the region for filmmaking activity, advancement may be difficult. Relocating for an opening in another region may be a necessity to move up the career ladder.

Education and Training

Having a college degree in business or film will certainly be useful. A multifaceted educational background would include courses and training in advertising, promotion, management, contract negotiations, event planning, and festival organization. A Film Commissioner should have a knowledge of the film industry and filmmaking.

Experience, Skills, and Personality Traits

Working in a government agency or for a film company or studio would be useful for gaining the administrative, negotiating, and promotional skills that Film Commissioners need. A Film Commissioner should be friendly as well as clear in his or her commitment to bringing filmmaking business to his or her region. A genuine enthusiasm about the benefits of filming in the particular region under the province of the Film Commissioner will help in that selling process. Attendance at industry trade shows and major film markets, such as Sundance, American Film Market, and the Association of Film Commissions International (AFCI) annual trade show will also be helpful for the job.

Unions and Associations

The Association of Film Commissioners International, based in Cheyenne, Wyoming, is a membership networking association of Film Commissioners. Its informative Web site (http://www.afci.org) provides a directory of members with contact information as well as information on AFCI's *Locations* magazine.

Tips for Entry

1. Work in an administrative assistance capacity at a local or state film commission.
2. Go to the local, regional, or state film commission online and see if they have a bulletin board for job hunters.
3. Attend and network at the industry trade shows, such as Showbiz East and Showbiz West, Cannes, and the AFCI Locations Trade Show.

EXECUTIVE ASSISTANT

Duties: Provides clerical and, sometimes, creative assistance to whatever department the assistant is assigned to, such as production, publicity, or development; answering phones; handling scheduling; filing; creating or maintaining databases; and other duties, as needed by the department, company, or individual that the assistant supports

Alternate Title(s): Assistant; Administrative Assistant

Salary Range: Depending on the size and location of the company, as well as years of experience, from $15,000 to $60,000+

Employment Prospects: Excellent

Advancement Prospects: Fair

Best Geographical Location(s): Los Angeles/Hollywood, New York City, or wherever there is a film company with an executive requiring administrative support

Prerequisites:

Education and Training—High school diploma required; college degree preferred; courses in film and film production are beneficial; training in basic

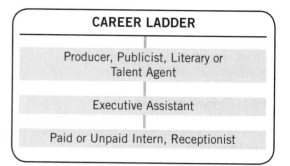

CAREER LADDER

Producer, Publicist, Literary or Talent Agent
Executive Assistant
Paid or Unpaid Intern, Receptionist

administrative tasks, such as filing and answering the phone, as well as computer software knowledge, including word processing, spreadsheets, and database software

Experience—Any clerical or administrative work at a company, especially a film company

Special Skills and Personality Traits—Being well-organized is essential as is having excellent time-management skills; having a pleasant personality and phone manner and the ability to take orders well and to be a self-starter

Position Description

Executive Assistant is a job category that can include entry-level assistants, for whom this is a first job in the industry or a stepping stone to a higher level creative or administrative job, such as a producer, development executive, or entertainment publicist, or a seasoned Executive Assistant who earns top dollar working as an indispensable right hand to a CEO or president of a major studio or production company.

What an assistant does at a company will depend on the size of the company; assistants at larger companies tend to be based in one particular department, such as marketing or development, versus those at smaller companies, where an assistant may be performing clerical and administrative duties for the president but also juggling multiple other film industry functions, such as development, publicity, script coverage, scheduling, and database maintenance.

Executive Assistants, also known as assistant, administrative assistant, assistant to . . . (talent manager, agent, CEO, producing partner, association director, etc.), perform a range of administrative duties, such as answering the phone; sending out faxes; typing correspondence;

arranging meetings, directly or through a travel agency; and handling the myriad of details related to travel. Added responsibilities, depending upon the emphasis of that particular assistant job, include filing; overseeing interns; assisting with the research for reports; taking, typing up, and distributing notes from meetings; performing multiple tasks for a variety of projects; and keeping track of expenses.

For more than a year, 25-year-old Mirembe Nutt-Birigwa, who likes to be called Mimi, has been Executive Assistant to Terry Lawler, who is the Association Director of Manhattan-based New York Women in Film and Television (NYWIFT). She was volunteering at different film festivals, working as a production assistant on several TV shows, including a season of *Law & Order: Criminal Intent.* Her current salaried Executive Assistant position at NYWIFT is an outgrowth of the month she spent being paid on a day-rate basis doing general office work there. Says Nutt-Birigwa: "I was working in the office when the previous Executive Assistant gave her notice. I was already hoping to be hired by the organization on a steady basis, so it was perfect timing, and I jumped at the opportunity. I was at the right place at the right time."

What is it like to be an Executive Assistant? Says Nutt-Birigwa, who also acts and writes, "It's like having to juggle and not tire. It's juggling all the time. I juggle scheduling, I juggle office supplying. I run the intern mentor program. Information flows through me to the office to the executive director. It's a great experience for networking because anyone who needs to speak to the executive director oftentimes has to speak to me first; therefore, I'm able to gain contacts that I might not have made in another position, even in the office. I have interns to answer the phones and do the filing who are rewarded for their 45-day internship service with a mentor in the film industry at the end of their internship here. I prepare materials for the board meetings, so I work closely with the board of directors. I also order all of the office supplies that the office needs to move smoothly. The executive director can't be bothered with replacing the toner in the copy machine. I haven't paid to see a movie in a year. A great perk. I attend the premieres of the latest films. Our programs take place in the evening, so I work fairly long hours, from 10 A.M. till 8 P.M. I definitely would recommend it as an entry-level position. It's a good springboard into other positions that will require organization and attention to detail, which are useful to anything. This job also allows me to continue studying acting. It's very flexible. My boss is quite supportive of my goals in the film and television industries. My long-term goals are producing my own material, as well as acting in television and features. And while I'm here, I'm networking in the industry and honing my organizational and professional skills. Over this past weekend, I shot a music video and a commercial, and it's all through contacts I made through the organization. We're a nonprofit film membership organization, so in that sense it makes it different from being assistant at, say, Sony Pictures, for example, where the work is more specific to film production alone."

Salaries

Salaries depend on the size of the company and its location (Los Angeles/Hollywood or New York City versus a suburban or rural area), and if it is an entry-level job or a career with seniority, from $15,000 to $60,000+.

Employment Prospects

The employment prospects for this job are excellent since this entry-level position has a lot of turnover as Executive Assistants, except for those who wish to have the job as a long-term career, typically moving up the ladder or to another company after one to three years.

Advancement Prospects

There are only fair advancement prospects because, with the exception of major production companies or studios, few companies have the budget for them.

Education and Training

A high school diploma and some college may be required; a college degree is preferred. Some graduate courses or an advanced degree related to film may be helpful but are not required. Having training in basic administrative skills, such as filing, as well as a working knowledge of using a computer, including proficiency with the Microsoft Office suite, which includes PowerPoint, Word, Excel, and Outlook software. There may also be additional computer skills required, depending on the procedures at each office, such as database management software, or scheduling software.

Experience, Skills, and Personality Traits

For the entry-level Executive Assistant job, experience at another film company may not be required, but it will definitely help your application if you have worked in any kind of office in an administrative capacity during high school or during college vacations. Internships during and after college will also provide helpful administrative assistant experiences. Some jobs may require that you already have had one or two years working at an agency, production company or network, or studio.

Depending on the type of department or office where you work, additional skills may be necessary, such as script reading/coverage, which demands a critical eye for what makes a good film, as well as excellent writing skills to communicate your ideas succinctly and clearly; being very organized, having superb time-management skills, and being able to multitask; being able to file or delegate filing to interns or others in the office; a pleasant phone personality; the ability to take orders and to work well under pressure; a combination of being a self-starter and a team player; a love of the film industry and being a hard worker and reliable; an ability to do research on the Internet for travel-related responsibilities, including scheduling or being able to work well with a travel agent.

Unions and Associations

Join associations that offer opportunities to meet those in the industry, or specific aspect of the industry, that you wish to work in, such as publicity, sales, production, or distribution. Find out the contact information for those associations in the Appendix of this book including IFP (Independent Feature Project), WIF (Women in Film), NYWIFT (New York Women in Film & Television), NATAS (National Association of Television Arts and Sciences), and others.

Tips for Entry

1. Take a paid or unpaid internship during or after your school years to gain experience doing administrative jobs. Let your boss know that you're interested in a fulltime salaried job upon graduating or when one opens up.
2. Network in the film industry through association memberships and attend association functions, such as awards events and benefits, or volunteer to be on a committee for an event that includes members from film companies.
3. Attend conferences, take a course, or go to a workshop with programs led by executives at companies where you would like to work and find out if anyone needs an assistant and who to contact with your résumé.
4. Visit the various industry career sites on the Internet, such as http://www.entertainmentcareers.net, http://www.showbizjobs.com, http://www.mandy.com, http://www.entertainmentjobs.com, http://www.mediabistro.com, as well as the Web sites for production companies or studios, such as http://corporate.disney.go.com/careers, and go to their lists for jobs.

PART II
PRODUCTION (PRINCIPAL PHOTOGRAPHY)

CAMERA

DIRECTOR OF PHOTOGRAPHY

Duties: Work as the eyes of the director; turns the words of the screenplay into visual images; oversee camera crews and equipment as well as all photography; work with lighting and set designers and others to make sure every shot in a movie works; be responsible for all technical aspects of filming a movie

Alternate Title(s): Cinematographer; DP

Salary Range: $0 to $200,000+

Employment Prospects: Good

Advancement Prospects: Good

Best Geographical Location(s): Los Angeles/Hollywood, New York City

Prerequisites:

Education and Training—Bachelor's or advanced degree in film or dramatic and visual arts recommended but not required

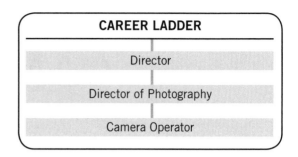

CAREER LADDER

Director

Director of Photography

Camera Operator

Experience—Working as a camera operator or assistant camera operator on feature films, industrials, or documentaries

Special Skills and Personality Traits—Strong visual sense; able to turn words into pictures; strong photographic skills; good photographer; well organized; detail oriented; excellent interpersonal skills

Position Description

The Director of Photography, or DP, is the person who directs the camera crew to create the moving image portion of the director's overall vision of the film. Also known as the cinematographer, the DP works hand in hand with the director to put on film or video what the audiences eventually see on the screen. He or she is responsible for everything involved in capturing the image to be used in the film, including selecting the camera, lenses, filters, lighting, and grip equipment. The Director of Photography also gets involved in setting camera positions, framing the shot, and controlling the overall quality of everything filmed or videotaped for the production. A Director of Photography must be able to lead her or his camera crew in order to get the vision she or he and the director share. It is an extremely demanding and important position and one that is crucial to the overall quality of the film being produced. The DP is responsible for how the movie looks on the screen.

The DP does all this without actually touching any of the equipment. He or she has a camera crew to do all that, and in the United States, the cinematographer is prevented by union rules from even operating the camera. In Europe, the Director of Photography, or cinematographer, is also the camera operator.

A typical day for the DP will involve working with three key crew members—the actual camera operator; the gaffer, or person responsible for lighting; and the key grip, the person in charge of moving the camera, lights, and all other equipment associated with the camera crew.

Prior to shooting, the DP will have selected the camera, film or video stock, lighting, and grip equipment and will have tested the sets, the set dressing, and any scenic art, such as matte backgrounds, props, actors, costumes, and makeup.

During the shooting, the cinematographer keeps track of camera positions and angles, as well as lighting and movement, so the shots will match from scene to scene. There are constant decisions to be made, involving everything from light readings and exposures to camera angles and film stock, all while supervising the camera operator, the focus puller (usually the first assistant camera operator), and the key grip (the person who moves the camera around).

The key to everything is the cinematographer's close relationship to the director. They must trust each other completely. The DP has to understand and connect to the director's vision. If she or he doesn't, then the director will find a DP who will; thus, the DP and director spend a lot of time together talking through what the film should look like before the first shot is taken.

Much of the DP's time is taken blocking out the shot, figuring out how to cover the action, whether the director wants a two-shot (two actors in the frame) or a close-up (usually the head and shoulders of one actor). Some directors take what are called cover shots, even if the script doesn't call for a close-up. The DP may or may not work from a storyboard, depending on the complexity of the shot.

Because the DP in the United States isn't allowed to touch the camera, it is important that they work with a camera operator who will give them the shot they ask for. This also goes for the gaffer and key grip. Therefore, the DP usually hires the camera crew.

A DP usually is hired during preproduction and gets involved in several elements of preparation, including choosing locations, set building and set decoration, makeup and wardrobe, and selecting the camera equipment and lights. This is the time when she or he usually hires the camera crew and goes over with the director about her or his vision for the film. He or she will have already read the script, but the way the DP sees the movie may not necessarily be the way the director sees it. Therefore, she or he has to learn the director's version of what's going to appear on the screen, which may not identically reflect what was on the page.

Throughout shooting, changes are constantly made, so the DP has to keep a continual line of communication with the director. Everyday, the DP has to handle an incredible amount of variables that go into every shot, especially on location shooting. She or he will try to eliminate as many variables as possible before shooting. For example, the DP can go to a location ahead of time and take test shots. That way he or she can tell what type of film stock is needed, whether he or she will be able to use natural or artificial light, if he or she will need a wide angle or telephoto lens, and if there will be room for a dolly or crane.

A major change sweeping the film industry that has a direct impact on the DP is the introduction of high-definition digital video, especially something called HiDef 24p, a digital video shot at 24 frames per second, the same as film. Despite this latest innovation, it is believed that the new medium still needs improvement before it replaces film as the medium of choice among professional industry cinematographers.

Salaries

Salaries vary widely, depending on one's standing in industry. The weekly average is $3,400, but annual salaries for some veteran DPs are more than $200,000.

Employment Prospects

The Director of Photography is a key position on any film, so employment prospects are good. As long as the film industry keeps making movies, there is a strong need for DPs. However, there are many aspiring cinematographers, so competition can be stiff.

Advancement Prospects

Advancement may be measured by getting higher fees, being able to work on bigger budget movies, or working with name directors or talent. However, prospects for advancement from DP to director are rare, since most directors go through the Directors Guild of America (DGA) training program, graduate from film school, or get into directing from screenwriting or producing.

Education and Training

There are hundreds of college and university film programs, as well as studio training programs, designed to help the would-be Cinematographer learn the necessary technical skills and land his or her first job. The camera operator's union has a training program that would also be helpful.

Experience, Skills, and Personality Traits

Work first as a camera operator, focus puller, and film loader on as many films as possible, or work as a DP on low-budget films where you may have to do everything. Shoot as much film or video as possible to get as much experience as you can and to learn about what works and what doesn't.

Skills include a strong visual sense and visual creativity; intimate knowledge of the movie camera and photography; ability to work with lighting, design, color to create drama; and many of the other skills that go into being a director.

The Director of Photography should be able to follow orders but should also be willing to speak up when something isn't working.

Unions and Associations

Directors of Photography may join the American Society of Cinematographers (ASC: http://www.theasc.com). Being a member of ASC is an honor for a Director of Photography and is helpful in networking for future assignments.

Tips for Entry

1. Learn the ropes, beginning with the union's training program for camera operator.
2. Work on low-budget, independent feature films or student films.

3. Shoot as much film or video as possible, and make a showcase film of your work.
4. Make short films or music videos.
5. Work in television.
6. Since the director usually hires the Director of Photography, get to know as many directors as you can. Go to networking functions sponsored by the local chapter of the Directors Guild of America (DGA), as well as any other associations or get-togethers that attract directors to their ranks, such as film festivals or conferences.
7. Read *American Cinematographer,* the publication of the ASC (the American Society of Cinematographers).

CAMERA OPERATOR

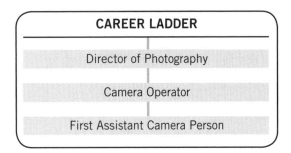

Position Description

Since the director of photography is not allowed to touch the camera, it's up to the Camera Operator to do the actual filming. When the director yells, "Roll film, then Action!," it is the Camera Operator rolling the film behind the camera, not the director of photography.

The Camera Operator is responsible for actually getting the shot the director and the director of photography are seeking. The Camera Operator, often working with one or two assistants, frames the shot, focuses it, moves the camera, changes filters, sets the f-stop, makes sure the correct film stock has been loaded, and maintains the camera and accessories.

In many cases, especially on big budget studio films, the Camera Operator has his or her own team to assist in loading the film, changing the focus, and moving the camera. The DP puts a lot of trust in the Camera Operator to get the shot she or he has told the director she or he is going to get. And while the job of the Camera Operator is mostly technical, he or she has to be in touch with what's going on in each scene.

A Camera Operator has to know how various film stock reacts to different light and colors. It's his or her eye that is seeing what the film sees, so it is up to the Camera Operator to understand how the film will look when it is developed and shown on the screen. Since the Camera Operator is the only one who sees what the camera sees, it is up to him or her to call for another take if he or she fails to get the shot the DP or director wants.

The Camera Operator is usually hired by the director of photography and begins work on the first day of principal photography.

A typical day for a Camera Operator begins with blocking the set. The director of photography, working with the director, has positioned the cameras. Once that's done, the DP calls for a run-through with the camera and lighting team to determine how she or he wants to light the shot and to figure out camera movements.

After a couple of rehearsals with the actors, lighting is set, and tracks are placed if needed for a dolly shot. Operating the camera is usually a team effort, with the Camera Operator looking through the lens and moving the camera on its tripod; the first assistant Camera Operator pulling the focus; the second assistant handling the film stock; and the dolly grip moving the camera, tripod, and Camera Operator on a dolly, when required.

Salaries

Salaries vary widely. Most Camera Operators earn between $70,000 and $110,000. The average weekly rate is $2,100. According to the rate card for the International Cinematographers Guild (ICG), the average daily rate is $414 to $531 for work either at a studio or a distant location; $2,052 to $2,280 for weekly rates for Schedule B weekly employees, depending on whether work is at a studio or distant location; and $2,007 to $2,230 for Schedule C weekly employees, depending on whether work is performed in a studio or at a distant location. Since these rates usually increase regularly, check with the ICG for the most recent rates and other factors influencing the pay scale.

Employment Prospects

The Camera Operator is a key position on any film, so employment prospects are good. However, there can be a lot of competition for desirable jobs.

Advancement Prospects

Prospects for advancement are good. By word of mouth, Camera Operators will be assured steady work, especially since a director of photography will often want to work with the same Camera Operator over and over again if they work well together. Camera Operators may advance to bigger budget films or go on to become directors of photography.

Education and Training

There are hundreds of college and university film programs, as well as studio training programs, designed to help the would-be Camera Operator land his or her first job. There is a Camera Operators' union apprentice training program too. The program focuses on field training on union films. Trainees are required to work on at least six productions for a minimum of 120 days to become familiar with a variety of camera systems. They learn about the latest technology and cutting-edge skills.

Special Requirements

Professional certification or state licensure is not required, but you may be required to become a member of the International Cinematographers Guild, Local 600 of International Association of Theatrical Stage Employees (IATSE), especially if you are working on a union film, which most studio productions are.

Experience, Skills, and Personality Traits

Working first as a focus puller and film loader on as many films as possible will give a would-be Camera Operator experience, as will working as a Camera Operator on low-budget, independent, or student films.

Skills include a strong visual sense and visual creativity; intimate knowledge of the movie camera and photography; ability to work with lighting, design, color to create drama, and many of the other skills that go into being a director of photography.

Those with the kind of personality comfortable following orders will find it easier to be part of the team, but the Camera Operator also needs to speak up when he or she knows something isn't working.

Unions and Associations

Membership in the International Cinematographers Guild, Local 600 of IATSE (http://www.cameraguild.com) is not only beneficial but required if a Camera Operator is hired to work on a studio or union film. Once you are a member of the union, it is also important to be inducted into the American Society of Cinematographers (ASC).

Tips for Entry

1. Work on low-budget, independent, or student films, commercials, or music videos.
2. Associate with camera rental houses and be available when work comes in.
3. Contact the directors of photography whose work you admire and ask for work as an assistant.
4. Take any job to get on a film set and work your way up.

FIRST ASSISTANT CAMERAPERSON

CAREER PROFILE

Duties: Maintain and assemble all camera equipment; make sure the focus is correct during the shots

Alternate Title(s): None

Salary Range: $1,600 to $2,000 per week

Employment Prospects: Good

Advancement Prospects: Fair

Best Geographical Location(s): Los Angeles/Hollywood, New York City

Prerequisites:

Education and Training—Bachelor's or advanced degree, with courses in filmmaking; film school is recommended but not required

Experience—Work on as many films as possible

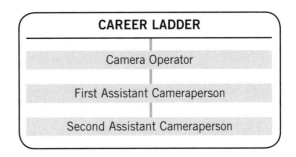

Special Skills and Personality Traits—Keen eye; working knowledge of camera equipment and elements of photography; able to follow instructions; good interpersonal skills

Position Description

The First Assistant Cameraperson works for the camera operator as part of the camera team. The First Assistant Cameraperson is usually in charge of the equipment, maintaining it and assembling it, and then acts as the focus puller during the shots. The focus puller makes sure the proper focus is used during the shots. This is an important part of the First Assistant Cameraperson's job, and he or she works closely with the camera operator to get the focus just right, especially during mobile shots when both the camera and actors are moving in and out of a designated depth of field. Sometimes, it takes four people working in conjunction to keep a shot in focus—the First Assistant Cameraperson, the crane operator, the dolly grip, and the camera operator.

On larger studio films, a second assistant cameraperson loads the camera and supports the First Assistant Cameraperson. He or she also handles any paperwork, works the slate at the start of the shot, and alerts the production manager when more film is needed.

Salaries

Salaries for assistant camera operators are usually set by the camera guild, which is a unit of the International Alliance of Theatrical Stage Employees (IATSE). The average weekly pay is $1,600 to $2,000 per week, depending on such factors as whether work is at a studio or distant location and whether one is hired as a Schedule B-1 or C-1 weekly employee or at an hourly

rate of $302 per hour. Since rates do change based on the negotiation of a new contract, check with the International Cinematographers Guild for the most recent salary rate card.

Employment Prospects

Studio films, as well as independent movies with budgets of $10 million or more, will have at least one First Assistant Cameraperson, so employment prospects are good. Some films, such as action movies with complicated stunts and explosions, may use more than one camera to get different angles of the same shot. In that case, each camera operator could have a First Assistant Cameraperson.

Advancement Prospects

Prospects for advancement from First Assistant Cameraperson to camera operator are very competitive. It's important to develop the right skills and a good reputation.

Education and Training

A bachelor's degree with a major in film is recommended but not required. Assistant camerapersons can get on-the-job training by working on student or low-budget nonunion films, or through the union's apprentice training program, where trainees learn about the latest technology and master a variety of camera systems. They are required to work on at least six productions for a minimum of 120 days.

Experience, Skills, and Personality Traits

Assistant camerapersons need a strong visual sense, visual creativity, and an intimate knowledge of a variety of camera systems. They should be comfortable following orders, happy to work as a team, and be physically fit.

Unions and Associations

Membership in the camera operator's union (http://www.cameraguild.com) is beneficial.

Tips for Entry

1. Develop contacts with DPs and camera operators.
2. Work as a second assistant cameraperson.
3. Take any production assistant job.

KEY GRIP

CAREER PROFILE

Duties: Supervises the crew responsible for all the equipment used by the director of photography (DP), including the camera and accessories, lights, rigging, dollies, cranes, booms, and scaffolding

Alternate Title(s): None

Salary Range: $36.35 and hour minimum per basic agreement with IATSE Local 80

Employment Prospects: Good

Advancement Prospects: Good

Best Geographical Location(s): Los Angeles/Hollywood, New York City

Prerequisites:

Education and Training—Bachelor's or advanced degree is not required

Experience—Get experience as a grip, then participate in the International Alliance of Theatrical Stage Employees (IATSE) training and advancement

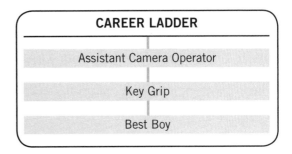

CAREER LADDER

Assistant Camera Operator

Key Grip

Best Boy

program and work on low budget films, industrials, and documentaries

Special Skills and Personality Traits—Strong mechanical abilities; able to move heavy equipment; working knowledge of equipment used by grips; knowledge of lighting, electricity, and colors; ability to handle cranes and dollies

Position Description

The Key Grip works primarily for the director of photography and is in charge of the crew that handles and takes care of the camera equipment, lights, and everything associated with the camera operation. Working closely with the gaffer, or key electrician in charge of lighting setups, the Key Grip will supervise the positioning of the lights and the scrims and the reflectors that diffuse those lights. During the filming, the Key Grip will supervise the camera movements, such as dolly shots, and the crane and boom operations.

A Key Grip has an assistant called the best boy (even if it's a woman), who takes care of the equipment, hires extra crew members if needed, orders supplies, and supervises the prerigging.

On any given day during production, it's up to the Key Grip to oversee the moving, rigging, positioning, operating, and striking of all the equipment used by the crew reporting to the director of photography.

The Key Grip has a copy of the shooting script that includes camera directions and movements, as well as locations (interior or exterior) and the time (day or night). Working with the DP and gaffer, he or she will supervise any necessary rigging for the lights or backgrounds. Then, when the shooting starts, the Key Grip supervises any dolly or crane movements. On larger productions,

there will be grips assigned to each piece of equipment. But on low-budget films, the Key Grip may have to be his or her own dolly grip, so it is desirable for a Key Grip to also know how to operate a dolly and a crane.

Salaries

Salaries vary widely, from $60,000 to $100,000 a year. International Alliance of Theatrical Stage Employees (IATSE) Key Grips have a basic hourly minimum rate of $36.35.

Employment Prospects

A Key Grip is on all studio films, so employment prospects are good.

Advancement Prospects

Prospects for advancement are good. An experienced Key Grip may go on to become a camera assistant and continue moving up from there.

Education and Training

There are hundreds of college and university film programs, as well as studio and union training programs, designed to help the would-be grip. You can find more information about the training program at the IATSE Web site (http://www.iatse-intl.org).

Experience, Skills, and Personality Traits

Working first as a grip on as many union films as possible is the only way you can advance to Key Grip. There is an apprentice program sponsored by the union, which gives grips experience in working as trainees on a variety of union films.

Skills include agility, comfortable with heights, strong mechanical ability, leadership abilities, and the strength to be able to move heavy equipment.

A Key Grip should like manual labor, traveling, and working long hours.

Unions and Associations

Membership in IATSE is required for studio or union films. Local 80 (http://www.iatselocal80.org) is the local branch of IATSE whose membership includes Key Grips.

Tips for Entry

1. The best way to becoming a Key Grip is through the union training program.
2. Work on low-budget, student, and nonunion films.
3. Take any grip job to get on a film set and work your way up.

GAFFER

Duties: Acts as the chief electrician in charge of all lighting setups; reports to the director of photography

Alternate Title(s): Chief Lighting Technician (CLT), Key Electrician

Salary Range: $36.35 an hour

Employment Prospects: Good

Advancement Prospects: Good

Best Geographical Location(s): Los Angeles/Hollywood, New York City

Prerequisites:

Education and Training—High school diploma

Experience—Take any job available on any film being shot; work on commercials and music videos

Special Skills and Personality Traits—Strong mechanical abilities; be able to move heavy equipment; working knowledge of equipment used by gaffers; knowledge of lighting, electricity, and colors; ability to work with people

Special Requirements—Union membership may be required

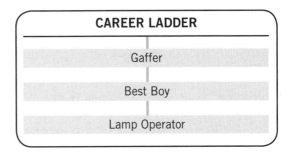

CAREER LADDER

Gaffer

Best Boy

Lamp Operator

Position Description

The Gaffer, the chief electrician in charge of all lighting setups, works with the key grip in the selection and positioning of lights and lighting equipment. As chief electrician, the Gaffer also maintains and supervises the use of all electrical equipment, as well as the loading, transportation, rigging, operation, and striking of all lighting equipment. It's the Gaffer's job to make sure working conditions are safe.

The Gaffer, the key grip, and the best boy all work together to light a set. While the key grip focuses on the rigging, the Gaffer is responsible for the lights and the electrical power supplying those lights. Like the key grip, the Gaffer's second in command is also called a best boy (regardless of gender). The Gaffer usually gives the best boy instructions on where to put the lights, and the best boy supervises the actual positioning of the lights.

Lighting a set can be complicated. First of all, there are different kinds of lights, such as key lights, fill lights, and backlights. The key light, usually the brightest, lights the crucial elements of the action. A fill light is used to remove shadows caused by the key light, and backlight is added to provide different effects. Each light must be focused and diffused, using reflectors or scrims.

A typical day of production begins with the grip and Gaffer crews preparing the set. The grips prerig the scaffolds where the lights will go, and then the gaffing crew lays cable wherever lights are going to be needed.

Lighting is an expensive part of the budget, so the Gaffer has to work with the director of photography and the production manager to select equipment they can afford but still give the DP the lighting he or she needs to get the shot the director wants.

Salaries

International Alliance of Theatrical Stage Employees (IATSE) Gaffers have a basic hourly minimum rate of $36.35.

Employment Prospects

A Gaffer is used on all studio films, so employment prospects are good.

Advancement Prospects

Prospects for advancement are good. The union (IATSE) has an apprentice training program.

Education and Training

Training as an electrician is required. There are also specific union (IATSE) requirements; members must complete training and safety programs sponsored by the locals. Apprenticeship periods have been shortened, which makes these safety programs even more important, since new members begin work on a set that requires them to have knowledge of voltage, amperage, and lighting capacity.

Special Requirements
Professional certification or state licensure is not required, but you may be required to become a member of IATSE, especially if you are working on a union film, which most studio productions are.

Experience, Skills, and Personality Traits
Working first as a best boy or lamp operator on as many union films as possible is the best way you can advance to Gaffer. Skills include a firm knowledge of electricity and lighting, strong mechanical ability, leadership skills, and the ability to move heavy equipment.

Gaffers should like manual labor, traveling, and working long hours.

Unions and Associations
Membership in IATSE (http://www.iatse-intl.org) is not only beneficial but is also required if hired to work on a studio or union film. Gaffers may be members of IATSE Local 728 (http://www.iatse728.org), which is based in Panorama City, California.

Tips for Entry
1. Take any job on a film production.
2. Work as a lamp operator.
3. Get experience working on low-budget features, nonunion films, or student films.
4. Study *Variety* for lists of productions just starting and see if an internship is available.

BEST BOY

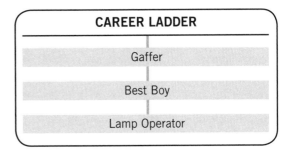

Position Description

The Best Boy (so-called regardless of the gender of the person performing the job) is the second in command, after the key grip and the gaffer. The Best Boy is the person who actually supervises as the rest of the crew, takes care of the equipment, hires extra people, orders supplies, and prerigs the set.

On the set, the director and the director of photography (DP) will decide how to shoot a scene. The DP, gaffer, and key grip will work out how to light it. The Best Boy will then carry out their decisions about where to position the lights and scrims.

The Best Boy and lamp operators, working for the gaffer, are responsible for all the lights and the electricity. The Best Boy is the real leader on the lighting crew.

A typical day on the set involves a lot of moving very heavy lighting equipment and cable. A Best Boy has to know exactly what gaffers want when they ask for a specific light, because different lights provide different effects. A Best Boy has to know about voltage and whether enough power is available for any lighting needs.

A Best Boy also has to know about diffusion. Various types of material are used to soften and diffuse the light on a set. The thicker the material, the softer the light.

The heavy lifting usually happens when you have to prerig the set. That involves building scaffolds, installing heavy lights and generators, laying cable, and moving camera equipment around.

The origin of the term *Best Boy* is unclear. Some say it started in the days of hand-cranked silent cameras, when the camera operator would have his most dependable crewmember, or "best boy," help in lighting the shot.

Salaries

International Alliance of Theatrical Stage Employees (IATSE) Best Boys have a basic hourly minimum rate of $32.40.

Employment Prospects

Since most studio films, as well as major independent features, require the services of a Best Boy, employment prospects are good. As the actual crew leader for grips and gaffers, this position has become essential during the production phase of filmmaking.

Advancement Prospects

Advancement from the grip or gaffer crews to Best Boy continues to be good because turnover is fairly steady. Advancing from Best Boy to key grip or head gaffer also appears to be good, as these positions are in constant need of being filled during production, and more films continue to be made each year.

Education and Training

Training as an electrician, lighting specialist, or lamp operator is essential. There is a union (IATSE) training program that teaches Best Boys important safety procedures.

Experience, Skills, and Personality Traits

Working as a lamp operator on as many union films as possible is an excellent way to advance to Best Boy.

Skills include knowledge of electricity and lighting; strong mechanical ability, leadership ability, and the strength to move heavy equipment. Best Boys should like manual labor, traveling, and working long hours.

Unions and Associations

Membership in the International Alliance of Theatrical Stage Employees (IATSE) (http://www.iatse-intl.org) is beneficial. Membership in IATSE is required if hired to work on a studio or union film.

Tips for Entry

1. Take any job on a film, so you can observe a film being made and get exposure to the technical aspects of filmmaking.
2. Work on low-budget, nonunion, or student films.
3. Study *Variety* and *The Hollywood Reporter* for lists of productions just starting and see if they have an unpaid internship available.

HOW THE FILM LOOKS

PRODUCTION DESIGNER

CAREER PROFILE

Duties: Work closely with the director to create the overall look of the film

Salary Range: For features adhering to the pay scale of Local 800 of IATSE, salaries range from $20.53 an hour (for low-budget features below $4 million) to $2,876 a week (for union movies budgeted at $9.8 million or higher)

Alternate Title(s): PD

Employment Prospects: Good

Advancement Prospects: Fair

Best Geographical Location(s): Los Angeles/Hollywood, New York City

Prerequisites:

Education and Training—Optional but useful is a bachelor's or advanced degree, with a concentration in film, theater, or fine arts

Experience—Working in as many design positions on a production as possible, such as costume design or set design

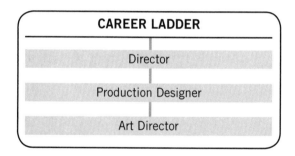

CAREER LADDER

Director

Production Designer

Art Director

Special Skills and Personality Traits—Artistic; strong sense of design; visually acute; able to re-create reality; able to create the director's vision of the film; interested in history

Special Requirements—Union membership may be required

Position Description

The Production Designer, in conjunction with the director, will design the set; help select the locations; choose the colors, textures, and tone of the film; and then supervise the drawing of blueprints, the construction and dressing of sets, and the coordination of any department involved in the artistic design of the film, including set design, construction and decoration, costume design, hair and makeup, props, and special effects.

The Production Designer is hired to design the director's vision of the way the film should look. In order to do this, the Production Designer has to spend a lot of time with the director, so that he or she is able to create from the script what the director wants to see on the screen. This includes the colors, textures, shapes, the look of the sets, locations, costumes, brightness, darkness, tone, and whether the director wants reality or fantasy.

A Production Designer is brought in at the start of preproduction and given a design budget, which will determine what can and can't be done.

While working on the film *Bonfire of the Vanities*, based on the Tom Wolfe novel, veteran Production

Designer Richard Sylbert had to re-create a huge bond trading floor. The script placed the trading floor at Solomon Brothers, but when Sylbert visited the actual trading floor, it didn't look "huge" enough. The cost of building such a floor would have been prohibitive, so Sylbert visited trading floors at other investment banks and chose Merrill Lynch, whose massive bond trading floor seemed perfect for scenes showing bond traders as "masters of the universe." An agreement was reached with Merrill Lynch to allow filming on weekends when the floor wasn't in use.

Working with an assistant known as an art director, the Production Designer does sketches of what some of the key scenes will look like. These sketches will show the set, costumes, props, makeup, and other important features, which then allows the Production Designer to oversee the creation of these sets, costumes, and props.

Typically, depending on the film's budget, a Production Designer will work for two to three months of preproduction and three months of production. The Production Designer will hire an art director, set designer, costume designer, and property master. On the set, he or she will work closely with the director, the production manager, and the cinematographer or director of photography, who will be interested in what colors will be used.

Once he or she has the sketches, the Production Designer can begin working with the director or production manager on selecting locations and building sets. If the PD doesn't have time to make the sketches, he or she may be able to work off storyboards, which are illustrations of key scenes.

Salaries

Salaries vary according to a film's budget and standing in the film community. Beginners working on low- or no-budget films may earn little or nothing, while established Production Designers can earn well over six figures. For features adhering to the pay scale of Local 800 of IATSE, salaries range from $20.53 an hour (for low-budget features below $4 million) to $2,876 a week (for union movies budgeted at $9.8 million or higher).

Employment Prospects

Employment prospects for Production Designers are good. Every studio film has a Production Designer, as do many independent films. The PD works closely with the film's director and hires the various members of the art department, such as the property master, set designer, and costume designer, who all contribute to the look of the film.

Advancement Prospects

Advancement from Production Designer to either director or producer is difficult. Production Designers who are at the top of the ladder rarely want to go on to something else.

Education and Training

Besides film or art school, the best training for a Production Designer is a major in history, literature, or the theater. Study as if you were going to be a director. Drafting and design courses are also helpful.

Experience, Skills, and Personality Traits

Have a background in the theater and fine arts. Be able to read blueprints, draw plans, sketch scenes from words written on a page, and translate a strong visual creative sense into reality.

Unions and Associations

Membership in the International Alliance of Theatrical Stage Employees (IATSE) is required if a Production Designer is hired to work on a studio or union film. Membership in IATSE is also beneficial for networking. The local that covers Production Designers is IATSE Local 800 (http://www.artdirectors.org), also known as the Art Directors Guild (ADG), based in Studio City, California.

Tips for Entry

1. The broader your background, the better, although having an artistic sense as well as training working with color, shapes, and light will always be helpful.
2. Take any position in the art department and begin working up the ladder.
3. Make a name for yourself as a Production Designer in the theater.
4. Work on low-budget or student films.
5. Go to film school.

ART DIRECTOR

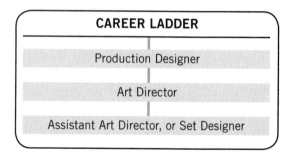

Position Description

The Art Director assists the production designer in creating the look of the film. It is often left to the Art Director to sketch out key scenes so that set and costume designers have an idea of what they need to create. These drawings are like architectural designs, and they can be anything from rough sketches to elaborate paintings. Often, the Art Director will work with an artist or illustrator if he or she doesn't do the drawings. It is from the designs of the Art Director that sets are built, locations found, actors dressed and made-up, the film given a "look." On low-budget films, Art Directors also fill the role of Production Designer.

It is up to the Art Director to give the set its character and its underlying vitality. Art direction is a key element to the look and tone of the movie, and an Oscar is awarded each year in recognition of this contribution.

As second in command of the art department on major studio films, the Art Director does most of the hands-on designs for sets and locations, working closely with the production designer and director. An Art Director helps the production designer and director select colors, textures, and the combinations of both to render specific effects.

The Art Director is responsible for making sure that the set or location works thematically within the overall structure of the film. Is the director striving for reality,

or is this a fantasy film? If the director suddenly changes her or his mind and wants a set stricken or replaced, it's often up to the Art Director to make it happen.

In order to become a production designer, one must first work as an Art Director. In fact, it is the Art Director who will probably manage, budget, and schedule whatever the production designer needs. It is the Art Director who deals with the construction coordinator in charge of building sets. The Art Director is also responsible for keeping costs within the production designer's budget.

Salaries

Salaries vary according to a film's budget and the Art Director's standing in the film community. The International Alliance of Theatrical Employees (IATSE) sets a minimum fee; the weekly average is $2,600 to $3,000. (Check with the union for current minimum salaries since contracts are renegotiated regularly.) Beginning Art Directors may work on low-budget, nonunion, or independent films for little or nothing in order to get experience.

Employment Prospects

Employment prospects for Art Directors are good. Every studio film has an Art Director. On low-budget films, they may also double as the production designer.

Advancement Prospects

Prospects for advancement from Art Director to production designer are good. Many Art Directors are promoted to the production designer level.

Education and Training

Besides film or art school, the best training for an Art Director is a major in fine arts or the theater. Drafting and architecture courses are also helpful.

Experience, Skills, and Personality Traits

Have a background in fine arts. Be able to draw blueprints, read plans, sketch scenes from words written on a page, and have a strong visual creative sense.

Unions and Associations

Membership in the union IATSE is beneficial. Membership in IATSE Local 800 is required if an Art Director is hired to work on a studio or union film. For more information, go to their Web site: http://www.artdirectors.org.

Tips for Entry

1. Take any entry-level position in the art department and begin working up the ladder.
2. Take a job as an illustrator or storyboard artist.
3. Be patient. Persistence is needed, because it can take time for the right opportunity to come along.
4. Network with established Art Directors, production designers, directors, and other film professionals.
5. Work on low- or no-budget films to gain experience.

LOCATION SCOUT

CAREER PROFILE

Duties: Find the appropriate place to shoot specific locations on a film; secure the necessary permits or licenses from local authorities, such as fire or police departments

Alternate Title(s): Location Manager

Salary Range: Varies based on union membership as well as location; in California and 12 other western states, $2,423 per week plus $70 a day for car use, according to Teamsters Union Local 399

Employment Prospects: Good

Advancement Prospects: Fair

Best Geographical Location(s): Wherever a film is being shot, especially Los Angeles/Hollywood and New York City

Prerequisites:

Education and Training—Studying film in college or film school provides a useful background

Experience—Working on a film or in any job in the film industry, such as assistant to a producer or director

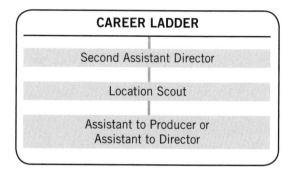

CAREER LADDER

Second Assistant Director

Location Scout

Assistant to Producer or Assistant to Director

Special Skills and Personality Traits—Able to work as part of the production team; capable of breaking down a script into the necessary locations; detail oriented; able to work under time and budget constraints; able to take still photographs or videotape locations; widely traveled; strong research skills

Position Description

In the real estate business, there's an expression about what to look for in an apartment or a house: "Location. Location. Location." After the screenplay and the choice of director and actors, where the movie will be shot is one of the most important decisions to the creative and even financial success of a film. Some films that might be too expensive to shoot in one location might work out in a very different setting. The Location Scout not only handles details about lining up a place to shoot each scene in a movie but also how those choices will impact the look of the final film.

A Location Scout may be affiliated with a local or state film commission or he or she may be hired by a director for a particular movie. The Location Scout will get the script from the director. He or she will then break down the script into locations. Having traveled throughout the United States and internationally and having a photographic record of those trips allow the Location Scout to call upon all that firsthand and secondary research to choose just the right location for part or all of the entire film. A Location Scout must work within the budgetary constraints of the movie. Is there

$2,000 available to rent a restaurant for a shot, or just $200? Is it possible to take the entire cast and crew out of state to shoot the movie, or is it necessary to stay near the production company's headquarters? The Location Scout will also find out what permits or licenses have to be secured and what fees have to be paid.

Salaries

Location Scouts who are members of Teamsters Union Local 399 (http://www.ht399.org), which includes California and 12 other western states, have a feature rate of $2,423 per week plus $70 a day for a car. (This rate is through July 31, 2009 and will probably change when a new contract is negotiated.) Those who are successful and in demand may earn considerably more.

Employment Prospects

Every film needs someone to find locations for shooting, so there is an ongoing need for Location Scouts. The job requires a lot of research and legwork, as well as travel and detail work. Since this often is a job embarked upon at the beginning of a film career, as the opportunity to produce or direct develops, the Location Scout moves on. This means openings will occur more regularly than in other film industry jobs.

Advancement Prospects

Advancement will depend on where the Location Scout lives, as well as whether or not specific directors or producers begin requesting the services of a specific Location Manager. A successful Location Scout can rise to the top or use the position as a stepping stone to directing or producing jobs.

Education and Training

In college or graduate school, take courses in film and producing so that you know what a location manager is supposed to do. Develop excellent research skills and photography skills to record potential places for shooting a film.

Experience, Skills, and Personality Traits

Working at a film company or studio, as well as working at a local or state film commission, offer opportunities to learn about the film business and what a Location Scout needs to do. Traveling extensively and keeping mental and physical records of particular settings and even restaurants or locales that could be in a film is useful knowledge for this job.

Unions and Associations

In California, as well as in 12 other western states, Location Scouts are members of the Teamsters Union. In New York, they are members of the Directors Guild of America. Other states are nonunion. However, studios will only hire union Location Scouts. Nonunion Location Scouts may work on smaller films and commercials.

Tips for Entry

1. If you know a student or independent filmmaker who is planning to shoot a movie, ask if he or she has a Location Scout. If not, volunteer to scout locations.
2. Get an administrative assistant position with a film company and offer to accompany the Location Scout when he or she scouts a film to observe how it's done.
3. Travel and make notes and photographic records of your trips.

STORYBOARD ARTIST

CAREER PROFILE

Duties: Draw a series of sketches and illustrations that show in pictures what the script shows in words and that help the director and director of photography visualize and set up a shot; help the production manager create a budget; help the editor get a better feel for pacing; and help the production designer visualize sets and locations

Alternate Title(s): Production Illustrator

Salary Range: $461 per day is the minimum fee for Storyboard Artists who are members of the IATSE Local 800

Employment Prospects: Good

Advancement Prospects: Fair

Best Geographical Location(s): Los Angeles/Hollywood, New York City

Prerequisites:

    Education and Training—Bachelor's degree in film or art is helpful but not required

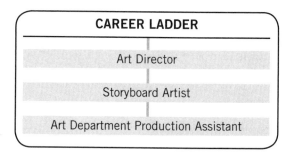

CAREER LADDER

Art Director

Storyboard Artist

Art Department Production Assistant

    Experience—Working as a Storyboard Artist on student or low-budget films; work in commercial art or comic book illustration

    Special Skills and Personality Traits—Creative; artistic; able to illustrate action and movement; have strong visual interpretive skills

Position Description

The Storyboard Artist illustrates the movie in a series of sketches, similar to pictures in a comic strip. Taking his or her cue primarily from the director, the Storyboard Artist draws key scenes or action sequences to help in the preparation of the actual production. Storyboards are also used to prepare a budget, and they assist in production design and art direction and even editing.

A typical day for a Storyboard Artist might include meeting with the director, who has an idea for a particular shot but wants to see what it looks like. The director talks to the Storyboard Artist; he or she makes notes and then draws a variety of sketches to help the director visualize the scene. These are usually simple pencil or pen drawings.

A Storyboard Artist may be asked to make 15 to 60 separate drawings a day. Sometimes she or he will be asked to include more detail, which takes longer.

On expensive, big budget studio films, there may be a team of Storyboard Artists, while low-budget, independent films will have one, if any at all.

On films that involve special effects, a Storyboard Artist may be asked to draw something that doesn't exist, except in the mind of the screenwriter or director. In that case, a more detailed drawing may be expected.

Today, there is computer software to help in drawing storyboards. In complicated films like *The Matrix,* three-dimensional storyboards are created on a computer and then printed out as a computer-generated image for use in the film.

Salaries

Salaries vary according to one's standing in the industry. The International Alliance of Theatrical Stage Employees (IATSE) Local 790 sets the minimum fee, which is $461 a day or $2,035 a week.

Employment Prospects

More and more films are using Storyboard Artists and relying heavily on computer graphics and special effects, making employment prospects good.

Advancement Prospects

It can be difficult to go from Storyboard Artist to the next level, which could be art director. The competition is stiff, and there are fewer openings as one moves up.

Education and Training

A bachelor of arts degree in film is helpful but not required. General training in art is always a plus, as is an understanding of film production. Courses in illustration, graphic design, and film production are useful.

Experience, Skills, and Personality Traits

Storyboard Artists must be visually creative and able to tell stories with drawings. They must be comfortable taking instruction and criticism from the director. They need a lot of enthusiasm and energy, since they may be called upon to do multiple drawings in a short time or re-draw finished pieces.

Unions and Associations

Membership in IATSE Local 800 is required for working on a studio or union film. Film industry associations such as Women in Film are helpful for networking purposes.

Tips for Entry

1. Produce storyboards for student or nonunion films.
2. Work as a production assistant, so you can show the director your storyboard talents.
3. Use film school acquaintances to find opportunities.
4. Storyboard a movie on spec and show it to directors.

MATTE PAINTER

CAREER PROFILE

Duties: Paint a background to be used whenever it is deemed too expensive, difficult, or impossible to shoot the actual background, such as that used in a science fiction space adventure

Alternate Title(s): Matte Artist

Salary Range: $54.02 per hour for union scale minimum computed on a daily basis

Employment Prospects: Good

Advancement Prospects: Fair

Best Geographical Location(s): Los Angeles/Hollywood, New York City

Prerequisites:

Education and Training—Bachelor's degree in art is helpful but not required

Experience—Working as a landscape artist, a scenic painter, or an artist; any work with computer graphics

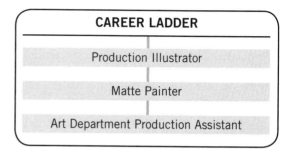

CAREER LADDER

Production Illustrator

Matte Painter

Art Department Production Assistant

Special Skills and Personality Traits—Creative; artistic; able to illustrate landscapes and backgrounds; understanding of depth of field; a passion for art and a vivid imagination; excellent computer skills

Position Description

The Matte Painter provides the background for a scene when the actual background is not available for any number of reasons. The best Matte Painters are truly artists, because they have to create something that looks so real that the human eye and brain will not notice the difference between art and reality. This takes a special skill with design and composition, as well as a keen insight into shadows and light, depth of field, and perception.

Matte drawings have been created to duplicate almost every background, either real or imagined. They may be completely static, or they may give the illusion of movement. They may even contain people, drawn so lifelike they seem real in the background. The key to filming a matte painting is to never hold on it too long. More than a few seconds of focusing, five at the most, may break the illusion of reality.

With the digital revolution, matte drawings are being completed more and more on computers, with three dimensions and real movement. It is known as CGI, or computer-generated imagery. Industrial Light and Magic, George Lucas's company, Pixar, and Blue Sky Studios are just some of the companies that are creating whole worlds in a digital realm.

Salaries

Salaries vary according to one's standing in the industry. The ballpark earnings for a Matte Painter working on a union shoot of a low-budget movie in the $1 million to $5 million range is $500 to $600 a day. Members of IATSE earn a minimum of $54.02 per hour for union scale minimums computed on a daily basis.

Employment Prospects

Films still need Matte Painters, even if the paint is a pixel and the canvas is a computer, so prospects are good for those with the right skills.

Advancement Prospects

Matte Painters can advance to production illustrators. Some move on to become art directors and production designers.

Education and Training

Art training is helpful but not required. Courses in computer graphics are a definite plus. Matte Painting is often a skill acquired on the job, perfected by assisting Matte Painters on large projects.

Experience, Skills, and Personality Traits

Matte Painters must be visually creative and have a keen sense of design and composition. They need strong interpersonal skills and should be comfortable taking instructions.

Unions and Associations

Membership in the International Alliance of Theatrical Stage Employees (IATSE) Local 800 is required to work on a studio or union film. Film industry associations such as Women in Film can be helpful for networking.

Tips for Entry

1. Get hired to produce matte paintings for student or nonunion films.
2. Be a scenic artist.
3. Let fellow students and teachers at art school, college, or film school know that you are interested in being a matte painter.

SET DESIGNER

CAREER PROFILE

Duties: Create the blueprints from which the sets will be built; work closely with the director, cinematographer, and special effects department; help determine how parts of the set are used and shot

Alternate Title(s): None

Salary Range: Union minimums range from $34.35 for a junior to $37.65 an hour for a senior

Employment Prospects: Good

Advancement Prospects: Good

Best Geographical Location(s): Los Angeles/Hollywood, New York City

Prerequisites:

Education and Training—Bachelor's or advanced degree in art; courses in design and architecture are optional

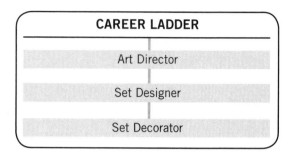

CAREER LADDER

Art Director

Set Designer

Set Decorator

Experience—Working as an architect or designer
Special Skills and Personality Traits—Artistic; strong sense of design; visually acute; good interpersonal skills

Position Description

The Set Designer is hired by the production designer to carry out the ideas and vision set forth by the director and production designer. He or she is responsible for the drawings from which the sets will be built, as well as for overseeing their construction.

A typical day in preproduction or production for the Set Designer would begin with getting rough sketches from the art director about what the director wants for a set. The Set Designer takes the sketches and adds all the details needed to bring the set to life, from a detailed blueprint to elevations, even to some prop specifications.

The Set Designer also creates any period details. For example, if a film is futuristic or set in ancient Rome, it is up to the Set Designer to render the characteristics necessary to express the period. This could include anything from having simple moldings on the walls to elaborate dressings on the windows.

A Set Designer also has to keep in mind that she or he only has to design what the camera is going to see. Instead of creating a skyscraper, maybe all she or he needs is the front portion of the lower floors.

It is also up to the Set Designer to create a feeling of depth to an otherwise two-dimensional medium. This is done in a variety of ways, such as making a set larger, so things in the back are out of focus, or building doorways and openings into other rooms.

A Set Designer may also be asked to design airplanes, cars, and futuristic vehicles.

Salaries

Salaries vary according to a film's budget and the Set Designer's standing in the film community. High-profile Set Designers command high salaries. The minimum hourly pay for union members is $34.35 for a junior to $37.65 for a senior, depending upon experience. The union contract is renegotiated periodically, so check with IATSE Local 800 for the new rates after July 31, 2009. Novice Set Designers may work on nonunion low-budget or student films for little or no pay in order to gain experience. Set Designers working on union low-budget films (budget of $1 million to $5 million) may earn around $3,000 a week.

Employment Prospects

Employment prospects for Set Designers are good since every studio art department employs a number of set designers, ranging from junior to senior Set Designers. In addition, Set Designers create more than just sets. They also design cars, planes, and trains as well as other vehicles.

Advancement Prospects

Advancement from junior or entry level Set Designer to senior Set Designer is good but requires patience and perseverance. Advancement from senior Set Designer to Art Director is more competitive because a film may require many Set Designers but only one Art Director.

Education and Training

Degrees in architecture and design are helpful. On-the-job training in the art department of any major studio or independent production company is the best preparation. A background in theater, photography, or art is also helpful.

Experience, Skills, and Personality Traits

Have a talent for drawing and drafting, as well as for architectural design. A strong knowledge of history is extremely helpful, especially on period films. Set Designers must be able to communicate well and take direction.

Unions and Associations

The union for Set Designers is Local 800, part of IATSE. Membership in industry associations, such as Women in Film, may be helpful for networking.

Tips for Entry

1. Take any entry-level position in the art department to get your foot in the door.
2. Get experience as a set decorator, illustrator, or storyboard artist.
3. Work on low-budget or student films.

SET DECORATOR

CAREER PROFILE

Duties: Supervise the crew that will decorate the set similar to an interior decorator

Alternate Title(s): None

Salary Range: $2,224 per week is the minimum set by the union (IATSE Local 44)

Employment Prospects: Good

Advancement Prospects: Good

Best Geographical Location(s): Los Angeles/Hollywood, New York City

Prerequisites:

Education and Training—Bachelor's or advanced degree in film, theater, art, or design is optional

Experience—Working in film or the theater as a carpenter

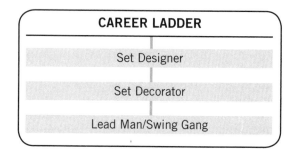

CAREER LADDER

Set Designer

Set Decorator

Lead Man/Swing Gang

Special Skills and Personality Traits—Artistic; strong sense of design and lighting; well organized; good management abilities; excellent communication skills

Position Description

The Set Decorator is in charge of the "set dressing crew"—the men and women from various craft unions that decorate and furnish the set with furniture, carpeting, drapes, plants, appliances, paintings, lamps, and, basically, anything that isn't nailed down or part of the construction of the set or props, which are devices used by the actors and handled by the director of props.

The Set Decorator is in charge of designing and decorating the set with furnishings. By the time the Set Decorator gets involved, the set is already built and painted or wallpapered. Following directions from the production designer and set designer, the Set Decorator manages what's called the dressing crew, which is made up of a lead man and a swing gang, a group of union craftspeople, such as electricians, painters, upholsterers, carpenters, furniture movers or refinishers, and landscapers.

The Set Decorator takes her or his cues from the script, the director, the production designer, and the director of photography, or cinematographer. Often, the scene description in the script will offer little guidance; for example, the phrase, "Mary enters her bedroom," says nothing about the type of furniture or bed in the bedroom, what paintings or prints are on the wall, or even what the room generally looks like. It is up to the art director, set designer, and Set Decorator to make it look like Mary's bedroom.

Once a "look" is established, the Set Decorator must make sure there's enough time or sufficient stock to furnish the room the way the director and production designer have chosen.

Once the set is dressed, the director of photography may issue her or his own requests for extra lamps to match the actual light source.

Set Decorators, according to their union, the International Association of Theatrical Stage Employees (IATSE), are not allowed to move or repair anything involved in the dressing of the set. They must give instructions to the Lead Man, who then assigns the appropriate task to someone on the Swing Gang.

A typical day would involve the Set Decorator researching what type of furnishings should go onto the set. For example, if the scene called for a certain historical look, the Set Decorator might make arrangements to furnish the set with antiques, either renting them from an antique store or borrowing them from the studio property department.

The Set Decorator will give instructions to the lead man/swing gang to gather and move the objects onto the set. Often, the Set Decorator will have to use the studio's refurnishing department to adapt a piece of furniture to the set designer's specifications. He or she will also tell the lighting fixtures department what lights are needed where, and if a certain fixture isn't available, they'll find out where one can be acquired for the least amount of money.

It is said that the "devil is in the details," and a good Set Decorator will go that extra step to decorate the set with as much detail as possible to give the set character. If you compare old movies or many low-budget films with contemporary studio productions, you can see the difference in the details in the set.

Salaries

Salaries vary according to a film's budget and one's standing in the film community. Basic minimums are set by the International Alliance of Theatrical Stage Employees (IATSE). The weekly minimum set by the union, IATSE Local 44, is $2,224, through July 31, 2009.

Employment Prospects

Employment prospects for a Set Decorator are good. Most studio films have one.

Advancement Prospects

Prospects for advancement from lead man or member of the swing gang to Set Decorator are fair. Competition to advance to Set Decorator is stiff, but many Set Decorators rise up through the studio ranks, while others enter the field after being commercial or residential directors. Many work as set dressers or crew leaders first.

Education and Training

Degrees in film, drama, or decoration are helpful but not necessary. Training as an interior decorator or interior designer would be extremely helpful.

Experience, Skills, and Personality Traits

Have a talent for design. A strong knowledge of history is useful, and a background in decoration is helpful.

Unions and Associations

Membership in IATSE is required for work on union or studio movies. The local for Set Decorators is IATSE Local 44 (http://www.local44.org), based in North Hollywood, California, and Local 52 in New York. Joining an association called the Set Decorators Society of America is valuable for educational and networking opportunities.

Tips for Entry

1. Take any entry-level position in the set-dressing department.
2. Get experience as a Lead Man on a Swing Gang.
3. Work on low-budget or student films.

MODEL AND MINIATURE BUILDER

CAREER PROFILE

Duties: Design and create scale duplicates of imaginary or real artifacts when, because of cost or practical considerations, the actual object is unavailable

Alternate Title(s): None

Salary Range: $36.85 per hour for members of IATSE Local 44

Employment Prospects: Fair

Advancement Prospects: Fair

Best Geographical Location(s): Where filmmaking is a major activity, such as Los Angeles/Hollywood or New York City, although being affiliated with a company that is hired by the studio is more important and that company might be based in other locations

Prerequisites:

Education and Training—Artistic ability; bachelor's degree; classes in architecture or landscape architecture may be helpful

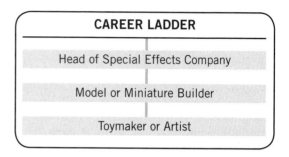

CAREER LADDER

Head of Special Effects Company

Model or Miniature Builder

Toymaker or Artist

Experience—Practice creating models from kits and from scratch; make models and miniatures

Special Skills and Personality Traits—Patience; ability to work as part of a team; attention to detail; dexterity; good eyesight and sense of proportion

Position Description

Model or Miniature Builders create real or imaginary objects when it is either too expensive or not possible to film the actual object. The Model and Miniature Builder, working closely with the director and production designer, handles all aspects of the model or miniature that a film requires. Sometimes, a model will be created for a movie and used to shoot just certain scenes, even if a replica of some or all of the original object is also used, as was done with the ship in James Cameron's historical epic, *Titanic*.

As Greg Jein, Model and Miniature Builder on *Close Encounters of the Third Kind*, points out in *Working in Hollywood*, Model and Miniature Builders are part of Local 44, the carpenters' union, in Hollywood. In San Francisco, those who work for Lucasfilm are under the Bay Area Local, with each local having its own guidelines about what aspects of model and miniature building someone is able to do, such as whether or not it is permissible to paint or mold one's models, or if someone else has to carry out that task. This means that specific duties will vary, depending on your location.

Basically, Model and Miniature Builders are sophisticated toymakers. They make toy boats, toy planes, toy space ships, and toy monsters. Sometimes, they make toy cities and mountains. For the movie *1941*, Greg Jein built director Steven Spielberg a toy Hollywood Boulevard, as well as a miniature amusement park and Ferris wheel.

Models have to be made to scale so that people watching the movie will not be able to tell the difference between a real battleship and the model that just blew up and sunk in a water tank.

Salaries

Model and Miniature Builders who are members of the union, IATSE Local 44 have a minimum salary of $36.85 an hour.

Employment Prospects

This is a very competitive and specialized field that is difficult to break into. Although there is still a need for models or miniatures in some films, the growth of computer-generated images (CGI) has narrowed the field.

Advancement Prospects

Working on a successful film that attributes its acclaim to the models or miniatures built for it will help advancement. Model and Miniature Builders can move on to higher level special effects jobs or even become art directors or production designers.

Education and Training

Practical training in the building of models is useful, as is taking related courses in film, special effects, architecture, and sculpture.

Experience, Skills, and Personality Traits

On-the-job training as an apprentice or intern working with a Model or Miniature Builder is the fastest way to achieve the experience and skills to make it in this unique aspect of filmmaking. Patience, attention to detail, and the ability to work as part of the film production team are also helpful. Being able to make deadlines and to work within a budget are also crucial.

Unions and Associations

Working on studio movies requires that the Model and Miniature Builder be in the carpenter's union. In Los Angeles, it's IATSE Local 44 (http://www.local44.org). But in San Francisco, there's the Bay Area Local.

Tips for Entry

1. Perfect your skills as a Model and Miniature Builder, and have samples of your work to show.
2. Get a job as an apprentice or intern working for a model or miniature builder who has film companies as clients.
3. Work for student, low-budget, or independent feature films to get experience and to gain entry to the union so that you can be considered for a studio film.

PUPPETEER/SCULPTOR

Duties: Create puppet creatures, controlled by a Puppeteer, for films; create clay sculptures of creatures, either in miniature or full-size format

Alternate Title(s): Creature Designer

Salary Range: Annual salary ranges from $31,000 to over $100,000

Employment Prospects: Poor

Advancement Prospects: Poor

Best Geographical Location(s): Access to a filmmaking center, like Los Angeles/Hollywood or New York City, or to a special effects company with ample film work

Prerequisites:

    Education and or Training—Art courses or specialized training in puppeteering, drawing, or sculpting

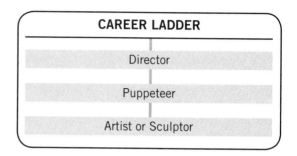

CAREER LADDER

Director

Puppeteer

Artist or Sculptor

Experience—Making puppets or sculptures; being part of the moviemaking process on student films and studio projects

Special Skills and Personality Traits—Imaginative; independent self-starter; able to work as part of a team; art and sculpting skills; detail-oriented

Position Description

The Puppeteer creates puppets to be used in movies. He or she may also sculpt miniature creatures that represent what the final creature will look like. The late, great Puppeteer Jim Henson, famous for the puppets he created for the long-running *Sesame Street* television series, as well as the Muppets, along with Frank Oz, collaborated with filmmaker George Lucas to create Yoda for *The Empire Strikes Back*. At www.stampede-entertainment.com, Amalgamated Dynamics Inc. (ADI) co-founders Tom Woodruff and Alec Gillis list more than 10 kinds of puppets that are used in filmmaking, such as the articulated puppet, the hand puppet, the hydraulic puppet, the hero puppet, and the maquette, which is the miniature clay sculpture presented to the director for approval "before time and money are invested in the development of full-scale puppets."

A special category within this group is Creature Design. Anyone working in puppeteering needs to know about the anatomy and biology of humans and animals, as well as have a vivid imagination, since most of these models and miniatures only exist in the imagination.

Carlo Rambaldi created the being ET for *E.T.* and the aliens for *Close Encounters of the Third Kind*. Rambaldi says in the book *Working in Hollywood* that the secret to his work is knowing human anatomy—even ET had to have mechanisms to make it similar to the human body. For *E.T.* he created a miniature capable of 85 movements.

For the 1975 remake of *King Kong*, Rambaldi had to construct a giant gorilla, so he visited zoos, searching for the right look. He found what he needed at the San Diego Zoo, and he reproduced that gorilla's face for the face of King Kong. Unlike the original film, in which the ape was a miniature model less than three feet tall, for the remake, Rambaldi created giant mechanical arms and hands, while the rest of the body was done to human scale, using a man in a gorilla suit.

The Puppeteer works closely with the director to match as closely as possible the director's vision of what the creature should look like. While working with Spielberg on *E.T.*, Rambaldi was instructed to make a creature that looked ugly enough to scare a little girl but innocent enough to appeal to a wide audience.

There is a concern that digital computer graphics will replace the need for a Puppeteer. For example, in a recent *Star Wars* movie, the character of Yoda was computer generated, whereas in earlier films, he was a puppet.

Salaries

The International Alliance of Theatrical Stage Employees (IATSE) minimum is about $30 per hour. Earnings may be determined by one's reputation and the budget of the film. Veteran Puppeteers and Creature Designers, such as Carlo Rambaldi, command much higher salaries. Annual salary can range from $31,000 to over $100,000.

Employment Prospects

This is a highly specialized type of artistry, dependent upon imagination, creativity, and artistic ability, plus the practical knowledge of puppetry and sculpting. There are limited openings, and competition can be heavy.

Advancement Prospects

Puppeteers and Sculptors are artists, so their advancement will be determined by the success or failure of their work. Beginners often start out as part of a team of sculptors working on a major project and advance to head their own crew of artists.

Education and Training

College is not necessary, but a knowledge of the film industry, such as that gained in film school, is helpful. Also needed is a mastery of the necessary artistic skills required to create a puppet or to sculpt a miniature or full-scale model. Get the artistic training as a Puppeteer or Sculptor, as well as on-the-job training, by working in the creature workshop of someone who

regularly works for film as well as commercials and music videos.

Experience, Skills, and Personality Traits

Internships or apprenticeships are extremely useful as a way of observing the techniques of accomplished Puppeteers and Sculptors and for the opportunity to create works. Sculptors must be creative, resourceful, and dedicated. They must be comfortable taking instructions from the director or special effects supervisor. They must also have a sense of form and anatomy.

Unions and Associations

Membership in IATSE may be beneficial. Membership in industry associations, such as Women in Film, is good for networking opportunities.

Tips for Entry

1. Apply for an apprenticeship program in the creature department of a studio or a special effects company.
2. Take art courses at a school that also offers film courses. See if you could develop a project with a filmmaker using puppets.
3. Get any kind of job, paid or unpaid, creating puppets for live theater or for a movie.

PROPERTY MASTER

CAREER PROFILE

Duties: Responsible for the design, selection, acquisition, placement, and disposal of all props used in a motion picture

Alternate Titles(s): Prop Master, Director of Props

Salary Range: $37.44 per hour is the union minimum

Employment Prospects: Good

Advancement Prospects: Good

Best Geographical Location(s): Hollywood/Los Angeles, New York City

Prerequisites:

Education and Training—Bachelor's or advanced degree not necessary but helpful

Experience—Working as an assistant Property Master or in the prop department

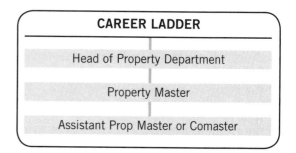

CAREER LADDER

Head of Property Department

Property Master

Assistant Prop Master or Comaster

Special Skills and Personality Traits—Able to get anything anytime anywhere; well organized; detail-oriented; reliable

Special Requirements—Special licenses may be required

Position Description

The Property Master is responsible for the purchase, design, manufacture, and acquisition of all props, which generally means all those items used by actors, including food, guns, toys, household items, office supplies, and so forth.

A "prop" is defined as anything other than actors or animals that moves or anything handled by an actor. For example, if a dinner setting was used as background but no one actually ate dinner, then the dinner setting would be considered a set decoration. But if an actor sat down and picked up a plate for whatever reason, that plate just became a prop.

A Property Master gets involved in preproduction by doing a prop breakdown from the script. Sometimes, the prop is actually mentioned in the script, but the art director, director, or production designer will also sometimes add a prop that is not even mentioned in the script, mainly because the scene needed it. The Property Master also determines how much each prop is going to cost and produces a prop budget.

If a prop is not going to be easy to find, the Property Master will need as much time as possible to either find or have made the necessary prop before shooting begins. The Property Master must also be on the set during filming, because there are always last minute changes in the script, the set, and, especially, the props.

It's the Property Master's job to make sure that all the props are ready when the actors need them, that they are positioned properly, and that they are stored afterward in case a scene has to be reshot or the prop reused in a different scene. It's also up to the Property Master to instruct the actors on the proper and safe way to handle a prop, especially a weapon. The Property Master is responsible for maintaining a safe and secure environment whenever firearms or explosives are being used.

If cue cards are being used, the Property Master is responsible for them, making sure that they are placed so that the actors can see them clearly and that the correct card is facing the correct actor.

The Property Master usually has at least one assistant and may have a whole team on a big-budget studio film. If special requirements are needed, it is up to the Property Master to provide technical advisers for these special needs, such as animal handlers, food specialists (also known as food stylists), bartenders, weapons specialists, computer technicians, law enforcement and military advisers, medical technicians, and special mechanics.

The place on the studio lot where props are stored is called the "prop boneyard."

Salaries

Salaries vary according to a Prop Master's standing in the film community and the budget of the film. The basic minimum set by the International Alliance of

Theatrical Stage Employees (IATSE) Local 44 is $37.44 per hour.

Employment Prospects

Employment prospects for a Property Master are good. All studio films have one.

Advancement Prospects

Prospects for advancement for a Property Master are limited. A studio only has one head of the property department. However, one can go into set decoration, set design, or even acting, but these would be departures from the Property Master position. To meet union requirements, a Property Master must have logged 2,500 hours with IATSE signatories as an assistant Property Master or, if not in the union, work for 30 days as a Property Master on a IATSE film or television show.

Special Requirements

Property Masters or their assistants may need to have necessary licenses for handling conventional firearms, as well as short-barrel shotguns and assault weapons. Scuba certification may be required for underwater work.

Education and Training

There is a safety-training program offered by IATSE. Formal training at a film school can be helpful. Watch and study movies to be aware of the props. Observe and talk to Property Masters to find out what they do.

Experience, Skills, and Personality Traits

A Property Master should have a general knowledge of where to go to obtain any style of prop possible, including period, contemporary, or futuristic. As one Property Master put it, one of the best skills to have is a working knowledge of the yellow pages. Creative ability to make a prop that may not be available through other means, a good rapport with local law enforcement, strong research skills, good communication skills, a diplomatic personality, and a working knowledge of how colors will photograph and how different camera lenses affect an image are all useful skills. As for other personality traits, being a collector would be helpful, because Property Masters tend to collect just about everything—they never know when something may be needed.

Unions and Associations

Membership in IATSE Local 44 (http://www.local44.org), based in North Hollywood, California, is required to work on a studio or union film.

Tips for Entry

1. Take any entry-level position in the property department.
2. Work in the property department on a low-budget or student film.
3. Get any job related to props for commercials or music videos.

LEAD MAN/SWING GANG

CAREER PROFILE

Duties: Supervise the crew, known as the Swing Gang, used to decorate, or dress, the set

Alternate Title(s): Swing Crew

Salary Range: $1,800 per week for union films; less for nonunion features

Employment Prospects: Good

Advancement Prospects: Good

Best Geographical Location(s): Los Angeles/Hollywood, New York City

Prerequisites:

Education and Training—High school diploma is a minimum requirement

Experience—Working as a set dresser or production assistant

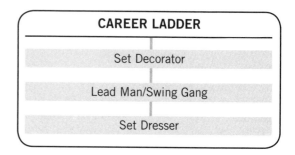

CAREER LADDER

Set Decorator

Lead Man/Swing Gang

Set Dresser

Special Skills and Personality Traits—Strong; able to move heavy objects; excellent leadership abilities; good communication and accounting skills

Position Description

The Lead Man leads. He or she supervises the Swing Gang, which is the crew assigned to dress the set. Other duties include assisting the set decorator in locating, acquiring, and arranging for the transportation, loading and unloading, and care and positioning of everything used in decorating the set, as well as preparing and filing all paperwork connected with the rental or purchase of set-dressing items.

In a sense, the Lead Man is an assistant set decorator because he or she will carry out the dressing of the set, but he or she will also coordinate the logistics and prepare all the paperwork and make sure that the furniture being delivered is what was ordered.

The Lead Man will supervise all the heavy lifting and moving, since the set director is not allowed to touch or move anything. It is the Swing Gang that physically decorates, or dresses, and takes down, or strikes, the set. It is the Lead Man who coordinates the dressing of the set with the set builders, painters, lighting personnel, grips, electricians, and prop masters.

It is his or her job to make sure that the set is ready when the rest of the production company arrives to shoot. Once the camera rolls, the Lead Man turns over responsibility of the set to the prop-

erty master. Once shooting is finished, the Lead Man and the Swing Gang take over again to undress the set.

Salary

Salaries are determined by experience, and the range is set by the International Alliance of Theatrical Stage Employees (IATSE). The average is $1,800 per week.

Employment Prospects

Employment prospects for a Lead Man/Swing Gang are good. All studio films have one.

Advancement Prospects

Prospects for advancement for a Lead Man to set decorator are good. From there, one may continue moving up to set decorator or set designer, as well as to other positions.

Education and Training

A minimum of a high school diploma is generally required. Acquire on-the-job training as a set dresser.

Experience, Skills, and Personality Traits

A Lead Man begins as a set dresser working on a Swing Gang. Skills include strength to lift and move heavy objects, leadership skills, and knowledge of where to go to get set decorations, whether it is from the studio's collection or the local antique store.

Unions and Associations

Membership in IATSE is beneficial. Industry associations, such as the Set Decorators Society of America (http://www.setdecorators.org), may be helpful for networking.

Tips for Entry

1. Take any entry-level position in the swing gang.
2. Work in the set-dressing department on a low-budget or student film.

COSTUME DESIGNER

Duties: Create or select from preexisting clothing or costumes the wardrobe for all the actors in a film

Alternate Title(s): None

Salary Range: $2,500 to $10,000 a week with an average of $4,500 a week for union feature films; $21.68 an hour is scale, according to the basic contract for members of IATSE Local 892, the Costume Designers Guild

Employment Prospects: Good

Advancement Prospects: Good

Best Geographical Location(s): Los Angeles/Hollywood, New York, Chicago, Orlando, and other major urban centers of filmmaking

Prerequisites:

Education and Training—A formal degree is not necessary, but a college degree with a specialization in costume design may help

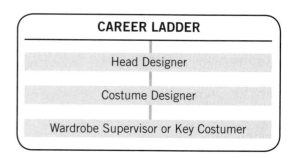

CAREER LADDER

Head Designer

Costume Designer

Wardrobe Supervisor or Key Costumer

Experience—On-the-job experience designing costumes in the theater and for movies

Special Skills and Personality Traits—Attention to details; creative; excellent communication and time management skills; artistic; team worker; able to delegate; responsible; excellent memory; fashion sense; research skills

Position Description

Whether it's for a historical feature requiring the re-creation of the period costumes for a diverse range of principal actors, supporting cast, and extras or it's for a contemporary drama requiring certain fashions, the Costume Designer plays a pivotal role in the look of a movie. From the color of the clothes to the fabric, style, and authenticity of each costume to the accessories that are chosen, the Costume Designer is a fundamental and critical part of every film. Some well-known Costume Designers, like the late Edith Head, have international reputations as wide as the best-known actors whom they designed costumes for in films. Costume Designers also supervise the seamstresses, dressers, and cutters, who transform their costume designs into actual garments.

The Costume Designer will work closely with the production designer and art department to come up with wardrobe ideas. He or she will also meet with principal actors to make sure that a particular costume is appropriate for that character. Sketches and designs are then submitted to the director for approval.

Once the director signs off on the costume designs, the designer prepares to build the wardrobe. Some costumes are designed from scratch, while others are either purchased, rented, or found in a studio wardrobe department. Recently, product placement has become a

factor in what a lead actor will wear. Clothing manufacturers will pay the film company if the principal actors wear their brands.

On the set, the Costume Designer makes sure the actors are dressed in their character's wardrobe and that they are comfortable.

Actor James Woods said in an interview with Fred Yager that he wasn't able to get into his character for the film *The Onion Field* until he put on a bolo tie as part of his outfit. He says it was that tie, which was part of the wardrobe created by the Costume Designer, that allowed him to become the character of a cop killer that won him an Academy Award nomination.

Salaries

Costume Designers earn an average of $2,500 to $10,000 a week, with the average earnings of $4,500 a week for union or studio films, depending on budget and what the Costume Designer negotiates. The minimum for Costume Designers who are members of IATSE Local 892 is $21.68 an hour. Wages are determined by one's reputation and the budget of a film.

Employment Prospects

Every movie needs a Costume Designer, even a low-budget feature, so there are as many employment opportunities as there are films. The budget to pay a Costume Designer, however, will vary greatly, depending upon the film's budget.

Advancement Prospects

After getting that initial foot in the door, additional jobs and advancement will be based on praise for the costumes designed, as well as how easily someone works with the film's casting director, talent, director, producer, and screenwriter. Winning recognition, especially a major award, for costume design can ensure a Costume Designer's future in the movie business. Advancement usually comes with working on higher profile, bigger budget films.

Education and Training

Degrees or formal training are not required, but studying costume design at a college or university is a useful path to this specialized job in the film industry. Studying drawing, illustration, and art, including color as well as theater or history could be helpful. Even more important is gaining on-the-job experience, through an apprenticeship, internship, or entry-level position, as a Costume Designer for a professional, regional, or amateur theater company or doing similar costume design work on a feature film, documentary, or music video. Costume Designers usually have an art or fashion background. They may get to design costumes for a film by way of high fashion or theater costume design.

Experience, Skills, and Personality Traits

A Costume Designer translates the vision of the screenwriter and director into fabric and dress, which help advance the plot and develop the characters in the movie. Yet, the wardrobe cannot be so overwhelming that the costumes get more attention than the film itself. Costume Designers need to be detail-oriented, since color and fabric can have as much bearing on whether or not a costume works as overall design and style. Costume Designers must be very creative and have an eye for fashion and design. They must have patience designing dozens or hundreds of costumes for major characters as well as minor ones, and the ability to stay with one project for as long as it will take, sometimes a year or more for a major studio film. The Costume Designer also has to be organized, stay within a fixed budget, and utilize available inventory for non-principal actors, if possible.

Unions and Associations

The Costume Designers Guild (http://www.costume designersguild.com) was founded in 1953; it became affiliated with the union International Alliance of Theatrical Stage Employees (IATSE) in 1976 and is part of Local 892 (http://www.costumedesignersguild.com). Membership in IATSE Local 892 is mandatory for Costume Designers who are working on a studio or union film.

Tips for Entry

1. Work in a paid or apprenticeship capacity for a Costume Designer in a music video, play, or film.
2. Network with casting directors, directors, and talent. Let them know about your work as a Costume Designer.

KEY COSTUMER

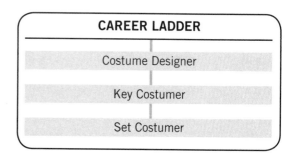

Position Description

The Key Costumer is the wardrobe supervisor. He or she is in charge of the wardrobe on the set, fixing any problem involving costumes, assisting in the budget, and selecting the costumes the actors will be wearing. It is the Key Costumer's responsibility to make sure that each costume works, that it doesn't clash or look too much like another actor's wardrobe, and that it makes a statement about the character. He or she supervises all costume fittings and is responsible for choosing and acquiring the wardrobe to be used by the actors. In low-budget films, the Key Costumer may also be the costume designer.

The Key Costumer not only picks the costume, but he or she also has to either rent it, buy it, have it made, and then make sure that it survives the entire shoot.

It is up to the Key Costumer to supervise all fittings. He or she usually hires all the set costumers who do the actual fittings of the actors.

As head of the wardrobe department, the Key Costumer works closely with the production designer and director of photography to make sure that all the costumes work within the overall design and look of the film.

Another job for the Key Costumer is to take the costume designer's script breakdown and do a scene-by-scene analysis to figure out how many costumes are needed for principal actors and extras, as well as how many identical costumes to acquire for key performers whose costumes may get torn or otherwise affected during filming.

The Key Costumer also keeps track of all costumes for both continuity and maintenance.

Salaries

Salaries vary according to one's standing in the industry, but Local 705 of IATSE sets $30.64 an hour as the minimum rate for members of its union.

Employment Prospects

Since most films, whether they are studio films or independently produced, require the actors to wear costumes of one kind or another, employment prospects for the Key Costumer, or those people who provide those costumes, is pretty good.

Advancement Prospects

Key Costumers may advance to costume designer. From there, it is possible to move up to other art- and design-related positions. Advancement also comes through working on higher profile, bigger budget films.

Education and Training

Fashion training is helpful but not required. The best training is that acquired on the job at a costume house. A costume house is a business that specializes in providing wardrobes for film production companies. Although studios have their own Costume Department, they may need a specialized costume that can only be found at an outside costume house.

Experience, Skills, and Personality Traits

Key Costumers must be visually creative and have a keen sense of fashion and design. They should get experience working in a costume house. They must be diplomatic and able to deal with actors' reactions to costumes they may not want to wear.

Unions and Associations

Membership in the International Alliance of Theatrical Stage Employees (IATSE) Local 705 (http://www.motionpicturecostumers.org) is required to work on a studio or union film. Industry associations, such as Women in Film or the Academy of Motion Picture Arts and Sciences, are helpful for networking.

Tips for Entry

1. Get hired as a set costumer in the wardrobe department.
2. Work in a costume house.
3. Take a job as a tailor in the wardrobe department of a film.

MAKEUP ARTIST

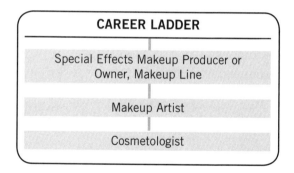

CAREER LADDER

Special Effects Makeup Producer or Owner, Makeup Line

Makeup Artist

Cosmetologist

Position Description

Makeup Artists apply makeup to principal actors and extras in a film to reflect the period, vision, or characters as conceived by the screenwriter and the director. Some Makeup Artists, such as the legendary George Westmore, go on to start their own business. Westmore started a makeup studio in 1917 at Selgi Studio and went on to create his own line of makeup. The late John Chambers, most well known for his makeup work on the first *Planet of the Apes* film series, for which he received an Academy Award in 1969, began his career designing the prosthetics that amputees need following reconstructive surgery, then moved to working in television and on feature films.

There is an intimate bond between Makeup Artists and principal actors. The Makeup Artist is usually the first person to see actors when they arrive on the set, often before sunrise. Some big-name talent have their own personal Makeup Artists, who follow them from film to film.

Most productions have more than one Makeup Artist, and they are hired by either the production designer or costume designer.

Depending on the character, some Makeup Artists may have to work on an actor for hours, getting a certain look just right, such as aging, or if the character has an illness, an unusual appearance.

On a typical day on the set, the Makeup Artist will be working long hours and usually on their feet. Between each take, they have to make sure the makeup they spent hours applying still looks good on the 34th take.

Each Makeup Artist has his or her own brushes and various types of makeup, such as old-age makeup or fashion makeup. There are two basic types of makeup: "street," or normal everyday makeup, and "character" makeup, which is needed for that particular part, such as aging makeup for an elderly character or makeup used to make a character look injured.

Makeup Artist Carola Myers grew up in Bolivia; she learned the basics of makeup artistry there and in Brazil. She moved to the United States and was hired by Trish McEvoy, a Makeup Artist from New York. For several years, Myers worked at a major department store, studying skin tone, blending color from all kinds of textures and pigment types, and working with different kinds of products while learning from beauty industry pros such as Guy Lento, Osvaldo Perez, Trish McEvoy, and François Nars. She has perfected her own makeup techniques, including high-definition airbrushing.

Now based in the Washington, D.C., area, Carola works in the film and television industries, and she also has a clientele of politicians, socialites, and brides who hire her to apply their makeup for special occasions. Her Makeup Artist film credits include the independent feature film *Again*, in 2003, and *Money Makers*, a Discovery Channel production by Leopard Films of England in 2004, as well as many corporate films, TV presentations, Internet shows, and live events.

Myers tries not to limit her experiences as a Makeup Artist; she finds that many things contribute to improving her craft. As she says: "One thing I've learned is to never limit myself to any specific work in the makeup artistry field. I learned so much when I did live events that helps in [doing] feature films. It's truly a team effort to make a production successful. When the filming crew communicates and discusses options or requests changes, makeup artists have to understand that producers or directors may have to tape the same scene over and over, and you might also be doing the makeup over and over. You have to maintain the same look to keep continuity in the film. If you put more eyebrow color or more blush definition, that will change the scene slightly. When they pick up on the scene and notice a difference, they will call you out, and say, 'It doesn't look the same as yesterday. What happened?' So you have to study and be aware of your work. Makeup artists shouldn't be sensitive [when that happens]."

Myers loves what she has been doing for more than 18 years. She suggests joining an association that will facilitate networking relating to who needs a Makeup Artist and about what films or videos are shooting in the area. She belongs to Women in Film & Video of Washington, D.C. (WIFV), a chapter of Women in Film & Television International (WIFTI).

She has other suggestions for how to get started or how to land jobs: "It's a good idea to send your résumé to a production company," Myers explains. "They usually don't have the budget for an in-house makeup artist. They only use freelancers." She also suggests helping other colleagues: "fellow filmmakers when they need you, when they're studying or with their documentaries if they have a low budget. If you help them to make their movie look better, they will definitely refer you to other filmmakers, and next time they're going to call you when they actually have a budget for a Makeup Artist."

"It's all about giving," says Myers. "In this industry, you have to be very friendly. You have to be very creative about how to get the business." Every spring, Women in Film & Television of Washington, D.C., has an awards dinner where women in the industry are honored. Myers volunteers her services and makes up the honorees. "It's a way of meeting the honorees but also of giving back to them for their service to the industry."

It's also vital that you train in and keep up with the latest techniques. "You have to be the full package," advises Myers. "You have to be reliable, on time, and [have] a good attitude, or they won't call you anymore."

The most exciting film job Myers has ever had? For a year, she worked on *Beauty in the Eye of the Beholder*, a 2006 documentary produced by Art Pallette Productions, Says Myers: "It's a documentary, but they're also doing a lot of reenactments. And actually it is all about real women issues. They will be presenting it this year at a California film festival."

Salaries

Earnings range from a minimum of $20 to mid-$40s an hour for studio or union films, based on the film's budget as well as the contract that is signed with IATSE. Earnings are determined by one's standing, the budget of the film, whether the position is for Head Makeup Artist or one of many assistants, and the complexity of the work.

Employment Prospects

Since makeup is considered one of the key elements of a film, employment prospects are good. However, if there are budgetary restraints, openings for a Makeup Artist, especially for contemporary settings and lower-budget films, may be less assured.

Advancement Prospects

Developing a reputation for excellent work is the best insurance for advancement. Directors, casting agents, and talent like to work with the same Makeup Artist over and over again if they are pleased with the results. A successful artist will go on to higher profile, bigger budget films. Those who become celebrities in their own right may launch their own line of makeup products.

Education and Training

There are Makeup Artist training centers that someone interested in pursuing this field could attend. One such course is the Master Makeup Course offered by the Westmore Academy, based in Burbank, California. (See their Web site for more information: http://www.westmoreacademy.com.) Taking makeup classes in college or beauty school helps as well. Learning about the film industry would also be useful. On-the-job training is crucial for an aspiring Makeup Artist, since the skills this specialized field requires can be taught, but practice helps to perfect the techniques.

Experience, Skills, and Personality Traits

Makeup Artists are just that—artists. They take a face and use products to create the effect that the screenwriter and director want for a character. For historical or futuristic movies, the Makeup Artist may do his or her own research to supplement what is in the script in order to conceptualize the right look for the actors, so research skills and a vivid imagination are useful.

Unions and Associations

Makeup Artists who work on studio or union films are members of Local 706 (http://www.local706.org) of the International Alliance of Theatrical Stage Employees (IATSE). The Hollywood Makeup Artist and Hair Stylist Guild holds annual awards.

Tips for Entry

1. Work in a makeup salon but also take specialized training to learn what is unique about moviemaking.

2. Get on-the-job training doing makeup in any performing arts setting, such as television or music videos, and any kind of filmmaking, from student, low-budget, or independent features to big-budget studio films.

3. Attend the International Makeup Artist Trade Show and network with feature film Makeup Artists who have their own companies and who could hire you or offer a training internship.

4. As Makeup Artist Carola Myers advises, offer to do the makeup for student films, documentaries, or independent feature films to gain opportunities to demonstrate the quality of your Makeup Artist skills. It will also provide a networking opportunity. You may be called later for a paying job or may be recommended to another filmmaker who needs a Makeup Artist.

SPECIAL MAKEUP EFFECTS ARTIST

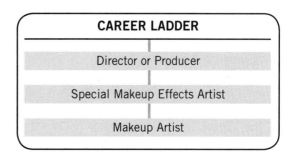

Position Description

The Special Makeup Effects Artist has been a key part of certain types of movies, going back to the very first films that had special effects creatures. Using the materials available at that time to the advanced computer technology and the standard latex materials and gels of today, they have to create the creatures in everything from *Frankenstein* to *Jurassic Park* to the cartoonlike characters in *Dick Tracy.* Special Makeup Effects Artists step in when more than the basic makeup used for beauty or standard characterization is needed. Special effects makeup artistry was first recognized as an official category for an Academy Award in 1981.

The Special Makeup Effects Artist will begin working with the director early in the development of a movie, since his or her decisions about what a film needs may dramatically impact on the film's budget. For certain movies, such as *Jurassic Park, Aliens, Terminator 2,* and *A.I.: Artificial Intelligence,* just some of the movies with special effects done by Stan Winston and his Stan Winston Studio in Los Angeles, the special effects are a pivotal part of why the movie works.

When a Special Makeup Effects Artist reads the script, he or she begins to decide what elements are needed to make whatever effects are needed as realistic as possible, even when such effects do not even exist in reality. Chris Walas, who did the special effects makeup for *Enemy Mine* and *The Fly,* is quoted in the book *Working in Hollywood* as saying, "I have to, in my own mind, build a biology behind whatever it is. How does he eat, how do the muscles form? Would he have mandibles? What kind of environment would he come from?"

During preproduction, Special Makeup Effects Artists camera test their creations to make sure the special makeup or molds hold up under sometimes harsh lights or various conditions called for in different scenes, such as rain or wind.

During production, the Special Makeup Effects Artist is on call constantly to make adjustments in between takes. For close-ups, they will actually stand behind the camera operator to make sure that each shot captures the effect or illusion the makeup is supposed to produce.

Salaries

Earnings range from a minimum of $20 to mid-$40s an hour for studio or union films based on the budget of the film as well as the contract that is signed with IATSE.

Employment Prospects

There is a regular need for the unique skills of the Special Makeup Effects Artist, especially those who master the traditional ways of achieving those effects, such as through makeup and gel or latex and molds, as well as the newer ways, such as CGI technology. More and more films are relying on special effects techniques to achieve their goals, so job prospects in this field are good.

Advancement Prospects

Developing a reputation for innovative special effects and being associated with movies that are commercial and critical successes, especially if the special effects, including any creatures that were developed, are credited for that success, will help advancement prospects. Advancement may come in the form of working on higher profile, bigger budget pictures or opening one's own studio. But the competition is stiff.

Education and Training

A college degree with a major in art or film is useful but not necessary. Knowledge of basic makeup artistry is key, as is a thorough grounding in the techniques of special effects and the technology of CGI. On-the-job training, such as becoming an apprentice in a design studio, is one way to learn necessary skills. Stan Winston started out as a makeup apprentice at Disney Studios.

Experience, Skills, and Personality Traits

Being involved in the production of a movie, from start to finish, will help the Special Makeup Effects Artist understand the demands of filmmaking. Mastering basic makeup skills for film, as well as the additional techniques of special effects, are crucial. A Special Makeup Effects Artist has to have the stamina to be on the set or location before everyone else in order to supervise or apply the makeup or devices that actors will wear that day. He or she must be available throughout the day in case any touch-ups are needed, as well as be available at the end of the day's filming to help or supervise in the removal of the special effects makeup. The Special Makeup Effects Artist must also be concerned with continuity issues, taking photographs throughout the day to study, so that the special effects are the same from day to day and frame to frame in a film.

Unions and Associations

Membership in IATSE Local 706 (http://www.local706.org) is required to work on a studio or union film. Associations such as Women in Film, the Academy of Science Fiction, Fantasy & Horror Films (http://www.saturnawards.org), and the Academy of Motion Picture Arts and Sciences may be helpful for networking.

Tips for Entry

1. Become an apprentice or intern in the studio of a renowned Special Makeup Effects Artist.
2. Become a makeup artist in the film industry and learn the additional techniques and skills of the Special Makeup Effects Artist.
3. Get a job working in any capacity on a horror or sci-fi film, whether a student, low-budget, independent, or studio film, and learn the movie-making process.
4. Attend seminars, film festivals, or conferences where Special Makeup Effects Artists are in attendance or speaking, and ask them if they know of any job openings or how to apply at their company.
5. Create a portfolio of special effects that you produce on your own or for a specific film, so that you have a record of your achievements.

HAIRSTYLIST

CAREER PROFILE

Duties: Responsible for the hair of the actors, including the style, cut, and color, as well as any necessary wigs

Alternate Title(s): Key Hairstylist; Hairdresser

Salary Range: Ranges from a minimum of $16 to low-$40s an hour for studio or minor films, based on the film's budget and the contract that is signed with the International Alliance of Theatrical Stage Employees (IATSE)

Employment Prospects: Good

Advancement Prospects: Fair

Best Geographical Location(s): Areas with access to constant moviemaking activity, such as Los Angeles/ Hollywood or New York City

Prerequisites:

Education and Training—Beauty school

Experience—Work in a hair salon; work on student films, independent movies, or music videos

Special Skills and Personality Traits—Able to get along with actors, directors, and the rest of the film's production team; willingness to work long hours; strong sense of style

Special Requirements—Current cosmetology license required; to work on a union film, a Hairstylist must also be a member of the Makeup Artists and Hair Stylist Local 706 of IATSE

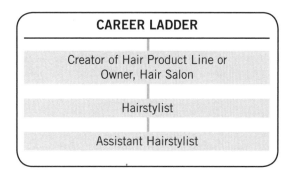

CAREER LADDER

Creator of Hair Product Line or Owner, Hair Salon

Hairstylist

Assistant Hairstylist

Position Description

The key Hairstylist is in charge of all the Hairstylists on a film. The director will provide the Hairstylist with the screenplay, and decisions will be made about the style, color, and length of hair for each character, including whether or not a wig will be used. The Key Hairstylist will oversee the daily hairstyling and continuity, so that hair looks the same in scenes shot over a period of time but supposed to take place at one point in time in the film. At the end of the day, the Hairstylist and his or her staff are responsible for brushing wigs in preparation for the next day's shooting.

In preproduction, the Hairstylist will research various hairstyles or periods of style, depending on the script, and then will make sure that he or she has the necessary supplies for the production. Reading the script also prepares the Hairstylist for special needs, such as a scene where it rains or snows.

During production, like the makeup artist and key costumer, the Hairstylist begins his or her job long before shooting begins and continues throughout the entire day to maintain hairstyles for each take. A key part of this job is making sure that the actor feels comfortable with the way she or he looks. Many top stars will have their own Hairstylist because they have developed a trust or friendship.

Besides the actors, the Hairstylist works most closely with the second assistant director, who is the stylist's liaison with the rest of the production. For example, the second assistant director will appear every five minutes to check on an actor's availability for a shot or to say that the director is ready to shoot.

Salaries

Salaries depend on the budget of the film. Earnings range from a minimum of $16 to low-$40s an hour for studio or union films, based on the film's budget and the contract that is signed with the IATSE.

Employment Prospects

Hairstyling is a pivotal part of each movie, along with makeup and costume. Union films require that a Hairstylist is a member of the union, and there are specific requirements that must be met in order to join. Once one qualifies, there will be a good number of opportunities.

Advancement Prospects

Once a Hairstylist becomes popular with specific actors, he or she will often be requested by the talent to be on his or her next film. This may help a Hairstylist move up to bigger projects. Hairstylists with a measure of celebrity in their own right can often open their own salon.

Special Requirements

Hairstylists need to have a current cosmetology license as well as be a member of the union to work on a union film.

Education and Training

Hairstylists attend beauty school and learn hairstyling techniques, including coloring, cutting, and styling. A college degree is not necessary. Becoming an assistant to a Hairstylist, at a salon or on a film, is an excellent way to learn.

Experience, Skills, and Personality Traits

Becoming a Key Hairstylist is the result of long, hard work and experience, working at a hair salon and on numerous films. In order to apply for union membership, a hairstylist has to work on nonunion movies or commercials for 60 hours. Hairstylists should be organized, efficient, friendly, and have a good sense of fashion.

Unions and Associations

To be eligible for membership in the Makeup Artists and Hair Stylist Local 706 (http://www.local706.org) of the International Alliance of Theatrical Stage Employees (IATSE), a Hairstylist needs to work 60 hours within an 18-month period. Membership in IATSE Local 706 is mandatory to work on a studio or union film.

Tips for Entry

1. Work in a salon and gain experience as a Hairstylist, so that you have the necessary skills to apply to work on a film.
2. Get work as an assistant to a film Hairstylist and observe what he or she does and what works and why.
3. Network with film Hairstylists, art directors, directors, or producers.
4. Work on nonunion films or commercials to get the number of hours necessary to join the union, then get work on union films.

SOUND

SOUND DESIGNER

Duties: Responsible for the overall design and shape of the entire sound track and all of the sound elements of a movie, from dialogue and sound effects to music

Alternate Title(s): None

Salary Range: $50,000 to $100,000+ for studio or union films

Employment Prospects: Limited

Advancement Prospects: Good

Best Geographical Location(s): Los Angeles/Hollywood, New York City

Prerequisites:

Education and Training—A broad liberal arts, music, and film background are recommended; any formal training with sound and recording equipment

Experience—Work in a range of sound areas, including mixing, recording, editing, radio, television, and music studios

CAREER LADDER

Film editor or
Supervising Sound Designer

Sound Designer

Sound Mixer

Special Skills and Personality Traits—Besides knowing everything there is to know about sound, should have knowledge of how sound affects emotions; be a team player; creative; musical; technically astute regarding sound equipment

Position Description

The position of Sound Designer can mean different things on various films. On some, the Sound Designer is an artist who joins the team early in preproduction to work with the director in creating the overall design and shape of the entire sound track to complement the theme and tone of the film. However, in many cases, a Sound Designer is given the task of creating and manipulating the necessary nonmusical sound elements, such as the sounds of battle, horses galloping, laser guns firing, or doors slamming. On other films, a Sound Designer might be hired to design nonmusical sound effects, such as the sound of a human turning into a werewolf or the sound of the devil after it has taken possession of a young girl.

Sound design is a relatively new area in the history of the film industry. Its name was coined by sound editor Walter Murch, who worked with Francis Ford Coppola on *Apocalypse Now*. Murch and others, such as Ben Burtt who designed sound for George Lucas's *Star Wars* movies, discovered that a film's sound had a dynamic impact on the film, even on the way it looked. For example, Gary Rydstrom designed the sounds of the dinosaurs for *Jurassic Park* before the dinosaurs were even created. Model dinosaurs were later built to match the sound of the roars.

Under the best conditions, the Sound Designers' work begins in preproduction, going over the script with the director to determine how sound is involved in the overall creation of the movie. The script will have specific references to sounds, either directly or indirectly, such as implied sounds of battle, running water, and so on.

During production, capturing the sound will depend on what's being shot that day and how. If you're on a soundstage, you will have more control over recording specific sounds. But when you're on location, it becomes more difficult to filter out unwanted sounds, such as traffic, birds, or crowds.

Even on the set, there are sounds that will have to be filtered out or rerecorded in postproduction, such as mechanical and electrical sounds, buzzing lights, running motors, and footsteps.

Much of the Sound Designer's work takes place in postproduction, which is probably why many Sound Designers are also sound editors. This is where everything is fixed, from bad shots to bad sound. Flubbed or mumbled lines are looped. Footsteps are enhanced by foley artists, who bring the sounds to life.

In movies such as the *Star Wars* series, a Sound Designer's work involves creating sounds that do not even exist in the real world. As noted in URL: http://

starwars.com/bio/benburtt.html, for the character of R2-D2—a droid that speaks in beeps and electronic crunches—whistles, water pipes, and electronic vocalizations were combined to make its sounds. The voice of Chewbacca, the tall Wookie, is a combination of walrus barks and those of other animals. Sound Designer Ben Burtt tapping the wires of a radio antenna with a hammer created all those signature laser blasts.

Salaries

Earnings may vary greatly from film to film, depending on what is needed in terms of sound design. A highly regarded Sound Designer can easily earn six figures a year. The average is $2,000 to $2,500 per week for union films.

Employment Prospects

Since this is a relatively new category and is often only available on high profile or big-budget studio productions, employment prospects for a Sound Designer are limited. On many films, this position is filled by the supervising sound editor or sound mixer.

Advancement Prospects

Advancing from sound editor to Sound Designer is getting easier as more and more films are including this category as a necessary position. Still, it is a highly competitive field.

Education and Training

Besides learning everything you can about sound, a diverse liberal arts background is recommended. Take training in music, sound, film, and anything through which you can express your audio ideas. Learn about microphones, as well as about recording and sound mixing equipment.

Experience, Skills, and Personality Traits

Work for a radio or television station. Be part of the sound crew for a play or low-budget film. Record sounds. Watch movies and cartoons—and listen. Be creative and musical. Think of sound as an art form in which ideas can be expressed. Sound Designers must be able to work closely with the director to create the kind of sounds they want.

Unions and Associations

There is no union for Sound Designers; however, some Sound Designers belong to either the Sound Technicians Local of the International Alliance of Theatrical Stage Employees (IATSE) or the Sound Editors Union. Others may belong to an association known as Screen Composers of America.

Tips for Entry

1. Work as an apprentice for the sound mixing or editing crew on a film.
2. Work for a radio or television station or recording studio.
3. Take any job on a film set. Network.

SOUND MIXER

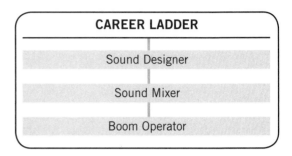

Position Description

The production Sound Mixer is in charge of hiring and supervising the production sound crew, which includes the boom operator and cable personnel, as well as obtaining and maintaining all sound recording and mixing equipment. Another key responsibility of the production Sound Mixer relates to the quality of all sound recorded during production and the mixing of the various sounds into the film's overall soundtrack. Have you ever been watching a movie in a theater or on DVD and found yourself wondering what the actor just said? With a DVD, you can always go back and listen again, but in the theater, this can be a frustrating experience. It's up to the Sound Mixer to make sure that this doesn't happen, or if it does, to make sure that it is corrected in postproduction.

Poor sound can ruin a good film. And, often, a well-mixed sound track can enhance or improve an otherwise mediocre movie.

Normally hired by the director, the Sound Mixer's job begins during preproduction, when he or she does a script breakdown to determine what equipment will be required to capture the best quality sound for each shot.

The Sound Mixer will maintain microphone levels to make sure the dialogue between characters is even and clearly heard. If an actor's voice is too soft or muddy, the Sound Mixer will alert the director, who will then decide whether or not to film another take. It is generally believed that it's better to capture dialogue during production, because it sounds the most natural. A viewer with a keen ear can usually tell when dialogue has been looped, or recorded later and then matched to the character's lips. There is usually a subtle or, in some cases, not-so-subtle otherworldly quality to the finished scene.

During production, a typical day will see the Sound Mixer overseeing the set up of the equipment, microphones, boom, and cables, then cueing tape in the recording gear to capture dialogue and background sound in the best way possible. Working with the director, the Sound Mixer will pass along instructions pertaining to sound, such as asking actors to speak louder or softer, to change an angle from a microphone to avoid popping "p" sounds. In between takes, the Sound Mixer will record something called "room tone," which is the natural way a room or location sounds when no one is talking. Even in silence, different places have different sounds, so room tone is recorded in case dialogue has to be looped later. The room tone will be mixed under the actor's voice so that it sounds as if it was recorded during production.

A recurring task is making sure that the boom mike or any other recording equipment is out of the shot. This isn't as easy as it seems, because in order to capture the best quality sound, the boom mike has to be as close to the actors as possible, and chances are the bottom tip will drop into the frame at least once during principal photography.

Another important element of the Sound Mixer's job is keeping track of the sound recorded on each take so that it can be synchronized to the picture. This is accomplished by using a clapboard and time code.

Often, the Sound Mixer would have started as a boom operator, which according to many production sound veterans is one of the hardest jobs during production. That's because the boom operator has to be aware of many factors other than sound, such as how the shot is being set up, where the lights will cast shadows, and whether it is a close-up or an establishing shot so that she or he will know how close to put the boom mike.

Meanwhile, the cable person is left to do everything else for the Sound Mixer, including running cables and wires, holding a second boom if needed, and being available for other odd jobs. There may also be a recordist who operates the recording equipment and, occasionally, a playback operator if music or dancing is involved on the sound crew.

Salaries

Earnings for a Sound Mixer can range from a low of $200 a day on nonunion films to more than $50,000 for an award-winning veteran Sound Mixer on a big-budget studio film. Salary minimum rates are set by the union and average around $56 per hour for sound technicians. Depending on the length and number of films worked on per year, salaries can range from $50,000 to more than $100,000 per year.

Employment Prospects

Employment opportunities are good, since every film needs a Sound Mixer. In many cases, the Sound Mixer will also double as the sound designer.

Advancement Prospects

Advancement prospects are good. The need for high quality sound is becoming more and more important as technology makes everything more noticeable, including how well a film's sound is recorded and mixed.

Education and Training

A college degree or film school is recommended but not required. Some training in sound technology is important. Sound Mixers should be proficient in all aspects of the recording equipment used to make movies.

Experience, Skills, and Personality Traits

Gain experience as a boom operator apprentice or cabler. Sound Mixers must have strong audio skills and a keen understanding of sound, similar to that of a musician. The Sound Mixer must be ready to follow the director's lead and work around the circumstances of every shot.

Unions and Associations

Membership in the Production Sound Crew Local of the International Alliance of Theatrical Stage Employees (IATSE) may be beneficial. Industry associations, such as the International Association of Audio/Video Communicators, or Women in Film, may be helpful for networking.

Tips for Entry

1. Work as an apprentice to a cabler or boom operator.
2. Work in a television or music studio.
3. Take any job on the set to get a foot in the door.

BOOM OPERATOR

CAREER PROFILE

Duties: Responsible for operating and placing the microphones to capture the best sound for the sound mixer

Alternate Title(s): Boomman, Boomperson

Salary Range: $35 per hour; $250 and up per day for union shows

Employment Prospects: Good

Advancement Prospects: Fair

Best Geographical Location(s): Los Angeles/Hollywood, New York City

Prerequisites:

Education and Training—Degree in film or theater helpful but not required

Experience—Work as a sound assistant or cabler, work on student or nonunion films

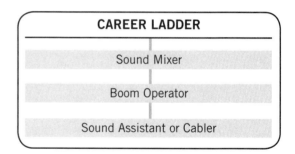

CAREER LADDER

Sound Mixer

Boom Operator

Sound Assistant or Cabler

Special Skills and Personality Traits—Have working knowledge of film production and dynamics of sound and lighting; patient; reliable; able to follow directions; physically fit and strong enough to hold microphone boom for long periods of time

Position Description

The Boom Operator works with the sound mixer. He or she is responsible for placing and operating all the microphones in order to get the best quality sound. He or she is also responsible for making sure that none of the microphones are visible during the shot.

To do his or her job effectively, a Boom Operator should be on the set at all times, following the director closely as he or she sets up the shot, which will often determine where to place the microphone. For example, if the director is shooting an establishing shot, the boom mike will have to be far away from the talent to stay out of the frame.

A Boom Operator also has to be aware of the lighting to determine whether a mike will cast a shadow. It is usually up to the sound mixer to choose which type of microphone to use. Does she or he want an omnidirectional mike, which picks up sound from a wide area, or a shotgun mike, which has a narrow field and is used to capture dialogue from a distance? The Boom Operator has to know the different types of mikes and how they perform.

One of the main problems the Boom Operator has to deal with is keeping the boom mike from dipping into the frame. This seems to happen a lot. Normally, the camera operator will see it and tell the Boom Operator to move the mike. But once a scene is underway, if the boom begins to slowly move down, the cameraperson

might miss it. Sometimes, the scene worked so well the director decides to keep the take anyway.

Salaries

Salary minimums for a Boom Operator are about $35 an hour; 250 and up for union shows. Earnings are set by the International Alliance of Theatrical Stage Employees (IATSE).

Employment Prospects

Just about every film needs a Boom Operator, so job prospects are good.

Advancement Prospects

Advancement prospects to sound mixer are fair. There is heavy competition for this move. Once advancement is underway, one can go on to become a sound designer.

Education and Training

A college degree or film school is recommended but not required. Some training in sound technology is important.

Experience, Skills, and Personality Traits

Gain experience as a sound assistant or cabler. Have strong audio skills and a keen understanding of sound.

Unions and Associations

Membership in the Production Sound Crew Local (IATSE) may be beneficial. Industry associations, such as Women in Film, may be helpful for networking.

Tips for Entry

1. Work as a sound assistant or cabler.
2. Work as a soundperson in a television or music studio.
3. Take any job on the set to get a foot in the door.

MUSIC

MUSIC SUPERVISOR

Duties: Responsible for finding music and songs for the sound track; hiring and supervising the film composer; and finding songwriters to compose new songs for the film

Alternate Title(s): Music Director

Salary Range: $2,000+ per week

Employment Prospects: Fair

Advancement Prospects: Poor

Best Geographical Location(s): Los Angeles/Hollywood, New York City

Prerequisites:

Education and Training—Bachelor's degree, with a major in music recommended but not required

Experience—Work as an A&R or music talent scout or for a radio station; work on television programs, events, or productions that require music to be played in the background; work at a music publishing company

CAREER LADDER

Producer

Music Supervisor

Director of music licensing; Rights and music clearance manager

Special Skills and Personality Traits—Love for music; a strong knowledge of various music genres and types throughout history; a working knowledge of licensing and the music industry

Position Description

Finding the right songs for a movie's sound track has become increasingly important as more and more movie sound tracks are released on CDs as promotional tools for the film and as an another way to make money. In other words, movie sound tracks have become big business; the person responsible for finding the songs for the sound track is called the Music Supervisor.

Working closely with the director and producer, the Music Supervisor searches for the best music or songwriters to create the songs that become the theme songs or signature songs for a movie.

Unlike the composer, who comes in toward the end of postproduction, the Music Supervisor is usually hired early so that he or she can get a feel for what kind of music will work for this movie. They will often go to dailies and visit the set to increase this feeling. Often, the director or producer will know some of the music he or she wants for a film, but usually this idea is quite vague, such as "70s funkadelic type sound." It's the Music Supervisor's job to know what she or he is talking about.

As various songs that either already exist or are being written for the film are gathered, it must be decided

how these songs are going to be used in the movie. Are they going to be heard coming from a radio, played by a band, either onscreen or off, or added for dramatic effect instead of dialogue?

The Music Supervisor plays his or her ideas for songs for the director and producer to see if this is what they want. This can be a long process, and songs are often changed, switched or replaced at the last minute or even after the movie has been test marketed in theaters. Once the songs are selected, the Music Supervisor must then obtain permission to use them in the film and on the sound track.

Since licensing music can be expensive, the film's budget will often determine whether a particular piece of prerecorded music can be used for the soundtrack. Often, it is cheaper to use cover musicians (an unknown or less popular musician who sings a song made popular by someone else) or to write new music.

Maxine Kozler has been in the music industry since she was 19 years old, and she also has a degree in film production from Boston University. Now in her mid-30s, two years ago, when she started La La License, her New York–based music supervision and clearance company, she combined her backgrounds. Kozler, who is a Music Supervisor for film, got to this point through a variety of jobs and experience. She worked at a radio station initially, and she also interned at a recording studio, followed by working there for a year. Says Kozler: "The biggest thing that happened was that just by being there and hanging out and meeting everyone, I wound up meeting the songwriters who would write the songs. That got me to know about songwriting and publishing and what rights were involved." That led to being hired by a company called Avenue Music Group, where she spent four years, followed by working for four years at EMI, which is one of the largest music publishers in the world.

When she left EMI, Kozler had been running the company's licensing department. She recently worked on a student film being funded by a former congressman that is being submitted to film festivals now. What did she do on the film? Kozler explains: "I submitted songs to them for consideration for use in the film. I did the clearing of the songs for use in the film and negotiated all the rights. I worked . . . to find a composer to score the film. Then we decided to have some people cover songs, so we chose some artists to go into the studio and record new versions of older songs."

In terms of a time commitment, Kozler estimates that 80 percent of her time is spent on the film projects. But the bulk of her revenue is generated by the Music Supervisor work she does for TV commercials, music videos, and advertising companies. But she does the work on films because she loves doing it. "You should always do what you love. The only thing that's going to keep you doing any job is the challenge, and certainly any job within entertainment is challenging. If you don't love it, you're not going to stick with it."

Producing a movie might be in her future. "Music Supervisor is as close as it is to being the producer on the film," says Kozler. "That's why it's a very easy transition. It's a similar skills set. The topic or the script would have to be really well done, and I would want to make sure it came to fruition."

Salaries
Salaries vary, depending on the film's budget. Veteran Music Supervisors can earn six figures a year. The average is about $2,000 a week.

Employment Prospects
Prospects for entering this field are only fair. This is a competitive field, although demand is growing.

Advancement Prospects
There are only a few advancement prospects for a film Music Supervisor. Some have gone on to become producers.

Education and Training
It would help to be a music major in college or to train as an A&R person or music talent scout for a record company.

Experience, Skills, and Personality Traits
Get experience working for a record company, at a film studio in the music department, at a music publishing company, or for a radio station. Love music. Know music inside and out. Be familiar with various types and styles of music and what it sounded like through the ages. Network with songwriters to keep up with what's going on in the music industry.

Unions and Associations
There are no unions for Music Supervisors, but joining industry associations, such as the National Academy of Recording Arts and Sciences, or Women in Film, may be helpful for networking.

Tips for Entry
1. Take any entry-level job in the film or music industry.
2. Work on student films.
3. Work for record or music publishing companies that cater to the film industry.
4. Talk to film Music Supervisors and offer to be their assistants.

COMPOSER

CAREER PROFILE

Duties: Compose the music that will be heard through-out the movie, including background music, instrumental and vocal themes, the underscoring used for dramatic effect, and popular songwriting

Alternate Title(s): None

Salary Range: $0 to $100,000+

Employment Prospects: Fair

Advancement Prospects: Fair

Best Geographical Location(s): Los Angeles/Hollywood, New York City

Prerequisites:

Education and Training—Bachelor's degree in music recommended but not required

Experience—Work as a Composer to build a body of work that reflects a wide range of emotions

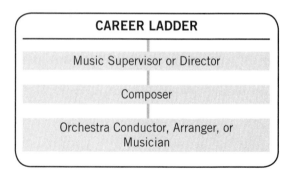

CAREER LADDER

Music Supervisor or Director

Composer

Orchestra Conductor, Arranger, or Musician

Special Skills and Personality Traits—Able to express emotions musically; a strong background in classical music and opera

Position Description

The primary job of the Composer is to create a music score that adds an emotional layer to the film. This includes both the dramatic underscoring and a musical theme or song. When it works well, the musical score of a movie can breathe life into an otherwise listless scene, whereas the wrong score can destroy a beautifully filmed and acted moment. In other words, the score can either help or hurt a movie's success, which is why directors and producers take great care in hiring the best Composer for their film.

While most of the Composer's work doesn't begin until the film is in its final editing stages, he or she may have begun composing themes or songs for the film. Still, it is not until a near final cut is ready that the Composer will begin actually creating the dramatic underscore used to heighten the drama, suspense, action, or comedy of a particular scene. The main reason for waiting as long as possible is primarily economic; the producer or financing entities do not want the Composer, orchestra, music editor, or scoring mixer to waste time and money on scenes that are not going to be in the movie.

To compose the score for a movie, the Composer first looks at a rough cut of the movie to get a creative sense of what kind of musical themes will be needed, as well as ideas for possible theme songs. Next, he or she does what's called a "spotting session" with the direc-

tor, where they screen the film and decide where music should come in and fade out.

When the director feels the editing is complete, the Composer, with the film playing on a screen, begins creating the music that will accompany each scene. The score will contain beats and measures to match the action on the screen.

Once the score is written, musicians are brought into a scoring session to work with the Composer, music editor, and conductor to perform the music on a scoring stage, which is comprised of a mixing console and a screen to show the movie. After the score is recorded, the music editor and Composer mix the music and then turn it over to a final mixing stage to be mixed into the final sound track.

Salaries

Salaries vary widely from Composer to Composer and depend on a film's budget. On no- or low-budget films, a beginning Composer may receive a deferred salary and use the opportunity to showcase his or her talents. A veteran established Composer, such as John Williams, will earn more than six figures a year.

Employment Prospects

Although just a few Composers seem to get most of the work on big-budget studio films, every movie needs music, so there is work out there. Competition is tough, but opportunities exist.

Advancement Prospects

There are only a few advancement prospects for a Composer. This position is at the top of the ladder for most. You can become a film music supervisor, the person who often hires the Composer.

Education and Training

It would help to be musically trained in the classics as well as opera. There are composing for film courses that one can take. Composers should have training on several musical instruments and in writing for an orchestra.

Experience, Skills, and Personality Traits

Any job as a Composer on a student or low-budget film will help you to prepare a sample CD or MP3 recording of your work. This should demonstrate an ability to create themes and musical stories that reflect a wide range of emotions.

Composers must be musically oriented and be able to create music that will form an emotional undertone for a visual moment.

Unions and Associations

Many composers are members of the American Society of Composers, Authors and Publishers (ASCAP). Other associations, such as the National Academy of Recording Arts and Sciences or Screen Composers of America, may be helpful for networking.

Tips for Entry

1. Prepare a CD or MP3 recording of your work.
2. Work on independent and student films.
3. Work as a traditional songwriter or Composer.
4. Work as a musician in a film score orchestra.

MISCELLANEOUS SUPPORT SERVICES

CATERER

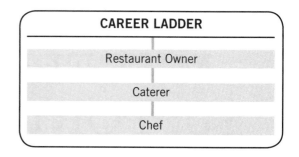

Special Skills and Personality Traits—Have good social skills; flexible; creative; fast worker; strong culinary sense

Position Description

When it comes to meals, a production company wants the food to taste good and be ready to eat as soon as lunch is called. It is the Caterer's job to provide meals for the entire cast and crew; on a big film, this could mean as many as a thousand people, all of whom have 30 minutes to eat.

The Caterer and her or his crew work closely with the second assistant director, who will let them know when the production will break for meals. He or she also has to find out from the transportation coordinator when they will have to provide catering trucks on location.

A typical day for a Caterer could begin with a request calling for 100 breakfasts at 6 A.M. at the Malibu location site for the following day, followed by 120 lunches at noon. The chef creates a menu for both meals, offering diverse selections of meat, fish, and vegetarian options, plus salads and desserts. The night crew will come on at 4 in the afternoon and work until midnight preparing the meals.

Many Caterers serving the movie industry use large trucks that are equipped with ovens and refrigeration units big enough to handle food storage and preparation. Once the meals are prepared aboard these trucks, they are loaded onto carts from which the crew is served. The number of meals being served will usually determine the number of servers needed. For 100 to 120 meals, two servers are required.

Salaries

The negotiated rate for Caterers who are members of Local 80 of IATSE is $30.20 an hour. A craft services leader earns an average $1,600 per week. Salaries vary, but some Caterers who own their own business earn more than $100,000 a year. Chefs earn $75,000 a year.

Employment Prospects

Employment prospects for Caterers in the film industry are good but competitive. All films, big and small, have catering needs. A film's budget as well as the size of the cast and crew will determine the number of craft services people needed to cook and serve meals.

Advancement Prospects

Advancement occurs once a Caterer establishes his or her own business. Success can depend on word of mouth and personal contacts. Dependability and affordability also play a role in determining advancement.

Education and Training

Training in food services, cooking, and food preparation. Any management or business education will prove useful too.

Experience, Skills, and Personality Traits

Caterers must be versatile and ready to respond to different orders. They should be able to prepare all kinds of foods, be patient, have good people skills, and be flexible and creative.

Unions and Associations

It may be helpful for Caterers to belong to the Teamsters Union. There is a contract covering craft services (including catering) as part of Local 80 of IATSE (http://www.iatselocal80.org).

Tips for Entry

1. Get a job as a dishwasher for a film Caterer.
2. Be a chef in a fancy restaurant.
3. Take any job available in craft services.
4. Drive the catering truck.

TRANSPORTATION COORDINATOR

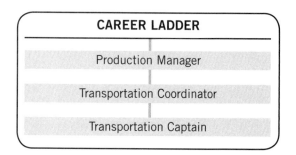

Position Description

The Transportation Coordinator is in charge of choosing and maintaining all vehicles used in the production of the movie. That includes all vehicles used to transport the cast, crew, and equipment wherever they have to go during production. He or she also finds any vehicle that may be used on camera; these are called "picture cars."

Working for the production coordinator, the Transportation Coordinator hires transportation captains and drivers and assigns the drivers to vehicles.

A Transportation Coordinator's job begins during preproduction when she or he does a script breakdown to determine what type and age of "picture cars" are going to be needed, what cars will be needed for stunts, and what cars will be used by principal actors. Once he or she determines what's needed, a budget and schedule are worked out with the production manager to come up with the most cost-efficient method of acquiring the vehicles to be used.

The vehicles needed for transporting the production team and equipment depends on the locations to which everything has to be moved. For example, if the film is shot entirely either on a soundstage or a studio back lot, the Transportation Coordinator may be able to get away with using fewer than a dozen drivers for everything. But if several locations are scheduled and they spread over a wide area of the country or world, then he or she could be coordinating a convoy of 40 to 50 drivers.

There are a variety of vehicles used to transport a film production company. They include a camera truck, which carries not only the cameras but the crew members who work them; a production van, which is a tractor trailer that carries the lights, rigging, and generators; a wardrobe trailer filled with clothing; a makeup trailer equipped with hot and cold running water, lights, mirrors, counters, hair dryers, and its own generator; a prop truck for all the props and special effects; and, finally, the mobile homes used by principal actors.

The primary function of the Transportation Coordinator is to make sure that everything moves smoothly and that everything arrives on time and in good shape. A film in the middle of principal photography could be spending an average of $100,000 a day, so even a flat tire is going to cost the production a lot of money. That's why one of the key jobs for a Transportation Coordinator is to ensure that the vehicles are well maintained, inspected constantly, and cared for to avoid breakdowns before they occur.

Salaries

Salaries are negotiable and vary according to many factors including size and length of shoot and whether it involves location shoots.

Employment Prospects

Employment prospects for Transportation Coordinator are fair, since any film that uses vehicles or shoots on location will need one.

Advancement Prospects

Advancing from driver to Transportation Coordinator tends to be very political. There are many drivers but few captains and coordinators. Competition is tight.

Special Requirements

Transportation Coordinators must have a driver's license and may be required to have a chauffeur's license or higher. A clean driving record may also be required.

Education and Training

Training in driving tractor trailers and recreational vehicles is required.

Experience, Skills, and Personality Traits

You must be a safe, careful driver; courteous; able to work long hours; punctual; reliable; conscientious, and able to make minor repairs and properly maintain vehicles. Have good social skills.

Unions and Associations

Being a member of the Teamsters Union, Local 399 (http://www.ht399.org) is a requirement in California and 12 other western states. In New York, membership in the Teamsters Union, Local 817, is a requirement.

Tips for Entry

1. Be available when needed.
2. Get to know Production Coordinators and transportation captains.
3. Work on low-budget, independent or student films.

PART III
POSTPRODUCTION

FILM EDITING

EDITOR

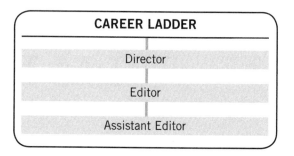

Position Description

Like the Editor of a newspaper, magazine, or book, a film Editor shapes the content and assists the writer and director in telling a story. In this case, the story is told in film, and it's up to the Editor, working hand in hand with the director, to assemble the hundreds of thousands of feet of footage, often shot out of sequence, into a coherent, entertaining movie.

Other than the director, the Editor probably has more to do with the way a film looks and feels than any other participant. He or she does this by balancing the assembled shots in terms of cinematography, consistency of performance, and timing; supervising the sound and voice synchronization; and overseeing the sound and music editing. The Editor is also responsible for the film's pacing. There's a huge difference in the way a film is paced depending on whether it's a comedy, a drama, a thriller, or an action adventure. Getting the pacing right is one of the Editor's main duties.

You might think the Editor's job begins after the director calls the last "it's a wrap," and principal photography is completed. In truth, the Editor's job begins long before the first inch of film or video is shot; the actual physical editing of the film usually starts at the end of the first day of shooting when the Editor receives the dailies and begins putting together what's called a "rough cut" of the movie. This process takes about three months for a studio film, less for an independent or low-budget film. A final cut could take just as long or

longer, depending on what's needed in postproduction, such as special effects, computer graphics, voice-over looping, music editing, and the other elements that are added to the film once principal photography is completed.

Actually, the Editor is hired before principal photography commences so that he or she can read the script and make suggestions that will affect the shooting schedule, from eliminating unnecessary shots or scenes that may not work to adding shots that may be needed to make a scene work better. In fact, Editors are usually the only members of a film team, other than the producer and director, to be a part of the film from the beginning to when it is released in theaters.

Throughout production, the Editor works closely with the director and cinematographer to make sure that the necessary shots are filmed in each scene. If you look closely, you'll notice that each scene is actually made up of many individual shots, such as close-ups, medium shots, establishing shots, two shots, over-the-shoulder shots, and reaction shots. It would be costly to have to return to a location or set up to reshoot shots needed to make a scene work in editing.

Because of cost, it is often left to the Editor to fix these problems. For example, once the picture is shot, an actor may have given a less than stellar performance in a particular scene, or the director of photography couldn't get the best lighting for a key scene, but that actor has left to make another movie and is no longer available for reshoots, even if they are affordable. A good Editor should be able to cover bad performances and weak shots by being creative. This is where visual storytelling prowess is put to the test.

No two Editors would cut the same footage together the same way. In fact, in editing classes in film school there's often an exercise in which each student is given the same raw footage from an old television series and told to edit the footage. If there were 20 students in the class, the result would often be 20 different shows.

The process of editing continues to change as technology both improves and complicates the Editor's ability to do her or his jobs. While some Editors may still use the Steenbeck flatbed editing machine, it has become more common for the dailies to be transferred to nonlinear or digital image and the actually editing and assembling of shots to be done on a computer. Two of the more popular systems for studio features are AVID and Lightworks; however, some low-budget or independent films are being edited on Final Cut Pro, so would-be film Editors may have to learn all three digital editing systems.

Salaries

Salaries vary widely. A top award-winning Editor can easily make six figures. But there are strict minimums set by the Motion Picture and Video Tape Editors Guild, which is a unit of the International Alliance of Theatrical Stage Employees (IATSE) (http://www.editorsguild.com). There is a wide variation in salaries, based on whether or not the project is a union film, the location, and the budget of the film. There are set union minimums, but individuals are able to negotiate a higher rate based on their skills set. Contracts are also renegotiated frequently, and minimums may also change, so it is best to check the Web site for the up-to-date minimums. Until August 2009, the minimum weekly rate for a motion picture editor based on the Motion Picture Editors Guild Motion Picture Editors Guild majors postproduction West Coast agreement is $2,653 and $2,557 for the East Coast major features agreement. Low-budget films may employ nonunion Editors, who will have to negotiate their own salaries.

Employment Prospects

The film industry is a growth business, and since the Editor is a key position on every film, employment prospects for Editors are excellent. Feature film Editors are basically in two employment groups: union and nonunion. To work on a studio film, you have to be a member of the Editors Guild of IATSE.

Job security for Editors depends on how well they work with the directors, who tend to use the same Editor because of the close collaborative relationship between Editor and director. If the Editor fails to deliver the film the director expects to see, then it's unlikely the director will use that Editor again.

Advancement Prospects

Most Editors stay in that category because it's so demanding, as well as rewarding. Prospects for advancement from Editor to either director or producer depend on many variables. However, being an Editor is one of the best ways to learn about directing. Martin Scorsese was an Editor before he became a director. While a good director has to be a good Editor, a good Editor may not necessarily be a good director.

Education and Training

Most good film schools have courses in editing. The Motion Picture and Video Tape Editors Guild has training programs designed to help the would-be Editor land his or her first job. These programs also keep members trained in the latest editing equipment and software programs. The American Cinema Editors society offers an internship program to college graduates who have majored in film.

Experience, Skills, and Personality Traits

One of the key skills for an Editor is to be a visual storyteller. Another is the ability to reorganize information to tell the same or different stories in different ways. Editors have strong creative and artistic abilities, both visual and auditory; are able to communicate well; and have excellent judgment.

As for personality, you have to be able to work well with strong egos. A director or the talent may be counting on you to fix a scene or improve on a performance—in other words, to make him or her look good.

As for experience, veteran film Editor Peter Honess (*L.A. Confidential*) said you should "cut anything you can get your hands on. No one can teach you how to do it. You have to sit down and do it yourself." Work on student films, at cable television companies, and small production companies.

Unions and Associations

Membership in the Motion Picture Editors Guild (Local 700, IATSE) is not only beneficial but also required if an Editor is hired to work on a studio or union film. The American Cinema Editors, or ACE, is an honorary society of film Editors; membership is through invitation only.

Tips for Entry

1. During middle school, high school, college, and graduate school, get involved in any aspect of filmmaking available to you, such as creating student films with a video or digital camera. Edit as many films as possible.
2. Edit short films or music videos.
3. Attend seminars that are given by successful Editors and listen to how they got started, what books they read, how they trained, and how they got their first break.
4. Discipline yourself to edit whenever possible.
5. Attend film festivals and meet directors. Directors usually hire the Editors. Get to know as many of them as possible. Meet other Editors who may be looking for assistants. Network.

NEGATIVE CUTTER

CAREER PROFILE

Duties: Accurately splice together the film's negative, from which positive prints are made for distribution to movie theaters; add visual effects and titles; supervise the person or persons responsible for breaking down, splicing, cataloging, filing, and storing the negative; take care of the film's negative

Alternate Title(s): None

Salary Range: $35 to $40+ per hour

Employment Prospects: Poor

Advancement Prospects: Poor

Best Geographical Location(s): Los Angeles/Hollywood, New York City

Prerequisites:

Education and Training—High school diploma helpful but not required

Experience—Work in film labs

Special Skills and Personality Traits—Precision; excellent vision; steady hands; understand basic editing; detail-oriented; able to work in isolation

CAREER LADDER

Assistant Editor

Negative Cutter

Breakdown Operator

Position Description

While an enormously monotonous job, the work of a Negative Cutter is critical and has virtually no room for mistakes. If the Negative Cutter makes an error, the only way to correct it is to reshoot the footage and this may be impossible or too costly.

Even though final editing may not take place until after principal photography is completed, the Negative Cutter's job begins on the first day of shooting. Negative Cutters have to break down and catalog the negatives of all the dailies into individual scenes. That way, when the director and editor decide which take or takes to print, the shots will be available.

Every foot of the negative is coded with numbers. Negative Cutters use these numbers to locate where to cut the beginning and end of shots in a scene. The film editor has marked where to cut on a work print by noting the number on the film. The beginning cut number is called the head key, and the end is the tail key. The Negative Cutter has to follow these cuts precisely. Two minutes of film time could have more than 300 cuts.

After all the cuts are complete and the negative matches the editor's work print, the Negative Cutter sends it to the lab, where it is physically spliced together, and then sends it to color timing to set the color balance so that the color of each scene matches.

While Woody Allen may joke that "the projectionist has the final cut," it is actually the Negative Cutter who has that distinction. If a negative is destroyed, it cannot be replaced—the film is lost forever. This is one reason more and more filmmakers are moving away from film as the medium of choice. High-definition video has reached the quality of film, and as this becomes the standard, the position of Negative Cutter may become obsolete (since there is no negative to cut).

Salaries

Salaries for Negative Cutters are set by Local 683 of the Film Technicians Union. Hourly minimums start between $35 and $40 per hour, not counting overtime, which is set at time and a half or double time. Some Negative Cutters may earn more.

Employment Prospects

Prospects for Negative Cutters are poor. While studios continue to shoot most of their movies on film, there has been an increasing trend to use high-definition video instead of film. This eliminates the need for a Negative Cutter.

Advancement Prospects

Prospects for advancement from Negative Cutter to assistant editor have always been competitive. The Motion

Picture and Video Tape editors film technician (Local 683 of IATSE) has mentoring programs as well as editor-in-training programs that Negative Cutters can enter to increase their chances.

Education and Training

A college degree is not required. On-the-job experience working in a film lab is recommended.

Experience, Skills, and Personality Traits

One of the most important traits of a Negative Cutter is to be a perfectionist, for if there is any job in film-making where there is virtually no room for error, this is it. Experience in editing is also helpful, because in order to cut the negative properly, you need to know the difference between a straight cut, a dissolve, and a fade-out/fade-in. This is a tedious job, so you have to be able to work in assembly line fashion, often alone, and be able to maintain concentration for long periods of time. Dexterity is an often overlooked skill, but

here it is a requirement. You will be handling different-sized pieces of film. Excellent eyesight is a must, and an understanding of the artistic elements of the editing process is essential, even though the Negative Cutter's job is precise rather than creative. You also have to be able to follow directions exactly.

Unions and Associations

Membership in the Film Technicians Union (Local 683 IATSE) (http://www.ialocal683.com) is required for studio films and many independent films as well.

Tips for Entry

1. Work in a film lab.
2. Work on student, low-budget, or nonunion films.
3. Take any production assistant job and work your way into the editing room.
4. Participate in the film technician IATSE internship program.

COLOR TIMER

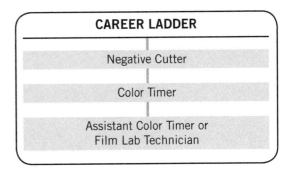

Position Description

The Color Timer's job is necessary for a number of reasons: Film stock varies from roll to roll, lighting shifts during shooting, and the camera might capture different takes differently. Any time a piece of color film is exposed, it takes on a particular tone, hue, density, and contrast. Since a movie is made up of thousands of different pieces of film spliced together, there's a fairly good chance that each shot will look slightly different from the one next to it. Therefore, the color variations, or grades, have to be adjusted so that the movie looks like one continuous image, with each scene consistent in look and tone with the one before and after it. It's the Color Timer's job to balance the various color qualities so that what you see in the final film is a seamless image flickering across the screen.

Working hand in hand with the director of photography, the Color Timer will determine the density, contrast, and color from scene to scene. Once the changes in color gradation are decided, the Color Timer gives the film to the person operating the Hazeltine machine, which is used to make the actual color changes on the negative.

The work involved can be somewhat tedious, since each movie contains more than a thousand scenes, all of which have to be color-timed to look consistent. For example, one scene may be two grades brighter than the next, or the hue in one scene doesn't match the one that follows, so more yellows or reds have to be added.

Salaries

Color Timers generally earn between $37,000 and $51,000 a year. Those with experience could earn more.

Employment Prospects

This position could become a victim of the digital revolution. But as long as film stock is used as the primary distribution medium, a Color Timer will be needed to balance it, so prospects for employment are fair.

Advancement Prospects

Once you get a job in a lab, it isn't that difficult to advance from one job to another. Color Timers may go on to become negative cutters, and from there to assistant editors. However, increased use of digital high-definition video could make this position obsolete.

Education and Training

On-the-job training is best. They don't teach color timing in film school. Get an entry-level job in a film lab and work your way up.

Experience, Skills, and Personality Traits

A Color Timer's most important skills are knowing color and understanding what effect the cinematographer was trying to achieve. Good communication skills are key too, because a Color Timer may have to talk to various creative people, such as the director, the editor, and the director of photography about what they want in terms of color.

Unions and Associations

Membership in the International Alliance of Theatrical Stage Employees (IATSE) may be beneficial.

Tips for Entry

1. Work as an assistant in a film lab.
2. Become an apprentice Color Timer.

SPECIAL EFFECTS

VISUAL EFFECTS PRODUCER

CAREER PROFILE

Duties: Responsible for all special visual illusions that re-create an on-screen reality designed to help tell the film's story

Alternate Title(s): Special Effects Producer

Salary Range: $2,000 to $2,500+ per week

Employment Prospects: Good

Advancement Prospects: Good

Best Geographical Location(s): Los Angeles/Hollywood, New York City

Prerequisites:

Education and Training—Bachelor's degree with a major in film, graphic arts, or photography helpful but not required

Experience—Working as an apprentice in a special effects company for experience in computer-

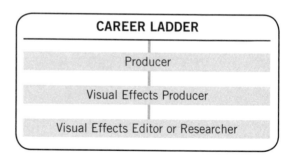

CAREER LADDER

Producer

Visual Effects Producer

Visual Effects Editor or Researcher

generated imagery (CGI), photography, matte painting, and blue screen; training as a visual effects researcher to gain an overall knowledge of how various effects work

Special Skills and Personality Traits—Creative; artistic; able to visualize things that may not exist in reality and then create them; an eye for photography

Position Description

As advances in technology impact the way movies are made, filmmakers are relying more than ever on the Visual Effects Producer to create images on the computer that once either had to be filmed at great time and cost or could not even be created. This may include computer-generated imagery (CGI); digital video effects; special effects makeup; mechanical effects, such as rain and snow; and blue screen, a technique in which actors are filmed before a blue screen and later placed in front of another background shot at a different time. This creates such illusions as people driving in cars when they are actually on a stage in a fake vehicle, and living in faraway exotic locations when, in reality, they haven't left Los Angeles. The Visual Effects Producer is responsible for more subtle optical effects as well as effects such as freeze frames, fades, dissolves, and wipes. Pyrotechnics, including explosions and gunfire, also fall under the Visual Effects Producer's domain.

Today, if you can think it up, someone can create it through computer-generated imagery, or CGI, technology.

It is up to the Visual Effects Producer to work with the film's director and producer to figure out which special effects images are needed. The Visual Effects Producer will then create those images through a variety of

methods. The film's budget will often determine which of these methods can be used to create the illusion.

The Visual Effects Producer is usually hired during preproduction or before so he or she can do a script breakdown to estimate how much the special effects are going to cost. If it is not within the budget, the script may have to be rewritten so that the scene can be eliminated or created without using special visual effects. During preproduction, the visual effects team will work with storyboards to decide how to re-create a particular visual image. Some might lend themselves to miniature models, while others will need blue screen or CGI.

During production, members of the visual effects team will be on the set whenever shooting involves a special effect, such as rain, snow, or an explosion.

It is during postproduction when much of the special visual effects are created. Often, during production, actors will perform before a blue or green screen and interact with people in blue costumes so that they can be replaced later with creatures or animals.

Today, digital images of actors are being used to make it appear as if an actor is actually in a burning building or shooting across the sky. Some even argue that we are getting close to the point where actors may not even be needed, because they can be replaced by their digital images.

Salaries

Salaries vary, according to the visual effects budget. The average weekly salary is $2,000 to $2,500 per week. Visual Effects Producers will earn more working on big studio films or if they are well known and in demand. Top artists in this field may earn more than six figures.

Employment Prospects

More and more films are using special visual effects, so opportunities are plentiful.

Advancement Prospects

As the need for visual effects grows, advancement opportunities in the field should grow accordingly. However, the field is crowded and competition is stiff. It pays to keep up with the state-of-the-art and new cutting-edge techniques.

Education and Training

It would help to be a film major in college, but any work in a special effects lab is helpful. Get training in the latest CGI technology. Any formal training in animation or illustration is also useful.

Experience, Skills, and Personality Traits

Visual Effects Producers must be visually creative, technologically astute, and able to tell stories with images created from illusions. They must also be good team players, ready to follow instructions from the director. They should be comfortable working long hours.

Unions and Associations

Membership in the International Alliance of Theatrical Stage Employees (IATSE) may be beneficial. Industry associations, such as the Academy of Science Fiction, Fantasy and Horror Films, and Women in Film, may be helpful for networking.

Tips for Entry

1. Get into a visual effects company as an apprentice.
2. Attend film school. Make and maintain contacts.
3. Work on low-budget, nonunion, or student films.

TITLES AND OPTICAL EFFECTS COORDINATOR

CAREER PROFILE

Duties: Responsible for the titles seen at the beginning and end of the movie, as well as the optical effects in between shots, such as dissolves, fades, wipes, and superimpositions

Alternate Title(s): Titles and Optical Effects Supervisor

Salary Range: $32 per hour

Employment Prospects: Good

Advancement Prospects: Fair

Best Geographical Location(s): Los Angeles/Hollywood, New York City

Prerequisites:

Education and Training—College degree in computer graphics is helpful

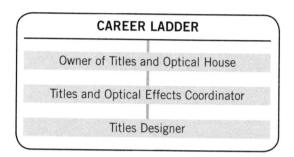

CAREER LADDER

Owner of Titles and Optical House

Titles and Optical Effects Coordinator

Titles Designer

Experience—Work in film labs

Special Skills and Personality Traits—Precision; excellent vision; steady hands; understanding of basic editing techniques; graphic design; artistic

Position Description

Working closely with the editor and director, the Titles and Optical Effects Coordinator will supervise the design of the titles and end credits; make a layout of what the titles should look like in terms of color, style, design, and animation; and then coordinate the production of the optical effects from simple fades and dissolves to complex computer generated special effects graphics designated by the editor and director.

End, or closing, credits have grown longer every year and tend to include everyone who had anything to do with the movie; it's not unusual now for credits to last more than five minutes after the actual movie ends.

Optical effects have also become more complex with the introduction of computer digital effects. Unlike any special effect shot during production, an optical effect is usually created in a computer or optical laboratory. The basic difference is that an optical effect is produced in a controlled setting and can be easily and cost-effectively repeated, whereas there may be only one chance to get a take right when those effects are shot on a soundstage or on location.

Today, most optical effects are done on a computer, even the simple dissolves, fades, and supers (superimposing one image over another). With sophisticated Avid technology as well as other new systems being designed, some films can almost be entirely created on

computers. Actors' faces are even digitally placed on computer-generated bodies.

There may come a time when actors will just have to license their image and voice and not even have to report to the set to put in a full day's work—the digital effects wizards will create their performance for them.

Salaries

The International Alliance of Theatrical Stage Employees (IATSE) sets hourly minimums. In most cases, a film's budget will determine the amount spent on titles and opticals. A Titles and Optical Effects Coordinator earns an average hourly wage of $32.

Employment Prospects

The Titles and Optical Effects Coordinator works for a film lab, such as Pacific Title. Since all movies have titles, prospects for employment are good. However, with digital video becoming more popular, the way titles and opticals are produced is changing, and these changes and new technologies could impact future employment.

Advancement Prospects

Advancement for a Titles and Optical Effects Coordinator is limited. It is usually the top job at the lab.

Advancing to this level from titles designer is highly competitive.

Education and Training

No formal education is required, but apprentice work in a film lab is almost always required. Formal training in computer graphics, filmmaking, or graphic design can be helpful.

Experience, Skills, and Personality Traits

Learn computer skills. Master the latest technology affecting this area. Have an eye for details and graphic design. A basic knowledge of how the film development process works and how to manipulate it for various effects is required.

Unions and Associations

Membership in the International Alliance of Theatrical Stage Employees (IATSE) may be beneficial. In California, Titles and Optical Effects Coordinators are members of Local 659, the cameraperson's local.

Tips for Entry

1. Work at an optical house, which produces the titles at the beginning and end of movies, in addition to any optical or computerized digital effect used in the film.
2. Become an apprentice in optical effects.
3. Take any job available in the optical effects lab.

SOUND

SUPERVISING SOUND EDITOR

Special Skills and Personality Traits—Have strong audio sense for sounds and dialogue; understanding of rhythm and pitch; working knowledge of how sound functions as well as the role it plays in film

Position Description

The Supervising Sound Editor oversees the postproduction of a film's sounds, which includes work done by the sound editor and foley artists, dialogue, sound effects (FX), and looping, or ADR, which stands for automated dialogue recording. This is then coordinated with the music editor and recording mixers. He or she is responsible for the quality of all the sound on the final sound track, excluding music. His or her job is supervising the postproduction sound process from both a creative and managerial perspective. That means coordinating the sound editing and mixing; making the final decision as to what goes into the final sound track; and working closely with the director, editor, and producer.

On a typical day, you will be working with various tracks of recorded sound and dialogue on both analogue tape and digital files. It will be up to you to oversee the way these tracks are edited and mixed together.

You will also have to decide whether recordings from principal photography are clear enough or have to be looped. Any number of problems can occur during filming, such as background sounds drowning out the dialogue or the mike being positioned too close to an actor and picking up unwanted pops, hisses, and lip smacks.

The Supervising Sound Editor also oversees the work of the foley editor, the dialogue editors, any looping sessions, the sound designer, and any special effects recordings. In the end, it is his or her responsibility to turn in the best sound track possible.

Salaries

Earnings vary greatly, depending on the film's budget, but a top Supervising Sound Editor can easily earn more than $100,000 a year. The average is $2,000 per week.

Employment Prospects

Since every film made today has sound, job prospects for a Supervising Sound Editor are pretty good.

Advancement Prospects

Advancing to Supervising Sound Editor may be a bit more difficult, because, while there are many sound editors, there is only one Supervising Sound Editor on a film. Competition is therefore stiff.

Education and Training

While it's not required, training in a film program at college or studying at a good film school is very helpful. You should learn all you can about various editing systems being created and using new digital technology.

Experience, Skills, and Personality Traits

Have a strong knowledge of computers, mixing consoles, digital audio work stations, audio recording, sound theory, and basic concepts of analog and digital audio technology. A knowledge of film history and a musical background are helpful. A Supervising Sound Editor should be a team player and a firm leader.

Unions and Associations

Membership in the Sound Technicians Local of the International Alliance of Theatrical Stage Employees (IATSE) may be beneficial. Industry associations, such as Women in Film, may be helpful for networking.

Tips for Entry

1. Work as an assistant sound editor.
2. Take any job in the postproduction sound crew.
3. Work in a music or sound studio.

FOLEY ARTIST

Duties: Re-create and enhance sound effects, such as doors closing, shoes walking, or storms raging; match the re-created sound effects with the action in the movie

Alternate Title(s): None

Salary Range: $400 per day

Employment Prospects: Good

Advancement Prospects: Fair

Best Geographical Location(s): Los Angeles/Hollywood, New York City

Prerequisites:

Education and Training—Bachelor's degree and training from film school are not required but helpful

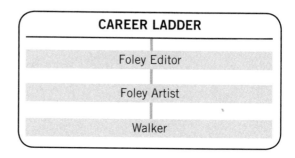

Experience—Work on a foley crew

Special Skills and Personality Traits—Keen ear for sounds and how to create them; sense of timing; hand-eye coordination

Position Description

Named after sound editor Jack Foley, the Foley Artist is part of the postproduction team. He or she matches re-created sound to the action on the screen, such as the rustling of leaves or the clacking of horses' hooves on cobblestone.

This is done because, during filming, much of the background sound is not recorded loudly enough. The boom mikes and other microphones are aimed at getting the clearest dialogue from the actors.

A Foley Artist will work on a foley stage, synchronizing a variety of sounds with what is happening on the screen. A number of different surfaces and props are used to simulate the actual sounds that would accompany the action on the screen.

The person in charge of the Foley Artist team is called the foley editor. He or she will screen the film and then direct members of the team to physically act out the sounds. This may include people walking, objects crashing or breaking, doors opening and closing—if it makes a sound, a Foley Artist should be able to re-create it.

The process of re-creating these sounds is called "walking the foley." In fact, the foley crewmembers making the sounds are called walkers, since many of the sounds they make replicate sounds of feet walking on a variety of surfaces.

Salaries

A good Foley Artist can earn $400 a day and $80,000 in a good year. Earnings depend on experience, reputation, frequency of employment, and the budget of the films.

Employment Prospects

Every studio film and most union pictures employ Foley Artists, so prospects for employment are good.

Advancement Prospects

Advancement to foley editor is very competitive, since there are few positions in this category.

Education and Training

No formal education is required, but film school can be beneficial. Musical training may prove useful, as might some training with sound equipment. Most training for this position, though, is on-the-job training.

Experience, Skills, and Personality Traits

Get work on any soundstage or assisting a sound editor or foley editor. Be able to create natural or unusual sounds, such as thunder and waterfalls, from everyday objects. Be able to follow directions quickly. Sharp audio skills are a must.

Unions and Associations

Membership in the Sound Technicians Local of the International Alliance of Theatrical Stage Employees (IATSE) may be beneficial.

Tips for Entry

1. Work as an intern on a soundstage.
2. Become a walker (someone who makes the sounds of walking).

PART IV
DISTRIBUTION, PUBLICITY AND ADVERTISING, AND EDUCATION

DISTRIBUTION

FILM DISTRIBUTOR

CAREER PROFILE

Duties: Responsible for getting the film into theatrical release in movie theaters

Alternate Title(s): Major Distributor; Mini-major Distributor; Independent Distributor

Salary Range: $0 to $10,000,000+

Employment Prospects: Good

Advancement Prospects: Fair

Best Geographical Location(s): Independent distributors may work in just one region or territory, but major or mini-major distributors will have an office where filmmaking is predominant, such as Los Angeles/Hollywood, as well as auxiliary offices in the 32 territories, or "exchanges," into which the United States has been apportioned for film distribution

Prerequisites:

Education and Training—College degree in film or business, with a knowledge of how a film is distributed in the United States and around the world

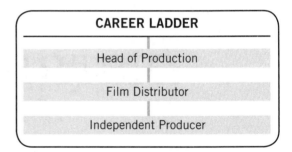

CAREER LADDER

Head of Production

Film Distributor

Independent Producer

Experience—Working for an independent producer or film company, especially in the distribution part of the business

Special Skills and Personality Traits—Good business sense; excellent at sales; detail-oriented; able to coordinate various advertising, marketing, and sales functions; willing to get involved in the creative part of filmmaking as needed

Position Description

The Film Distributor is a vital part of the making of a film planned for theatrical release. It is the Distributor who will get the film into cinemas throughout the country and the world. In *Making Movies,* John Russo, who helped "write, finance, film, and edit" the classic independent film *Night of the Living Dead* (made on a budget of $114,000 and grossing more than $50 million worldwide), notes that there are four basic categories of distributors: majors, mini-majors, independents, and producers, who choose to distribute themselves. Major Film Distributors include the major studios, like Paramount, Columbia, and Sony. According to Russo, the United States has been divided into 32 territories, or "exchanges," for the purpose of film distribution. The majors will maintain a central office in Los Angeles as well as distribution offices in most of those territories: The Mini-major Film Distributors are companies that have an office in only the key exchanges; subdistributors, paid a percentage (15 percent to 25 percent) of the box office receipts, handle the other territories.

Independent Film Distributors also only have an office in their one key area; outside of that area, subdistributors, paid a percentage, handle the distribution. Russo points out that *Night of the Living Dead* was

distributed in this manner: Independent film distributor Walter Reade Organization created 14 prints of the movie, distributed it in 14 neighborhood and drive-in theaters in Pittsburgh, and when it "played to packed houses," the Independent Distributor created several additional prints that were shown in Philadelphia and then Cleveland.

As Russo notes, as independent film producers also handle their own film distribution, they have actually become "first-time independent distributors." Although this may work within the producer's hometown or city, Russo explains, it may be hard to get distributed beyond that territory. If he or she succeeds, it may then be hard to get paid, since the producer lacks the track record and the promise of future product that make subdistributors or theater owners concerned about how they treat the independent distributor and the film.

With films intended initially for theatrical release, getting into theaters, and getting into the right theaters or territories, is crucial to the film's critical and financial success. For example, a character-driven film without major celebrity talent in the cast may need to be released in a few key territories at sites known to attract the right kind of audience, such as the Film Forum, an art house in New York City. Once favorable reviews and word-of-mouth are generated, the film can be moved to more and more screens for a wider distribution. If such a film was opened on thousands of screens right away, it might not attract audiences, and it would probably be pulled quickly without the chance to build support. It was just such a strategy that helped *In the Bedroom,* which opened in a very narrow release but expanded its distribution with positive reviews and word of mouth. It also earned awards for its cast, including Sissy Spacek who was nominated for the Academy Award for best actress, making the film one of the surprise hits of 2001.

While the type of Film Distributor discussed here represents those involved in distributing movies for theatrical release, there is a subset of the job of distributing that deals with nontheatrical distribution, such as licensing to television, airlines, video, and the Internet. Such licenses are normally handled between the production entity and television networks or syndication companies. There are separate distributors for video and other forms of electronic distribution.

Aleen Stein has been part of a unique aspect of film distribution for more than two decades. Instead of just distributing a DVD of a film, Criterion, the company which she cofounded, provides those who buy or rent the DVDs the context of the film, including filmmaker commentary and other elements. As Stein explains, "We're the ones who really pioneered that format. We started with laser discs in 1984. It's more like being a film publisher than a film distributor. It's more of a creative activity than film distribution implies, because we make an expanded, augmented film available to people that they can explore on their own."

Although she is the company's largest shareholder, Stein currently confines her activities with Criterion to special projects and outreach. In 1995 she started a new company, Organa, which digitally publishes DVDs and CD-ROMs, such as *Antarctica,* which has more than 1,500 photographs, and *The Book of Lulu,* an interactive fiction. Organa also publishes an imported line of films from Réunion des Musées Nationaux, France's official museum company, that commissions documentaries about the museums and artists of France. "We have a documentary film on Picasso and another one on Matisse and virtual tours of the major museums," says Stein, who studied journalism at the University of Oregon and anthropology and filmmaking at the University of California at Los Angeles. She is on the board of directors of the DVD Association, an international association with members from all over the world, and is a member of Women in Film and Television.

Says Stein, commenting about the feature film titles that she helped to create and distribute over the years,

such as *Citizen Kane* and *Taxi Driver:* "I feel lucky to have helped invent something that has transformed the film industry, making it possible for ordinary people to see behind the scenes, understand the creative process behind great filmmaking. Many famous directors and other filmmakers have told me that they really learned how to make great films from our discs, especially listening to the geniuses who talked about the process, their thinking and methods. I've always loved films and thought I would be a filmmaker, but there are many ways to make a significant contribution. I love the conjunction of new media and film. It's still a wild new frontier. For example, some new filmmakers are now filming on cell phone and editing on computers and distributing via streaming on the Web. My advice to new filmmakers is to look beyond the obvious; don't be constrained by what's been done."

Salaries

The Film Distributor's earnings are determined by a variety of factors. First, he or she negotiates a percentage of the grosses, somewhere between 15 percent and 30 percent. For this the Film Distributor pays for prints and advertising. If a film performs poorly or it fails to generate enough box office receipts to cover the distributor's expenses, he or she could actually lose money. Therefore, earnings could range from zero to several million dollars if the film is a blockbuster.

Employment Prospects

Distributing just one film locally may be a possibility for the energetic film producer who wishes to give his or her own film a hometown theatrical release. But employment at independent distribution companies, mini-major distributors, or majors will be more difficult, since distribution is such a specialized and complex aspect of the film industry. However, this is a major part of the industry, so opportunities do exist.

Advancement Prospects

Revenues from the percentage of the box office receipts paid to a distributor will be a key factor in whether or not a distributor advances. Independent distributors may grow to become mini-major or major distributors. Employees of major distributors may go on to work for movie studios in executive positions, while heads of distribution companies may go on to become heads of studios.

Education and Training

It will be helpful to have a college degree, with courses in filmmaking as well as business. Advanced specialized training in filmmaking and the business part of the film industry, such as producing and distribution, will also be useful.

Experience, Skills, and Personality Traits

Working in the film industry, at a production company, or for a film studio will provide experience related to becoming a Film Distributor. Even working part-time, summers, or full-time at a video rental store will provide exposure to part of the distribution process, albeit only the fifth step in the distribution chain (following theatrical, foreign, nontheatrical, and television distribution).

Unions and Associations

Film Distributors do not have a union. But membership in industry associations, such as the Academy of Motion Picture Arts and Sciences and Women in Film, may be helpful for networking.

Tips for Entry

1. Work for an independent film company so that you can see how a movie is made and distributed, from start to finish.
2. Take a job at an independent distribution company and learn how the decision is made about what films to acquire and how the distribution process works.
3. Attend trade shows and film festivals: Network with Film Distributors.
4. Start as an administrative assistant or in the mailroom and work your way up at a studio.

SALES AGENT

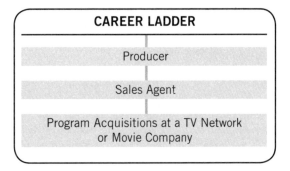

Position Description

A Sales Agent gets a commission or fee from a producer to sell movies internationally. The Sales Agent may have the finished movie to show and sell, or he or she may only have a title and cast. Such was the case when Sales Agent David Garrett, as he explained in an interview at http://www.filmfour.com, had to sell *Die Hard III,* a sequel to the Bruce Willis blockbusters. A Sales Agent may work independently with individual producers or may be part of a company dedicated to selling films internationally.

In addition to being able to pick the right international distributor or buyer for a particular movie, a Sales Agent needs to have a staff in place to track sales and future revenues or must be able to do it himself or herself. Most films are sold for seven to 20 years, so the job calls for someone who will maintain an interest over time.

Sales Agents spend most of their time either attending film festivals, such as Cannes, the American Film Market (AFM), and the international film and television market held each autumn in Milan (MIFED), or preparing for them. They meet with producers trying to sell their product, as well as with foreign exhibitors to assess what they're looking for.

When it comes to the festivals, Sales Agents will either screen films or hand out movie trailers and one-sheets, which are glossy, posterlike sheets of thick paper with a photo or design, an advertising line or slogan, and a list of principal cast members.

Sometimes, Sales Agents will get involved with presales, or preselling a picture in a market in return for an advance to be applied against grosses. Presales are often used as methods of financing the film's production. This is common among independent producers and is becoming more popular among majors seeking to offset production costs.

For example, a Sales Agent will presell the German market to a German distributor in return for an advance against ticket sales, because the picture being made appears to be one that will appeal to a German audience.

Sales Agents will know which stars perform well in certain markets and how much their names in the credits will mean to eventual box office receipts in those countries. In fact today, American-made movies often perform better in foreign markets than they do in the United States. For example, such hit films as *Titanic* and *Harry Potter and the Sorcerer's Stone* grossed nearly twice as much in foreign markets as they did in the United States.

Salaries

Sales Agents are paid on commission, typically 30 percent of the foreign box office receipts. This can range from very little or zero if no one wants it or the film is a flop, to several million dollars if it is a hit.

Employment Prospects

This is a very difficult field to break into and even harder to get established in. It is based almost completely on developing a detailed knowledge of filmmaking and distribution around the world, as well as knowledge of the right buyers and markets in each territory. Contacts and connections are everything, but with more and more films relying on foreign markets for their profits, opportunities do exist.

Advancement Prospects

Making excellent deals and placing the right movie in the right market so that it brings in additional revenues will enhance a Sales Agent's reputation. Advancement is based on word of mouth and referrals. Sales Agents can also move up by taking on bigger clients and films.

Education and Training

More important than credit or noncredit courses in business, selling, or the movie industry is on-the-job training at a television, cable network, or film company in program acquisitions. Learning how to read contracts and negotiate deals is crucial. Getting to know producers, distribution companies, and buyers in other countries is an important part of one's training.

Experience, Skills, and Personality Traits

Having a genuine positive feeling toward movies will help, since those who deal with a Sales Agent want to know that there is a concern for the product and not just for the deal. Having as wide an international base as possible will also be useful, as will an aptitude for many languages, or the ability to communicate effectively, through translators or other options, when language could be a barrier.

Unions and Associations

Sales Agents do not have a union, but membership in industry associations, such as the Hollywood Foreign Press Association or Women in Film, are good for networking.

Tips for Entry

1. Work in a paid or internship capacity in the program department of a television or cable company and learn how movies are acquired.
2. Work as an apprentice or assistant to a Sales Agent at a company that sells films internationally.
3. Attend two of the key markets for buying and selling films—American Film Market (AFM) and Cannes—and observe how films are bought and sold.

THEATER OWNER

CAREER PROFILE

Duties: Own and manage the theater where movies are shown

Alternate Title(s): Exhibitor

Salary Range: $0 to $1,000,000+

Employment Prospects: Fair

Advancement Prospects: Fair

Best Geographical Location(s): Anywhere there are enough people and, for suburban or rural locations, easy access by driving

Prerequisites:

Education and Training—Bachelor's degree in business administration; a knowledge of films; classes in selling, advertising, and marketing; management training

Experience—On-the-job, paid, or internship experiences working in a store or office setting; selling or

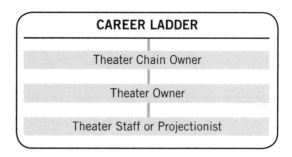

taking tickets and working at the concession stand at a movie theater

Special Skills and Personality Traits—Business skills; able to network within the community where the theater is located; organized; good communication skills; excellent interpersonal skills

Position Description

Theater Owners own or manage the building in which movies are shown. A Theater Owner may own or rent the actual space, especially if a multiscreen movie theater is part of an office building or a mall as opposed to a freestanding separate building.

It is the Theater Owner who is responsible for providing the surrounding activities going to the movies has to offer. He or she earns a living by selling tickets at the box office and food and drinks at the refreshment counter, so it behooves the Theater Owner to make these experiences as rewarding as possible.

To do this, the Theater Owner must ensure that the sound and picture are perfectly displayed, the seats are clean and comfortable, views are unobstructed, and audiences feel safe from fire, theft, and injury.

Perhaps most importantly, a Theater Owner has to exhibit movies people want to see.

Theater chains have virtually taken over the exhibition business, and they have their own buyers and bookers who attend screenings prior to a film's release. Theater Owners often have to make concessions with distributors to get blockbusters. They agree to show less desirable films in exchange for being allowed to show the movie that will fill their theater.

Today, most Theater Owners have multiplex screens. Depending on ticket sales, a Theater Owner may try to extend or shorten a movie's run, although this often isn't possible, due to contractual obligations with the distributor. In that case, the poorly performing film might be shifted to a smaller sized theater within the multiplex.

A Theater Owner has to know all aspects of the operation, from the projector to the popcorn machine. In fact, it is often the concession counter that keeps profits in the black—a typical Theater Owner will earn as much from the food and drinks sold as from ticket sales.

In addition to managing the staff of ushers, projectionists, and concession stand operators, the Theater Owner is responsible for tracking box office receipts. That means keeping the books as up-to-date as possible.

Another important responsibility is making sure that the local newspaper has the correct starting times for each picture. Nothing will anger a moviegoer more than to arrive at the theater in the middle of a movie they want to see.

Salaries

Theater Owners do not receive a salary but earn money from a share of the box office receipts, along with the distributor and producer, and from the concession stand. Since there are so many variables involved, earnings can range from very little to millions for owners of successful theater chains.

Employment Prospects

According to the National Association of Theatre Owners (NATO), since 1999 the number of movie screens has increased in the United States, from 37,131 in 1999 to 38,794 in 2007, but the number of movie sites has decreased from 7,477 in 1999 to just 5,928 in 2007. Being a Theater Owner is, therefore, a declining occupation, as fewer theater sites supply more screens.

Advancement Prospects

Being a Theater Owner is becoming more difficult for individual owners as chains of theaters become more predominant and as operating costs and overhead increase. Highly successful Theater Owners may start their own chain or move into the distribution arm of the industry. One of the most successful Theater Owners was Sumner Redstone, who became chairman of Viacom, one of the world's largest communications and entertainment empires.

Education and Training

Having an education in business, management, and film will help someone acquire the many business skills and film knowledge necessary to run a movie theater successfully. In addition to managing the people who staff the theater, a Theater Owner has to be able to deal with the customers as well as with the distributors from whom they rent each film. There is a lot of bookkeeping that has to be attended to, and a knowledge of advertising and marketing helps guarantee that customers choose to go to your theater instead of the ones owned by the competition.

Experience, Skills, and Personality Traits

Having a genuine love of films is definitely an asset for a movie Theater Owner. Business and management skills are also required. Theater Owners need to be adept at selling and marketing. They should be detail-oriented and focused on the current films being shown, as well as aware of what films may be offered in the future. This may require attending trade shows and reading the trade newspapers, such as *Variety* and the *Hollywood Reporter*.

Unions and Associations

The National Association of Theatre Owners, based in North Hollywood, California, is a membership association. Its Web site states that it is "the largest exhibition trade organization in the world, representing more than 26,000 movie screens in all 50 states and in more than 20 countries worldwide. Our membership includes the largest cinema chains in the world and hundreds of independent theater owners too." Their informative Web site (www.natoonline.org) also has statistics about the industry, as well as links to related associations, upcoming conventions, and information about their publication, *In Focus*.

Tips for Entry

1. Work at an independent or chain movie theater and develop the skills and capital necessary to eventually buy a theater or get promoted by the cinema chain.
2. Attend local, regional, or national conferences or conventions of theater owners.
3. Place or answer classified ads in your local community about movie theaters that are for sale.

PUBLICITY AND ADVERTISING

PUBLICIST

CAREER PROFILE

Duties: Create interest in a specific film through interviews with the stars of the movie; generate feature articles related to the film, the screenwriter, director, or talent

Alternate Title(s): Public Relations Executive

Salary Range: Varies widely

Employment Prospects: Good

Advancement Prospects: Fair

Best Geographical Location(s): Major urban centers with a concentration of filmmaking activities, such as Hollywood/Los Angeles, New York City, Toronto, and Orlando

Prerequisites:

Education and Training—High school diploma; college degree in liberal arts, business, communications, or film is helpful and may be required; training in public and media relations

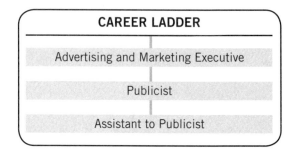

CAREER LADDER

Advertising and Marketing Executive

Publicist

Assistant to Publicist

Experience—Working in the publicity department, doing public relations, for individuals or companies, especially filmmakers, production companies, or studios

Special Skills and Personality Traits—Detail oriented; energetic; creative; able to work with different types of personalities and employees, from the director and talent to the producers; strong contacts and good relationship with the media or journalists

Position Description

Publicists help get the word out about a new movie by talking to journalists, writing press releases, planning a premier, organizing press junkets, attending industry trade shows, and contacting producers at television and radio stations to set up interviews for the screenwriter, director, or talent of a movie. A movie Publicist will carry out the campaign that has been created by the advertising and marketing executives and will submit the film to the appropriate film festivals. A Publicist will also make sure that there are production stills of all the principals in the movie and will coordinate the activities of the photographer for the film's shooting. Stills may be used for publicity purposes or possibly collected in a book about the film's production. If the film is going to have a Web site, a Publicist would be expected to work with a webmaster to make sure that the Web site effectively publicizes and promotes the movie.

Film industry Publicists work in a wide range of situations, from the publicity department of an independent or studio film company to working on a freelance basis for a specific film to running their own public relations firm, specializing in the film industry.

Michael Levine has been running his own film industry publicity firm, Levine Communications Office (LCO), for the last 25 years. Author of 18 books,

including *Guerrilla P.R., Charming Your Way to the Top,* and *Broken Windows, Broken Business: How the Smallest Remedies Reap the Biggest Rewards,* Levine's first clients were comedians Joan Rivers and David Brenner, who were touring together, "and it snowballed from there," he says. A self-made man, Levine grew up in New York City, left home at the age of 17, went to college for six months, quit, and "became self-employed at the ripe age of 18, and I've been self-employed ever since."

Levine's company, which currently has 15 employees, has a film industry client roster of A-list celebrities that includes, or has included, Sandra Bullock, Michael J. Fox, Cameron Diaz, Kirstie Alley, and countless others. Levine shares about his film publicist career:

"My job was to get Joan Rivers and David Brenner's tour publicity. At that time, I worked hard and I worked cheap. I was all self-taught. My story is that I never let school interfere with my education. I always used self-education as a tool. I have a very, very strong work ethic. I had no formal education, so I had to do it through hard work.

"I spend several hours a day networking. I go to a lot of events. I'm invited out a great deal—cocktail parties, screenings, private dinners. To succeed [as a film publicist], to a large degree you have to be obsessed with what you're doing. It's not enough to work hard [and] not everyone has that level of obsession."

What part of his job does Levine like the most? "It's different every day," he explains, adding, "It requires a lot of creativity and a lot of patience. PR, in essence, is a sales job. That's what it really is."

What publicity campaigns is he most proud of?

"Over the years, there are a lot of campaigns I'm proud of—Barbra Streisand, Nancy Kerrigan, Sandra Bullock, David Bowie, Jon Stewart. A vast number of people. I was very proud to get Charlton Heston to host *Saturday Night Live* in the '80s."

Salaries

Salaries vary widely, but for unit Publicists (publicists who work on a specific film) who are members of International Alliance of Theatrical Stage Employees, Local 600, the minimum hourly rate is $32.64. For Publicists who work at a studio and are members of IATSE, the salary ranges from the minimum rates for apprentice, $26.68 an hour, up to $32.64 an hour for senior publicist. Publicists who work as freelancers or for companies that are not covered by union agreements may earn far more or far less than these minimums, with some directors of publicity or those heading their own companies earning six figures a year.

Employment Prospects

Employment prospects are good. There is a high turnover rate in this type of position, since it is often seen as a stepping stone to other jobs with either higher pay or more power, such as a producer or advertising and marketing executive.

"I see a lot of opportunity for young women to excel in public relations," says Publicist Michael Levine. "That's a big change from 25 years ago."

Advancement Prospects

Helping to secure lots of exposure for a new movie, including movie reviews or feature stories about the principals in the cast, will help a Publicist's advancement prospects as her or his reputation spreads. Successful Publicists can go on to become advertising and marketing executives, open their own agency, or work on big blockbuster films. Some, like Martin Davis of Paramount, advance to chief executive officer of a studio.

Publicist Michael Levine comments on advancement prospects in this career: "Advancement is really a product of someone's own hard work and ambition. What does someone have to do to get noticed? Do a good job but also be available to do a lot of extra assignments that people don't want to do in the beginning. Three of the biggest things that sabotage careers are narcissism, fear, and irresponsibility. [Conversely] most people can be good at a lot of things, but the only thing they're going to be great at is something that they love. So figure out what it is that you love and want to be remembered for [and find a way to do that]."

Education and Training

A college degree with a major in liberal arts, business, communications, or public relations is helpful. On-the-job training in the basic skills needed by a Publicist, such as how to write a press release, how to work with the media, and how to develop and maintain a media contact database, will be useful.

Experience, Skills, and Personality Traits

Working as a Publicist in any type of company setting, especially for a television or movie company, will be beneficial. Computer skills, such as how to create and manage a database, will also be useful.

Publicists need to have upbeat, pleasant, and friendly personalities. They need to be good at initial communications, whether through phone, e-mail, fax, mail, or in-person meetings, as well as be good at follow-up. Being able to convey enthusiasm for a particular movie, without being so overly positive that it sounds like hype, is both an art and a necessary skill.

Unions and Associations

Publicists who work at the studios, as well as unit Publicists who work on specific union or studio films, are members of the International Cinematographers Guild, IATSE, Local 600. Membership in industry associations, such as the Academy of Motion Picture Arts and Sciences, the Hollywood Foreign Press Association, and Women in Film, may be helpful for networking.

Tips for Entry

1. Network at film festivals, industry trade shows, and conferences, letting everyone know that you want to be a Publicist.
2. Get a paid or unpaid job on a particular movie and learn, from start to finish, what goes into the promotion and publicizing of a film.
3. Create and maintain a wide network of contacts with film industry people, including film critics, entertainment writers at magazines and newspapers, entertainment and news producers and journalists at television and radio stations, and syndicated columnists.

STILL PHOTOGRAPHER

CAREER PROFILE

Duties: Take pictures (called "production stills") during production for later use by the publicist in press kits; maintain a photographic record of the production

Alternate Title(s): None

Salary Range: $300 to $463 per week or $1,500 to $1,700 per week, depending on whether it is a studio or distant location

Employment Prospects: Fair

Advancement Prospects: Fair

Best Geographical Location(s): Hollywood/Los Angeles, New York City

Prerequisites:

Education and Training—Bachelor's degree, with a major in photography is helpful but not required

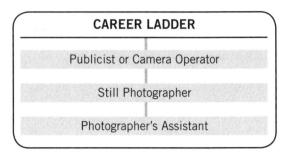

CAREER LADDER

Publicist or Camera Operator

Still Photographer

Photographer's Assistant

Experience—Working as a news photographer or for a magazine; working in a photo studio

Special Skills and Personality Traits—Talent for photography; a "photographer's eye"; organized; reliable

Position Description

Whenever you see a photo from a movie in your local newspaper or in a magazine, chances are it was shot by the film company's Still Photographer, whose job it is to take pictures during production of all principal cast members, important action sequences and special effects, key crew members, as well as the director, producer, writer, and director of photography, plus any other aspect of the film that could be used in promotion. The Still Photographer reports to the producer and the financing entity or studio.

The Still Photographer works in and around the actors and set without getting in the way or affecting the shot or actors' performances. He or she will sometimes use a special device called a "blimp," which is soundproof housing fitted to the camera to silence the sound of the shutter and motor drive, although newer digital cameras are silent.

Since it would be impossible to shoot every part of every take, the Still Photographer has to use his or her judgment as to what to shoot. Also, not every picture will lend itself to promotion, even if it captures a wonderful moment. Sometimes, an actor might feel that these moments are too private to be made public; in fact, many actors have in their contracts the right to destroy any still photo they do not want released.

The Still Photographer works most closely with the publicist, who will often request certain photos that he

or she thinks will have the biggest impact in terms of marketing. These are the photos the publicist uses in press kits, which are sent to the media to begin promoting the movie.

A member of the same union as the director of photography, the International Photographers Guild, the Still Photographer is supposed to be the only person on the set allowed to take actual photographs.

Besides publicity, the Still Photographer has other responsibilities. They take pictures of the set each day so that if it must be re-created for later reshooting, the crew can refer to the stills to make sure everything is placed in its proper spot. There will be some people from various departments shooting Polaroids from time to time, but these are used to maintain continuity in day-to-day shooting.

The Still Photographer's photos are also used as documentation of the production, which means every member of the crew will appear somewhere in a photo. If a star or celebrity visits the set, the Still Photographer may be asked to take his or her photo, unless he or she refuses. Sometimes, photos of actors in the movie are needed as props in a scene. It would be up to the Still Photographer to take those pictures as well.

Salaries

Salary minimums are set by the International Photographers Guild at $360 to $463 per day or $1,500 to $1,700 per week, depending on whether work is at a studio or at a distant location and whether one is hired as a Schedule B-1 or C-1 weekly employee. Since rates vary based on other factors, including holiday or vacation pay as well as the negotiation of a new contract, check with the International Cinematographers Guild for the most recent salary rate card.

Employment Prospects

This is not an easy position to break into. Though demand is steady, competition is heavy, and it can take time to build a reputation.

Advancement Prospects

There are only a few advancement prospects for a Still Photographer. One can strive to become a publicist, a camera operator, or even a director of photography.

Education and Training

It would help to be a photography major in college or to train as a photographer's assistant. On-the-job train-

ing at a newspaper, magazine, or television studio is useful.

Experience, Skills, and Personality Traits

Any job as a photographer at a newspaper, magazine, or ad agency is helpful. Build a portfolio. Have a photographer's eye. Be able to move quietly and remain still for long periods of time. Be trustworthy and sensitive. Know the latest equipment. Be creative.

Unions and Associations

Membership in the International Photographers Guild Local of the International Alliance of Theatrical Stage Employees (IATSE) may be beneficial.

Tips for Entry

1. Be patient, yet persistent
2. Work on student or nonunion films.
3. Work as a photographer's assistant.

ADVERTISING AND MARKETING EXECUTIVE

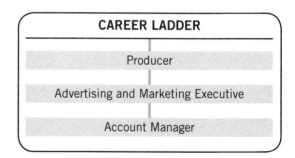

Position Description

Advertising and marketing have become pivotal elements in the success of a motion picture, regardless of the film's budget. The enormous prosperity of the surprise hit *The Blair Witch Project* was driven by the Internet. The Web site promoted the movie in a way that led scores of moviegoers to seek it out in the theaters, demonstrating how even a low-budget movie can make millions of dollars if the advertising and marketing campaign is effective. Generally, advertising is considered the exposure for a product that is paid for through advertisements in newspapers, magazines, or in television or radio commercials; marketing is the overall campaign, which includes advertising and publicity, such as interviews with the film's director or stars in magazines, newspapers, television, or radio. Whether or not a film will have a gala premiere or be entered in film festivals are some of the decisions that the Advertising and Marketing Executive will be making, either directly or through his or her staff.

Advertising and Marketing Executives will use a variety of strategies to get people to buy tickets to their movies. These vary from holding advance screenings for key journalists or opinion leaders to creating elaborate contests open to the public to see a movie before anyone else or even to be in it.

He or she spends a lot of money promoting a film, in hope of earning back a profit. A lot of the success or failure of big-budget movies are often determined within the first or second week of release. Therefore, release schedules become very important. Advertising and Marketing Executives play a key role in when a film is released, because if a movie opens at the wrong time, it can affect box office receipts. For example, several films that had terrorism as part of the plot were pulled from release following the September 11, 2001, attacks on the World Trade Center and in Washington, D.C.

At the studio level, hundreds of people are involved in a marketing plan for a major motion picture. Advertising and Marketing Executives have many factors to consider, including whether the release date is right, what the competition will be at that time, and the best way to market this particular movie.

If television advertising is involved, commercials have to be made. This is all tricky business, because in commercials, as in trailers, you want to give away just enough to entice people to see the movie without giving away too much.

An Advertising and Marketing Executive will get involved in producing the poster for a film and key art for newspaper ads. Marketing is almost as much of an art as filmmaking itself. There are many scientific reasons why one color or sound appeals to people, but marketing a movie has too many variables for this area to be entirely scientific.

A good Advertising and Marketing Executive works on gut instinct—and a lot of experience. He or she knows if a poster or commercial works or not. If it doesn't, then they'll change it.

Salaries

Advertising and Marketing Executives earn between $50,000 to $250,000 a year, depending on their standing within the firm or industry and the size and location of the company that employs them. Some top stars in this area can earn more than a million dollars a year.

Employment Prospects

Aside from the aspects related to the talent and the responsibilities of the producer, the job performed by the Advertising and Marketing Executive is probably the most important factor in a film's creative and commercial success. There is a definite need for someone to perform this function for each major film. Opportunities are out there, but so is the competition.

Advancement Prospects

Creating advertising and marketing campaigns that work will be the best insurance for advancement. Word of mouth about those successful films will reinforce the Advertising and Marketing Executive's status as an integral part of the moviemaking team. Advancement comes through increased responsibility, working on bigger movies, or opening one's own firm.

Education and Training

An undergraduate or graduate degree in business, including specialization in advertising and marketing, will be helpful, as will specialized training in the unique history and demands of the film industry.

Experience, Skills, and Personality Traits

Being able to work within a budget is essential for the Advertising and Marketing Executive. He or she must have a creative mind, capable of coming up with innovative advertising and marketing campaigns tailored to each unique film that he or she has to promote. Being a team player is essential, since the Advertising and Marketing Executive will be working with the creative and business participants in the film, as well as dealing with the media, the distributors, and the theater owners who will screen the movie for moviegoers.

Unions and Associations

There are no unions for Advertising and Marketing Executives, but membership in a variety of industry associations, such as the Academy of Motion Picture Arts and Sciences, the Hollywood Foreign Press Association, and Women in Film, may be helpful for networking.

Tips for Entry

1. Work in any advertising or marketing positions so that you gain the necessary skills that you will need to apply in the film industry.
2. Get a paid job, an internship, or an apprenticeship in the advertising and marketing department of an independent film company or studio. Study and become a part of a film's advertising and marketing campaign, from its inception to completion.
3. Network with Advertising and Marketing Executives at industry conferences and trade shows.

FESTIVAL ORGANIZER

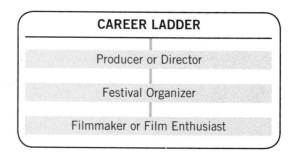

Position Description

Film Festival Organizers have to know a great deal about filmmaking, have to possess extensive contacts in the film community, and have to be able to organize a complex and demanding event. Usually, a film festival is more than just the screening of films. There are launch parties and press conferences, educational seminars and awards with judges and prizes. Coordinating the lodging, feeding, and transportation for the hundreds or thousands who attend a typical film festival requires a Festival Organizer who is able to delegate effectively as well as handle numerous details. Submissions for screenings have to be carefully logged and evaluated. Rejected submissions need to be returned; accepted submissions need to be carefully stored, displayed, and, after the festival, returned or forwarded according to the instructions provided with each submission. Attendees at the festival, whether industry insiders such as distributors, or the general public, need to be informed about the festival, whether through the mail, advertising, or a Web site developed just for the festival.

Some festivals are organized for the purpose of making money, but most are conceived and carried out of love for film. It is a way to organize in one place not only those who want to see new movies but also those who are involved in the moviemaking process, such as directors, producers, and seasoned and emerging tal-

ent. Furthermore, film festivals have become a cultural gathering that brings status and positive acclaim to a community. In recent years, film festivals have started in New York City as well as in many other locations around the country and world. Whether or not a film Festival Organizer continues to offer a film festival year after year may depend as much on how pleasant and rewarding an experience it was as on how profitable it was, since it is an enormous amount of work with many deadline, creative, logistical, and monetary pressures.

Salaries

Normally, there is no set salary for a Festival Organizer. Sometimes, they are wealthy individuals who volunteer their time free of charge. In other cases, they may take a percentage of ticket sales as compensation. Veteran film Festival Organizers can earn six figures a year, but most earn considerably less. At least initially, a Festival Organizer may also add that job to other job duties that he or she has at a company.

Employment Prospects

The film Festival Organizer often creates the position by deciding that his or her community or his or her cause, if it is a festival with a theme, would benefit from the event. Often, the film Festival Organizer is also in charge of raising the funds that will pay for the festival, including the Festival Organizer's salary. The entrepreneurial nature of the job limits employment prospects.

Advancement Prospects

Unless the film festival earns a profit or becomes an industry-wide institution, like Sundance or Cannes, organizing a film festival is more likely to be a onetime experience than a career. Successful Festival Organizers, though, may create long-term employment for themselves or go on to other positions in the industry.

Education and Training

A college or graduate degree in film and business will be helpful as background for becoming a film Festival Organizer. Courses in event organizing will also be useful.

Experience, Skills, and Personality Traits

Being involved in a film festival, in a volunteer or paid capacity, will help someone gain the necessary skills to work his or her way up to taking charge of and organizing the entire film festival. A film Festival Organizer has to be very detail-oriented as well as systematic, since the volume of submissions may be daunting. In addition to lots of paperwork, phone calls, and e-mail communications, there will be meetings with potential sponsors, as well as get-togethers with producers, directors, filmmakers, the media, and film distributors. Being able to raise money and being able to do follow-up whenever contacts are made are other skills that a film Festival Organizer will find valuable.

Unions and Associations

Meeting Professionals International (MPI) (http://www.mpiweb.org), an international membership association of meeting planners, offers information and trade shows about how to organize an event.

Tips for Entry

1. Attend film festivals.
2. Volunteer or work in many capacities at a film festival, from logging submissions to notifying filmmakers if their film has been accepted and to setting up screenings.
3. Take a course at an adult education program in film festival organizing.

FILM CRITIC

CAREER PROFILE

Duties: Evaluate movies from a critical standpoint; make recommendations about whether or not people should spend their money or time watching the movie

Alternate Title(s): Movie Critic; Reviewer

Salary Range: $0 to $100,000+

Employment Prospects: Poor

Advancement Prospects: Poor

Best Geographical Location(s): Those with access to screenings of new movies, usually the major urban areas and especially those active in the film industry, such as Hollywood/Los Angeles, New York City, Chicago, and Toronto

Prerequisites:

Education and Training—A college degree, with a major in journalism and credit or noncredit courses in film; courses in writing useful but not required

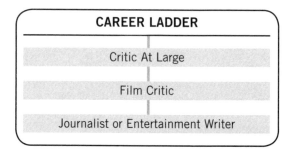

Experience—Writing film reviews for a high school or college newspaper or a community magazine or newspaper; attending educational seminars or lectures by filmmakers and about films

Special Skills and Personality Traits—Excellent writing skills; able to articulate thoughts and critiques about whether the plot, characterization, actors, setting, or direction contributes or detracts from a movie; comfortable working under deadlines and within space and length constraints

Position Description

Film Critics attend screenings of new movies and comment on the movies' good and bad points. Their reviews may appear in print, on the radio, on television, or over the Internet. As long as a Film Critic is able to get to the movies and file his or her stories electronically, by fax, or by mail, technically, any location is suitable. Being close to Hollywood/Los Angeles, New York City, and Chicago, where most of the new films are screened by the film companies, makes the job easier.

Film Critics must be comfortable writing negative comments about performers, directors, and writers when necessary. Critics for certain publications, Web sites, television or radio shows also have to be comfortable with the reality that a positive or negative review can directly contribute to the creative and commercial success of a new film. Thus, being a Film Critic can carry enormous influence and power, and a Film Critic has to be at peace with that situation.

There are few full-time Film Critics. Most Film Critics are also entertainment writers at a newspaper or magazine, and reviewing films is one of their many creative responsibilities.

Film critic and entertainment writer Susan Granger was born into a film family; her father, S. Sylvan Simon,

directed *Bud Abbott and Lou Costello in Hollywood* (1945) and produced *Born Yesterday* (1950), among dozens of other notable films, before he died at the age of 41 in 1951. Granger's stepfather, Armand Deutsch, worked in Hollywood as well, producing *The Magnificent Yankee* (1950) and numerous other movies.

Beginning at the age of three, Granger started acting in movies with such notable stars as Lucille Ball, Lassie, and Red Skelton. She began her studies at Mills College, graduating from the University of Pennsylvania with a degree in journalism. After relocating to Connecticut, where she and her husband raised two children, and working as a radio and TV anchor, she discovered that, most of all, she enjoyed writing and being a film critic. That was more than 25 years ago, and she hasn't looked back since.

In the United States, Granger is now self-syndicated; overseas, she has an agent who syndicates her reviews in newspapers and magazines in numerous countries. Granger is able to have a thriving film criticism career while still living and working in Connecticut without having to fly to the West Coast for screenings, although she does visit Hollywood to see her son, Don Granger, and his family (Don, also in the film industry, is president of Tom Cruise's company, United Artists) or her brother, Stephen Simon, who is a producer/director with credits that include *Somewhere in Time* and *Conversations with God.*

Granger sees more than 300 movies each year, commuting several days a week to Manhattan, where she views upcoming films at private "critics" screenings.

How did Granger become a film critic? "At first I went to work on radio," she says. "For around 10 years, I wrote and broadcast my own features. Then I became a TV news anchor at the ABC Connecticut affiliate (WNHC/WTNH). I started out reviewing movies as an adjunct to my anchor job. That took up so much time, so I had to make a choice. Anchoring was very depressing because, day-after-day, news is a 'death and destruction' report. As a movie critic, I could contribute something unique. Having a Hollywood background, I had a different point of view.

"For many years, I was film critic for WICC radio, then for CRN, Connecticut Radio Network. Around 10 or 15 years ago, I decided to self-syndicate. With the help of a lawyer and an agent, I created SSG Syndicate. Now, I have nobody to answer to but me."

What advice does Granger offer to anyone who wants to become a film critic? She replies: "Get a good liberal arts education. You've got to be a good writer. You've got to love what you're doing and have a great passion about it. I love movies—even bad movies. You can learn from them, observing the choices that filmmakers made. Cinematic creativity is all about making choices. All of life is about making choices. In this field, you just don't start out where you end up. A lot of it is taking advantage of whatever opportunities happen to come your way."

Allowing yourself to have a range of experiences is the way that you learn, notes Granger, who is also a professional speaker. Says Granger: "I've had enough chances to fail, and I've failed enough times. You learn by your mistakes. And you can actually have a great time along the way. Take your work seriously but don't take yourself too seriously."

Granger has found joining critics' associations beneficial. "These are professional organizations of people who have similar concerns," she explains, as she cites her memberships in the Broadcast Film Critics Association, New York Film Critics Online, American Women Film Journalists, Online Film Critics Association, Drama Desk, and Outer Critics Circle.

"Flexibility is so important," says Granger, noting the increased opportunities for online film critics and entertainment writers over the last few years because of all the new media, including video exposure at YouTube. com. Just take a look at Granger's extensive Web site,

http://www.susangranger.com, for an example of how one prolific film critic and entertainment writer provides a home for some of her thousands of reviews and selected entertainment writings.

Salaries

Film Critics may earn from nothing to more than $100,000 a year if they have a syndicated television show or write for a major newspaper such as the *New York Times.* Most critics are either entertainment writers who review movies as part of their jobs or who work as freelancers for a few hundred dollars per review. Some freelance critics may get two free tickets to a movie or free admission to a prerelease screening without additional pay. Some reviewers try self-syndicating, offering their reviews, for a small per review fee, to a certain number of local newspapers or publications that might not already get film reviews through a news syndicate.

Employment Prospects

Since there are just a few news syndicates that have full-time Film Critics and only a handful of television or radio shows that employ full-time Film Critics, the employment prospects are poor. Freelance Film Critics, however, or journalists who are full-time entertainment writers who also occasionally review films have better employment prospects.

Advancement Prospects

Full-time advancement as a Film Critic is extremely difficult, since there are so few critics associated with major publications or television shows. One moves up by increasing his or her reputation and drawing attention to his or her opinions.

Education and Training

A college education, a knowledge of film, and an excellent writing ability are helpful to a Film Critic.

Experience, Skills, and Personality Traits

Writing film reviews for a school or community paper, as well as honing writing skills in other types of journalism, are beneficial to a movie critic. Movie critics who work on a steady basis need to be able to write under deadline pressure, since there may be only a few hours or a few days, at the most, from when a movie is viewed until the review is due and published.

Unions and Associations

Some full-time critics may belong to various writer unions, such as the Newspaper Guild. Membership in industry associations, such as the Hollywood Foreign

Press Association or Women in Film, may be helpful for networking.

Tips for Entry

1. Write film reviews for any publication, whether or not there is a fee, to gain experience and exposure.

2. Attend film festivals and get invited to screenings so that you have the ability to write up movies in advance of the film's official opening. Offer those reviews to local newspapers or specialized magazines.

3. If you are a general writer, ask your boss or editor if you could add film reviews to your duties.

ENTERTAINMENT WRITER

Duties: Write magazine, newspaper, or Internet articles or books about the film industry, film companies, directors, actors, producers, or specific movies

Alternate Title(s): Film Historian; Film Biographer; Film Author

Salary Range: $0 to $50,000+

Employment Prospects: Good

Advancement Prospects: Good

Best Geographical Location(s): Because of the Internet and telecommunications, it is no longer necessary to be in a major urban filmmaking area or even near a library; as long as a writer can do the necessary research for a story or project, any location is possible

Prerequisites:

Education and Training—No formal educational requirements; college degree, majoring in film, film studies, or English and credit or noncredit specialized courses may be useful

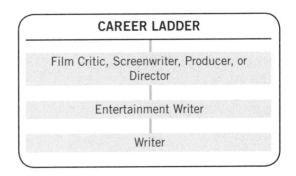

Experience—Working as the assistant to a Film Biographer or Historian may be helpful; journalism or writing experience; learning as much about film as possible; screening movies

Special Skills and Personality Traits—Able to conduct an interview; good research skills; diligence; a self-starter and highly motivated; able to work alone for long periods of time; willing to stick to a book-length project for the years that a film biography might take; excellent journalism skills; writing ability

Position Description

Entertainment Writer is a broad job title that covers those who write about the film industry, including film biographers and film historians, and those who write articles for newspapers, magazines, or new media about specific films or the film industry. The Entertainment Writer is different from the film critic in that he or she is not concerned with the criticism of just one film but of a filmmaker's entire career or the industry itself and all its directors, producers, or actors.

Entertainment Writers often work on their projects on a freelance basis in addition to a regular or full-time job, such as a film instructor at a school or reporter for a magazine, a newspaper, or the Internet. They may cover other topics as well, such as general features or business. It is rare to find a full-time position covering just entertainment or film or to get a book advance large enough for a film biography or film history that would support someone for the years it might take to research and write the book.

Salaries

Salaries for Entertainment Writers vary widely, depending upon whether or not he or she is freelance or full-time, whether or not he or she is writing articles or writing a nonfiction book, and whether or not he or she is writing about a person or aspect of the film industry. The range may be from zero to less than $10,000 for the average nonfiction book advance; from $25,000 to $50,000, for a staff Entertainment Writer position; to hundreds of thousands or millions for Entertainment Writers who have achieved celebrity and best-seller status.

Employment Prospects

Freelance work is much more plentiful than full-time positions. Selling a biography or film history based on a proposal may be difficult, since this type of book is perceived as having such a specialized market and audience.

Advancement Prospects

Moving up as an Entertainment Writer in a full-time position may mean waiting until a more visible or higher-ranking job is vacated. For entertainment nonfiction writers, selling enough copies to make back the advance for a book or getting critical acclaim helps an author's advancement prospects.

Education and Training

A college or graduate degree in writing or film is not necessary, but both would be helpful. If an Entertainment Writer also plans to combine writing with teaching, getting the necessary credentials and education to be able to teach is required. The best training for writing is writing, so Entertainment Writers should try to write about the film industry as often as possible for school or community newspapers or magazines. Courses, whether or not for credit, in the particular type of entertainment writing someone wants to pursue, such as books, magazine articles, newspaper articles, or Internet writing, may also be helpful.

Experience, Skills, and Personality Traits

Writing experience, especially if supervised by a respected author or editor, will be helpful, as will working in the film industry at a production company or studio. Having an understanding of the film industry will help someone write about it. Even if an Entertainment Writer does not wish to relocate or live in California, occasional or regular trips to Hollywood or other major film production centers to meet with and interview industry leaders will also be necessary.

Unions and Associations

Entertainment Writers may belong to a multitude of writer associations, such as the Authors Guild (http://www.authorsguild.org), National Writers Union (http://www.nwu.org), PEN American Center (http://www.pen.org), American Screenwriters Association (http://www.asascreenwriters.com), Organization of Black Screen-writers (http://www.obswriter.com), and Independent Feature Project (http://www.ifp.org), among others.

Tips for Entry

1. Improve and gain experience in your basic writing skills.
2. Interview members of the film industry. Get your interviews or articles published in the local newspaper, as well as in entertainment or general publications.
3. If you wish to be a film biographer or historian, read biographies and histories, especially exemplary film biographies or histories.
4. Become familiar with the newspapers, magazines, Internet sites, and syndicates that have Entertainment Writers. Contact the managing editor or the human resource department and see if they are hiring. Check if the publication has a Web site that posts job openings.
5. Write an entertainment article on speculation, and try to sell it as a freelancer to one of the publications that use entertainment articles. If they like your writing, and you let them know you are looking for a full-time staff position, they may keep you in mind when one opens up.
6. If you wish to write a film biography or history, and you read a book like that that you admire, look in the acknowledgements to see if the author thanked his or her literary agent or editor and publisher. If he or she did, contact those individuals to see if they would consider your book proposal.

EDUCATION

FILM INSTRUCTOR

CAREER PROFILE

Duties: Teach high school, college-level, or graduate-level courses in film, such as filmmaking, directing, acting, producing, and other technical aspects of making a film, or in film studies

Alternate Title(s): Assistant Professor; Associate Professor; Professor; Adjunct or Part-time Instructor; Lecturer

Salary Range: $25,000 to $50,000+

Employment Prospects: Good

Advancement Prospects: Fair

Best Geographical Location(s): Wherever there is a high school, college, university, or specialized school that offers programs or degrees in filmmaking or film studies

Prerequisites:

Education and Training—A bachelor's and master's degree with some courses or a degree in film or film studies; Ph.D. in film or film studies may be required for full-time college positions

Experience—Teaching college- or graduate-level courses; working in the film industry in the area you plan to teach

CAREER LADDER

Department Chairperson or Dean

↑

Film Instructor

↑

Graduate Assistant, Graduate School Student, or Film Professional

Special Skills and Personality Traits—Excellent speaking and communication skills; ability to inspire class discussion; attention to detail; self-starter; ability to get along with others, including students, fellow faculty members, and administrative staff; desire to perform and publish original research and work

Special Requirements—State teaching license or certification may be required to teach at elementary through high school

Position Description

Someone who teaches film courses or film studies at the college or graduate school level falls under the general title of a Film Instructor. Film Instructors may be directors, producers, or screenwriters who teach one course as an adjunct or part-time instructor, or a full-time assistant professor or full professor who devotes all her or his professional time to research activities and teaching related to film or film studies.

The two key approaches to teaching film that a Film Instructor might pursue are the practical, technical aspects of film, including the filmmaking techniques taught at film school or in a college- or graduate-level film program, and the critical approaches of a researcher and scholar who studies film as an academic pursuit, much the same as an English instructor might teach Victorian literature, or how to write an essay or poem.

Film Instructors may be expected to teach everything from the history of film to directing, acting, or producing. Organizing the program at a college or

graduate school or putting on a local film festival may be other duties of the Film Instructor. Grading exams, screening and discussing films, and exploring the business as well as the creative side of filmmaking with students are other job requirements.

For example, noted film scholar Wheeler Winston Dixon is the Ryan Professor of Film Studies, chairperson of the Department of film studies, and professor of English at the University of Nebraska in Lincoln, Nebraska. He worked in the 1960s and early 1970s, in New York, followed by Los Angeles and London, as an experimental filmmaker. Leaving Hollywood in 1976 after a career as a postproduction supervisor to pursue a career in academe, Dixon received a Ph.D. in English from Rutgers University.

Cynthia Wade, who has been directing and producing documentaries for 20 years, is the owner of four production companies, including Cynthia Wade Productions, Inc., and teaches an intensive course in advanced digital cinematography at the New School in Manhattan. She has taught documentary film production at Film/Video Arts in New York City and has been a guest lecturer for NYU, Smith College, and Marymount Manhattan College. Wade, who has made films for HBO, Cinemax, and PBS, sees herself as someone who makes "verb films as compared to noun films. [With] verb films, you are deep in the middle of chaos, shooting it from the inside out, following the action as it unfolds." She sees her brand as "unflinching looks at controversial social issues." Her works include *Shelter Dogs*, a documentary for HBO, and *Freeheld*, a 38-minute documentary that won her the Special Jury Prize in Short Filmmaking at the 2007 Sundance Film Festival, as well as 10 other film awards including an Academy Award for Best Short Documentary. For *Freeheld*, she lived with a dying New Jersey police lieutenant, Laurel Hester, who was racing against time to win the right to leave her pension to her female life partner. Wade makes the time to teach intensive digital cinematography courses despite her busy schedule and personal life—she and her husband are raising two young children—because it is fulfilling to her to be sharing her knowledge with the next generation of filmmakers.

A graduate of Smith College and holding an M.A. in documentary film production from Stanford University, Wade explains what teaching means to her: "As an independent filmmaker, I believe that I should also be a teacher, mentor, and consultant for the next generation of women filmmakers. Sharing the technical knowledge of filmmaking with emerging filmmakers, particularly young women, is important so that they can gain the confidence and skills to shoot their own films and not rely on crews to make their own films."

Salaries

Full-time salaries depend upon a Film Instructor's rank at a college or university, from $25,000 for an assistant professor to $50,000 or more for a full professor. Part-time adjunct instructors may get approximately $2,500–$3,000 for teaching one course. If a Film Instructor teaches full-time in high school, the salary is determined by the local or state standards.

Employment Prospects

Entry-level, especially nontenure track, positions are hard to find, but they are certainly more available than tenure-track positions, especially at the higher level of associate or full professor. At the high school level, film instruction is less common, and the instructor may also teach other courses, such as television production or communications.

Advancement Prospects

Unless someone is granted tenure, his or her position at a university may be short-term, even if it is full-time. Unless an instructor is tenured, advancement may be based on how much someone researches and publishes in the field, as well as on teaching ability and reputation. Adjunct faculty need a minimum number of students for a course to be offered.

Education and Training

A college or graduate degree in film or film studies, as well as a master's degree in film or education, is usually required. A Ph.D. will be required to teach higher academic levels.

Special Requirements

At the high school level, depending on the community or state requirements, education courses or a degree in education may be required, in addition to a teaching license. Teaching at the college level requires at least a master's degree, if not a doctorate.

Experience, Skills, and Personality Traits

Working in the film industry, or, for film studies, working at a company that researches film, such as the American Film Institute, may provide excellent background for a Film Instructor position. Any teaching experience is helpful. Film Instructors must have excellent communication skills and outgoing personalities. They should be well organized and dedicated to their students and studies.

Unions and Associations

At the university level, Film Instructors may be members of the American Association of University Professors (AAUP), which also includes adjunct and part-time instructors.

Tips for Entry

1. Combine practical training in the film industry with teaching experience in noncredit adult education situations and as a student teacher.
2. If someone is teaching a course and you know he or she has to take a trip or miss a class, ask if you could fill in or even team-teach the course.
3. Register for substitute teaching, which is often easier to obtain than a full-time, permanent position.
4. Become a member of teaching associations as well as film associations that have members who are educators.
5. Look for ads for teachers in the trade publications, such as the *Hollywood Reporter* and *Variety;* in

major newspapers, such as the *Los Angeles Times* and the *New York Times;* and on the Internet.

6. Apply directly to specific high schools, colleges, graduate programs, film schools, or specialized nondegree film or film studies programs.

7. Contact the high school, college, or graduate school you attended. Ask their job placement department to keep you in mind for any openings for a teacher in the film department or at other schools with which they have reciprocity.

ACTING TEACHER

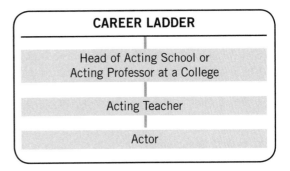

Position Description

Acting Teachers are usually senior performers who have reached a point in their career where they prefer to only teach acting or to combine teaching with a reduced acting schedule. Some of the great Acting Teachers, such as Stanislavski, Stella Adler, or Lee Strasberg, although highly regarded actors, are best known for their roles as teachers. Whether based at a university, teaching at a private acting school, or coaching one-on-one with individual students, Acting Teachers help performers master basic skills as well as fine-tune their approach to acting. They may also work on a particular role. Acting Teachers cover everything, including interpretation of a role, speech, voice, makeup, and movement, although some teachers may specialize in one or more of these areas.

Salaries

The salary for an Acting Teacher or Coach will vary widely, from an hourly rate for individual instruction to a staff teaching position at an acting school or a university. Hourly, Acting Teachers charge from $50 to $200 and up for individual training. If they are teachers at an acting school or university, they might earn from $30,000 to $50,000+ a year. If they have their own schools, they could earn much more, perhaps well into six figures.

Employment Prospects

There are fair employment prospects for Acting Teachers. They are usually expected to have some professional acting experience in addition to formal training. It is a very competitive field, where formal educational credentials and even advanced degrees may also be required.

Advancement Prospects

Having students who go on to great acclaim and who acknowledge their Acting Teachers help create the best chance of advancement. Another way for advancement is to receive accolades for your own acting abilities, since students will seek instruction from an acclaimed actor.

In terms of faculty positions, there may be little turnover in staff at academic acting departments or in private school settings. The necessity of combining teaching with professional acting experience makes it challenging to advance in both careers simultaneously.

Education and Training

A college degree, advanced degree, or specialized training in acting is expected, although celebrity status as a renowned actor would compensate for any deficiencies in formal education.

Experience, Skills, and Personality Traits

Acting Teachers are expected to combine excellence in acting with the skills and personality traits associated with a superior teacher. An Acting Teacher must have the ability to express what he or she is looking for in a performance, patience in dealing with students, and a commitment to teaching. An Acting Teacher should also be able to handle the business aspects of running an acting school or the pressures of being on the faculty of a private school, college, acting school, or graduate school.

Unions and Associations

Full-time college professors who teach acting may be members of the National Education Association (NEA), the teachers union. Participating in activities sponsored by the Screen Actors Guild (SAG) and Writers Guild of America (WGA) may expose the Acting Teacher to actors, producers, directors, and screenwriters who may know of potential students.

Tips for Entry

1. Let people know that you wish to teach acting. Act and network.
2. If you have an Acting Teacher, tell him or her that this is something you want to do. Intern or team-teach.
3. Apply directly to acting schools that may be hiring through word of mouth, alumni or career departments, or advertisements in trade or local newspapers.
4. Establish a reputation as an actor; it will be easier to teach acting if you are acclaimed as an actor.

DIALECT COACH

CAREER PROFILE

Duties: Help an actor to speak in a particular accent or dialect

Alternate Title(s): Accent and Dialect Coach

Salary Range: Varies widely

Employment Prospects: Good

Advancement Prospects: Good

Best Geographical Location(s): Major urban centers where there is extensive filmmaking activity, especially Hollywood/Los Angeles and New York City; on locations around the world during filming

Prerequisites:

Education and Training—College degree and advanced training in speech, phonetics, dialects, language, and acting

Experience—Being coached by and learning from a Dialect Coach

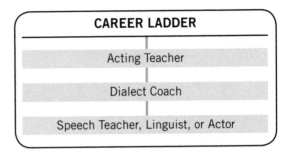

CAREER LADDER

Acting Teacher

Dialect Coach

Speech Teacher, Linguist, or Actor

Special Skills and Personality Traits—An ear for language and nuance; a talent for hearing and isolating what is unique about a language, dialect, or accent and an ability to teach that to others; patience; excellent communication skills

Position Description

Originally called a "dialogue coach" when silent movies became talkies, the role of the Dialect Coach has evolved into teaching actors how to speak for a particular part. In *Working in Hollywood,* famed Dialect Coach Robert Easton, who has been called the "Henry Higgins of Hollywood," describes how his coaching business began informally when his actor friends asked him to help with their speech for free. Easton, who studied speech at the University of Texas and phonetics at London University, notes that he not only knows "a hundred or so *actual* dialects," but that he also has "had to literally create new ones." Easton coached the great British actor Sir Laurence Olivier for a part that required him to have "the rural dialect of a small town in Michigan in the late 1800s."

Andrew Jack, a Dialect Coach, lists a range of accents and dialects on his Web site (www.andrewjack.com); these include Standard British, Cockney, Elizabethan, Chinese, Japanese, Canadian, and American, as well as many others.

Once well known, a Dialect Coach has to be open to the demands of travel that may be thrust on him or her, as well as the last-minute nature of some of the work, since a Dialect Coach may be called in if a new cast member needs emergency help with the role.

Salaries

The salary for a Dialect Coach will vary according to whether he or she is hired by an actor for tutoring or coaching or hired by the studio, director, or producer to work with the talent for a particular film. Dialect Coaches may also be film or acting professors at universities, earning $30,000 to $50,000 a year, depending upon their rank, how long they have been teaching, the school they are at, and its location. Many do dialect coaching as a source of extra income.

Employment Prospects

Any film set in a foreign country or historical period or using actors who have to sound like people of another culture may need a Dialect Coach. Employment prospects are good, but work can be irregular.

Advancement Prospects

Developing a reputation as an excellent Dialect Coach will help advancement prospects. Actors, directors, producers, and casting agents will recommend a Dialect Coach if they have been pleased with the results of that coaching and if the film critics or audiences have praised the results of the Dialect Coach's efforts, such as helping a British man or woman sound completely American. Advancement comes with higher fees and working with higher profile performers and stars.

Education and Training

Basic training in language, speech, phonetics, and dialects at the undergraduate or graduate level, acting training, and education training are useful. An enormous amount of research is required of the Dialect Coach, from listening to various languages and dialects to researching historical periods and times to using television or films from around the world as educational tools.

Experience, Skills, and Personality Traits

Working and living in a variety of countries will help, as will being observant of language and dialect differences. This is a highly developed skill, with few people able to achieve the necessary combination of the ability to hear the differences in dialect and accent and the personality and skill to communicate those contrasts to actors. Flexibility is also a useful personality trait, since a Dialect Coach may be called upon to teach in person, by phone, or even through audiotapes.

Unions and Associations

Dialect Coaches have no union, but membership in industry associations, such as Women in Film, may be helpful for networking.

Tips for Entry

1. Keep notes on all the languages that you hear or the dialects and accents that you are exposed to. What makes someone sound a particular way?
2. Study as many languages as possible and travel as widely as you can.
3. Become an intern to a Dialect Coach or become part of an apprenticeship program.

ASSOCIATION DIRECTOR

CAREER PROFILE

Duties: Management position that requires one to lead members in a film-related association; relevant duties usually include running an annual awards event and/or conference, offering career information and arranging job exchanges, networking among members, and providing educational opportunities, including guest speakers and/or teleconference events

Alternate Title(s): Association Manager; Executive Director; Arts Administrator

Salary range: $50,000 to $100,000+ depending upon the size (number of members) and budget of the association

Employment Prospects: Fair

Advancement Prospects: Fair

Best Geographical Location(s): Los Angeles/Hollywood, New York City, Washington, D.C.

Prerequisites:

  Education and Training—High school diploma is expected; college degree is highly recommended; graduate training in film or a master's of arts administration is helpful; attending courses or training in the film industry is useful

  Experience—Extensive management and administrative experiences are expected, such as working in an office setting while supervising one or more staff

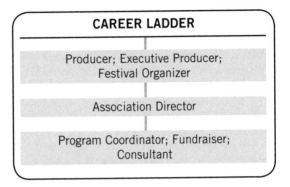

CAREER LADDER

Producer; Executive Producer; Festival Organizer

Association Director

Program Coordinator; Fundraiser; Consultant

members/employees; film industry jobs will also be very helpful

Special Skills and Personality Traits—Because so much of the job involves helping members to network as well as offering educational experiences, an Association Director has to be both a people person and good at organizing events. The association manager is required to have both excellent networking skills and be able to help people network who are not as skillful. Other necessary skills include being able to delegate as well as oversee financial considerations for the association, having a passion for movies and the film industry, being open to working more than nine-to-five if attendance at evening and weekend events is required

Position Description

This is an administrative job for someone who has a combination of management skills and a knowledge of the film industry. There are two key ways of becoming an Association Director for a film industry association: working your way up the ladder within a film association or getting experience in film or in association work in another industry and transfering those skills to an association in the film industry.

Terry Lawler has been executive director of the New York Women in Film and Television (NYWIFT) association for more than 10 years. NYWIFT is one of 40 chapters of an international association, Women in Film International (WIFI), which has more than 10,000 members internationally including such major chapters as Los Angeles–based WIF (Women in Film) and Washington, D.C.–based Women in Film & Video

(WIFV). Lawler, who grew up in New Jersey and who moved to New York City to go to film school, where she studied production, initially thought she was going to make films. Says Lawler: "I did love films. I was very interested in social issue films."

Lawler began as a film editor at a nonprofit company that was making films on social issues. But she found herself being drawn into arts administration, becoming program coordinator and, eventually, executive director of a nonprofit film fund. Says Lawler: "I like solving problems and supporting creative people," says Lawler, as she highlights some of the responsibilities of her position. Her association has approximately 1,600 members, as well as 250 active volunteers who help with everything from breakfast, evening, and occasional weekend educational and networking programs offered regularly to members (and nonmembers) to an annual awards luncheon, which is attended by around 1,200 members and guests.

Karen Rosa, director of the Film & TV Unit of the American Humane Association, became an Association Director through a different route than Lawler's. Rosa, who grew up in New Jersey and who studied art at Moore College of Art in Philadelphia, worked for more than a decade as a textile designer. She managed a design studio and style lines at Burlington Industries. "So I came to this position with some management background," says Rosa. After working in Florida as art director at an advertising agency that she co-owned, she became involved in designing theater sets. It was through a friend that she decided to relocate to California and try to get a job at the American Humane Association's Film & TV Unit. [For a more in-depth description of what the unit does, go to the entry for Animal Safety Representative in the Talent section of this book.] Rosa explains: "A friend of mine from the theater community in Tampa mentioned that the American Humane Association had representatives who go out on movie sets to oversee the treatment of animals. She thought it would be a good part-time job to introduce me to a brand-new city. She knew I had dogs and cats and that I knew how to ride [horses]."

Rosa did move out to California; she applied for the part-time job, was trained, and then she was asked if she could fill in for someone who was going on a leave of absence. "That was 15 years ago, and I never left."

Like Lawler, Rosa believes in the mission of the association that she heads. "I love the commitment of this program," she says. Association Director requires a wide range of skills. Having the ability to use a computer was initially one of the skills that helped her to get hired.

Rosa explains: "You need to be a multitasker. I have to be a grant writer, and I have to manage the grant. I manage people, and I have to stay informed and represent the organization. In preproduction, I read scripts to understand the animal action, and I do outreach to productions. We're actually scheduling people on the set who oversee the welfare of the animals and uphold extensive *Guidelines for the Safe Use of Animals in Filmed Media*. In postproduction, we screen to see if it's eligible for the end credit. There's staying abreast of research. It's an amalgam of being in the film industry as well as animal welfare."

Salaries

Ranges from $50,000 to $100,000+ depending upon the size of the association (number of members) as well as its annual budget.

Employment Prospects

The employment prospects are only fair because this is a specialized field with only so many associations serving the film industry. Association Director is the top job at an association, so the opportunities for that job will be much more selective than for the more plentiful entry-level association jobs.

Advancement Prospects

Since this is the top job at an association, there will be few advancement opportunities at a specific association, unless it merges with another association or two and becomes an even larger association with more members and staff reporting to the Association Director. If that does not occur, advancement may depend upon moving to another association or transferring the administrative skills to a for-profit situation, such as running a film company or becoming a film producer.

Education and Training

A high school diploma is expected and a college degree with courses in film, management, or business is recommended. Graduate courses in film and even a master's of arts administration with specialization in nonprofit administration considerations is useful and could give you a competitive edge today. Training in delegating and managing a staff will help for this top position. Knowing how a budget is put together as well as how to keep track of the association's fiscal health, even if there is an accountant or financial consultant responsible for those concerns, will be helpful training.

Experience, Skills, and Personality Traits

Having experience working at a nonprofit association, especially in the arts, including film, will be excellent background for this high-profile job. Being an excellent manager of your time—knowing how, when, and what to delegate—being able to stretch a budget as far as possible, as well as being able to juggle many projects and events are necessary skills. Having a passion for movies and film, as well as being a people person, are other skills and personality traits expected in this job. A love of travel is important because there may be a lot of local, as well as national or international, travel involved. A willingness to work long and nontraditional hours is also required, since so many of the association events may be offered before the workday begins, during the workweek evenings, and even occasionally over the weekend. Getting to know the association members as well as being able to handle a support staff are other requirements of the job. Association Director Lawler adds these personality traits for this job: "Being friendly, gregarious, really enjoying talking to people and hearing about their careers, being able to multitask, being well-organized, enjoying parties, social events, and being able to introduce people to other people."

Unions and Associations

Join associations that are tied to whatever specialty that is the focus of your association. For example, if your association is for film editors, join any associations that would be useful to film editors, such as IFP (Independent Feature Project) or the New York Production Alliance. You might also consider joining an association for association directors, whatever the specialty, such as the local chapter of the Society of Association Executives and its national association.

Tips for Entry

1. Become a member of whatever association you are interested in working at and work your way up the ladder at that association.
2. Get experience working at a nonprofit association or organization, since these will have dif-

ferent concerns than for-profit companies. If an opening at a film association becomes available, you will have the skills to transfer to a position in film.
3. Search for job openings at such online sites as http://www.mandy.com or http://www.entertainmentcareers.net.
4. Work in the film industry, getting experience in as many aspects of film as you can, from production to postproduction.
5. Especially for entry-level jobs, volunteer, particularly if you are a recent graduate. "Nonprofit groups always need help," says Lawler. (If you are working at an association, but it is not a film association, volunteering at a film association can help you to break into the film industry.)
6. Attend film industry events and network within the industry, letting others know of your arts administration background and skills and your interest in applying those skills to a film industry arts association directorship.

FILM ARCHIVIST/ PRESERVATIONIST

Duties: Responsible for managing the cataloging, preservation, restoration, storage, retrieval, or exhibition of moving-image materials, including film or video.

Alternate Title(s): Film Preservationist; Film Conservator; Film Curator; Film Librarian

Salary Range: $28,000 to $35,000/year depending upon experience as well as the size and type of film library (university, public, or corporate); may also be on a contractual basis

Employment Prospects: Good

Advancement Prospects: Fair

Best Geographical Location(s): Los Angeles/Hollywood, New York City, Washington, D.C., wherever film or video is being collected, categorized, stored, retrieved, or exhibited

Prerequisites:

Education and Training—High school diploma is expected; college degree with courses in film history, film production, data collection and exhibition is useful; University of California, Los Angeles, New York University, and George Eastman House offer a graduate degree program in film archiving; on-the-

CAREER LADDER

```
Executive Director of a Library or
Museum of Moving Images

        │

Film Archivist or Preservationist

        │

Librarian; Lab Worker; Researcher;
Writer; any position in postproduction
```

job training in data or film collection, cataloging, storage, retrieval, or exhibition

Experience—Working in the film industry, especially the technical side of it, including analogue film or digital media; data collection and exhibition experience, especially for moving images

Special Skills and Personality Traits—Attention to details; knowledge of how to categorize vast amounts of materials, including current materials as well as older products with an age of 50 to 100 years or more; a passion for film and preserving film or video for future generations

Position Description

Responsibilities include collecting, conserving, and categorizing film or video for its retrieval or exhibition, as well as working on the preservation of film or video for its availability to future generations. Film Archivists work for companies that produce film or video content, such as motion picture or TV companies, as well as universities or public libraries with film or video collections. The two key functions are that of archiving the film or video and preserving it for immediate and future retrieval. A Film Archivist needs to have knowledge of film and video as well as excellent computer skills, the ability to create as well as to search databases for information, attentiveness to detail, and the patience to constantly screen film or video footage. Some archivists also perform preservation tasks, such as supervising the transfer of moving images to more stable and long-lasting materials, as well as making sure

the materials are stored at the right temperature to avoid further decomposition. Some do only one or the other job function. Licensing for the use of film footage in videos, documentaries, or feature films may be part of the job in some instances.

Milton Shefter, who graduated from Syracuse University, is a Los Angeles–based Film Archivist and a Preservationist. He was a child actor at seven and later became a writer and booker for a weekly TV show. After working at a television station in Cleveland, Shefter moved to California with his wife. He went to work for an international media storage and distribution company. Shefter then formed his own company, Miljoy Enterprises Incorporated, which focuses on media asset preservation. Its first client in 1987 was Paramount Pictures Corp. Paramount recognized that it needed "asset protection" when it realized that all its holdings were in Los Angeles, and if a big earthquake came along, it could lose everything. So Shefter created a plan that included preservation vaults and archives for the company on the Hollywood lot and mirror-image vaults in an underground location in the eastern United States. He also built archival vaults in England, resulting in the very first motion picture studio worldwide with a total asset-protection program. In addition to working with other clients who own large libraries of moving images and recorded sound content, Shefter was selected to be the Moving Image consultant for the Library of Congress's National Audio-Visual Conservation Center. "Today," says Shefter, "there are a whole new set of questions regarding switching over to digital. We have always taken for granted that the film material we preserved had at least a 100-year life. But there is no standard in current digital systems, so there is no guarantee for continued and long-term access." This subject was recently published in a paper he cowrote and coedited for the Academy of Motion Picture Arts and Sciences, "The Digital Dilemma."

According to Milt Shefter, "There is a great cultural need to preserve what Dr. James Billington, the Librarian of Congress, has termed 'our cultural visual and aural heritage.'" Shefter agrees and thinks this is a great and challenging opportunity for those seeking a career in this field. Knowledge of the analogue photo chemical optical system has always been necessary, as has library science. To that, the archivist of the future must add computer skills and knowledge of digital systems.

Shefter points out that while some schools, such as George Eastman House in Rochester, New York; New York University, in New York City; and the University of California, Los Angeles, teach media preservation, the best education is practical, on-the-job training. Says Shefter: "A good source of information and job opportunities is the Association of Moving Image Archivists." (Shefter is past president.) Their Web site is www.amianet.org.

Salaries

Salaries range from $24,000 to $35,000 per year, depending upon someone's experience and the size of the collection and type of company; work may also be on a contractual basis.

Employment Prospects

This is a relatively new film career category, but as more and more companies and libraries realize the value of their moving image and recorded sound collections, they will need a specialist in film or video cataloging and preservation of the materials. Prospects are good. Employment opportunities include working at a film or TV studio or company, public or university library with film or video collections, or moving image museum or special collection.

Advancement Prospects

It is more difficult to move up in this field than to enter it because there are a limited number of senior managerial positions; advancement prospects are only fair. However, there are advancement possibilities, such as becoming dean of a university's film school or head Film Archivist and Preservationist.

Film Archivist/Preservationist Shefter points out that the way to advance is by getting more knowledge, moving into bigger arenas, and going with larger and larger collections.

Education and Training

A high school diploma and a college degree are expected; graduate training is available at UCLA, which offers a two-year, 72-unit graduate degree in moving image film archive studies. It is a full-time program with admission for the fall semester only. Some companies train entry-level film archivists through in-house training. Nondegree courses in film archiving or preservation are also available through the Association of Moving Image Archivists (http://www.amianet.org), a membership organization with more than 750 members that has an annual educational conference, symposiums, as well as regional workshops. There are also competitive fellowships and internship opportunities that offer training, such as the Kodak Fellowship, awarded to one student annually, which includes a $4,000 scholarship for the upcoming year, a six-week summer internship at the Kodak restoration facilities in Los Angeles, an internship through the Image Permanence Institute (IPI), and a visiting fellowship through AMIA and the Rockefeller Archive Center. For more information on film preservation, visit the Web site of the National Film Preservation Foundation (NFPF), a nonprofit organization created in 1997 by the U.S. Congress to help preserve U.S. films. At the organization's Web site, http://www.filmpreservation.org, you may download for free a 132-page illustrated publication, *The Film Preservation Guide: The Basics for Archives, Libraries, and Museums.*

Experience, Skills, and Personality Traits

Working in any aspect of the film industry, as well as in the field of library science, are useful experiences. On-the-job training is offered by some companies, and additional experience is available through summer or academic year-long internships offered through Kodak, the Image Permanence Institute (IPI), the AMIA, and the Rockefeller Archive Center. Skills include library science and cataloging competence, knowledge of film production as well as the particular storage, cataloging, or retrieval challenges of movies or TV programs made on film, digital video, or analogue video. Personality traits that a Film Archivist or Preservationist should have include being detail-oriented as well as the ability to work behind the scenes and in a technical capacity rather than in front of the camera. Finding the cataloging of data interesting and challenging is essential to this job, as is having an interest in the preservationist tasks and challenges that a Film Archivist/Preservationist deals with.

Unions and Associations

The key association for Film Archivists is the Association of Moving Image Archivists (AMIA, http://www.amianet.org), based in Hollywood, California. Another association is the Chicago-based Society of American Archivists (SAA, http://www.archivists.org), with more than 5,000 members.

Tips for Entry

1. Work for a company or library that does film archiving or preservation and get on-the-job training.
2. Join the Association of Moving Image Archivists and become active in its local and national activities, including attending workshops, symposiums, and the annual conference. Network with Film Archivists and Preservationists about what they do and about any job openings at their companies or libraries.
3. Become active in the Women's Film Preservation Fund, a New York City–based effort founded in 1995 by New York Women in Film and Television and the Museum of Modern Art. They are always looking for active members of their committee. For more information, go to: http://www.nywift.org.

APPENDIXES*

I. Educational Resources: Colleges and Universities

II. Colleges, Universities, and Schools with Relevant Graduate Degree Programs—MA (master of arts) or MFA (master of fine arts)

III. Selected Nondegree Acting, Directing, and Film Courses and Programs

IV. Professional Unions and Associations

V. Competitions, Fellowships, and Internships

VI. Film Festivals

VII. Film Commissions

VIII. Selected Agencies, Film Studios and Companies, and Libraries and Museums

*Throughout these appendixes, you will find street addresses, Web site addresses, and other contact information for schools, companies, associations, and organizations. However, since this information may change at any time, including even the name of an association or the existence of a Web site on the Internet, neither the publisher nor the authors take any responsibility for the accuracy of any listings. Being listed in these appendixes does not imply that the authors are recommending an association, company, product, school, or service, nor does omission from these lists, due to space and other considerations, imply disapproval. The publisher and authors shall have neither liability nor responsibility to any person or entity with respect to any loss or damage caused or alleged to be caused directly or indirectly by the professionals, associations, schools, or companies listed and/or their services rendered to the reader. Any corrections to any listings in this book or any suggestions for possible inclusion of Web sites, schools, associations, organizations, books, or resources for future editions should be sent to the authors at their mailing address: Fred and Jan Yager, P.O. Box 8038, Stamford, CT 06905-8038 or to their e-mail: fyager@aol.com *or* jyager@aol.com.

APPENDIX I
EDUCATIONAL RESOURCES: COLLEGES AND UNIVERSITIES

If you plan to pursue an undergraduate degree in film, you may be familiar with some of the better-known schools offering a degree program, such as the University of Southern California (USC), the University of California at Los Angeles (UCLA), New York University's Tisch School, or the University of Texas at Austin. However, there are also several graduate schools that are considered key film schools (listed in Appendix II), such as the American Film Institute, Columbia University, as well as selected nondegree programs (listed in Appendix III). Following is a more extensive list of colleges and universities that offer a major in film, and related areas, such as theater or digital media including cinema studies, because preparing for a career in film could include such a diverse range of jobs, from the actors in front of the camera to the director behind it, as well as the casting, talent, and literary agents who help bring everyone together. For that reason, it is difficult, at the undergraduate level, to point to just one course of study or major that will be right for everyone. If you want to be an actor after you graduate, you may wish to major in acting. Or you may want to major in philosophy, literature, physics, or art, and get a master's degree in acting or take nondegree or postgraduate acting courses.

The same is true for the dozens of other career options related to the film industry. At the undergraduate level, there are a wide range of majors that provide a solid foundation for the acting, directing, producing, technical, and business-related careers in the film industry embarked upon after graduation. Apprenticeships or internships during college or after graduation offer additional training for specific careers in filmmaking. (See Appendix V for a list of selected competitions, fellowships, and internships in the film industry.) For some, the time to specialize in film may be after graduating from college, pursuing a graduate degree or nondegree classes in a specific film area, such as cinematography, directing, screenwriting, acting, animation, or production.

It is a challenging decision: to major in drama or film or to garner a broad background by majoring in psychology, biology, chemistry or the myriad of other possibilities. For those who wish to pursue a costume or set design career in the film industry, you may want to major in art. Those who are considering a career in the film industry in the postproduction marketing, publicity, or distribution aspects of the business may wish to major in business, marketing, or communications.

The following list provides just a few of the hundreds of colleges and universities in the United States that offer majors or courses, through a film or drama department, which could prepare you for a career in the film industry. It is not intended to be comprehensive. You could also consult with your high school guidance counselor about other colleges or universities to consider, especially those in a geographic area not included in the following list. If a school you are interested in is not listed below, contact the admissions department of that school or go to that school's Web site to discover if they have a film, cinema studies, art, communications, or acting department. (To find the Web site for those colleges or universities omitted below, do a search on the Internet using a search engine, such as http://www.google.com.) An excellent resource on selected colleges and universities in general is the Princeton Review's *The Best 368 Colleges,* written by Robert Franek, Tom Meltzer, Roy Opochinski, Eric Owens, and Tara Bray, published by Random House, and updated annually.

Another way to find a college or university that might offer preparatory courses and training for a career in the film industry is to look through Appendix IV, Professional Unions and Associations, and find the union or association that is tied to your career interest. For example, the Directors Guild of America (DGA) would be helpful for future directors, as would the Producers Guild of America (PGA) for would-be producers. See if there is anything useful at their Web site or if someone at that union or association has any suggestions about colleges or universities that are especially noted for offering courses or even a major related to the specific career that interests you. (Appendixes II and III provides information about graduate and nondegree programs as well as adult education courses or workshops that offer specialized advanced training for the diverse career opportunities in the film industry.) Still another way to consider what college or university you may wish to attend is to read biographies of those who have been successful in your area of interest and see if you can find out where they did their undergraduate work. (Some schools list noted alumni right at their Web site, such as Boston University: http://www.bu.edu.) Or look at the undergraduate degrees listed for faculty members at universities or colleges with programs of study that you might wish to pursue; those schools might be other possibilities to explore.

ALABAMA

Auburn University
Department of Communication and
   Journalism
Radio-TV-Film
0326 Haley Center
Auburn, AL 36849
http://www.auburn.edu

University of Alabama
Telecommunication and Film
   Department
University of Alabama
Box 870172
Tuscaloosa, AL 35487
http://www.tcf.ua.edu

CALIFORNIA

California Institute of the Arts
24700 McBean Parkway
Valencia, CA 91355
http://www.calarts.edu

Loyola Marymount University
School of Film and Television
One LMU Drive
Los Angeles, CA 90045
http://www.lmu.edu/Page14955.
   aspx
Also offers a graduate MFA
   degree in film production and
   screenwriting.

Moorpark College
7075 Campus Road
Moorpark, CA 93021
http://www.moorpark.cc.ca.us
Offers an associate degree
   or certificate program in
   Exotic Animal Training and
   Management Program (EATM);

credits can be transferred toward
a degree.

San Francisco State University
College of Creative Arts
Cinema Department
Fine Arts Building
Room 245
1600 Holloway Avenue
San Francisco, CA 94132
http://www.cinema.sfsu.edu

University of California at
Los Angeles
Department of Film, Television, and
   Digital Media
School of Theater, Film and
   Television
102 East Melnitz Hall
Box 951622
Los Angeles, CA 90095-1622
http://www.tft.ucla.edu/dof.cfm

University of California at
Santa Barbara
Department of Film and Media
   Studies
Ellison Hall 1720
Santa Barbara, CA 93106
http://www.filmstudies.ucsb.edu

University of Southern
California
School of Cinematic Arts
University Park Campus
Los Angeles, CA 90089
http://www-cntv.usc.edu

COLORADO

University of Denver
Department of Theater
2199 South University Boulevard
Denver, CO 80208

http://www.du.edu/thea
Offers major and minor in acting
   with an emphasis on theater.

CONNECTICUT

Connecticut College
Department of Theatre
   (Film Studies)
270 Mohegan Avenue
New London, CT 06320
http://www.conncoll.edu

Quinnipiac University
School of Communications
Media Studies & Media Production
275 Mt. Carmel Avenue
Hamden, CT 06518–1908
http://www.quinnipiac.edu

Yale University
Film Studies Program
53 Wall Street
Room 216
New Haven, CT 06511
http://www.yale.edu/
   filmstudiesprogram

DISTRICT OF COLUMBIA

George Washington University
Film Studies
801 22nd Street NW
Suite 513
Washington, DC 20052
http://www.gwu.edu/~rgsll/filmstudies

Howard University
Communications
2400 Sixth Street NW
Washington, DC 20059
http://www.howard.edu
Offers programs in stage acting and
   directing.

FLORIDA

Florida State University Film School
University Center 3100A
P.O. Box 3062350
Tallahassee, FL 32306-2350
http://film.fsu.edu

ILLINOIS

Northwestern University
Department of Radio, Television and Film
1800 Sherman Avenue
Suite 106
Evanston, IL 60201
http://commweb.soc.northwestern. edu/rft/programs/undergraduate

INDIANA

Indiana University
Department of Communication and Culture
Film and Media Studies
Ashton-Mottier
1790 E. 10th Street
Bloomington, IN 47405
http://www.indiana.edu/~cmcl/ filmstud.html

IOWA

University of Iowa
College of Liberal Arts and Sciences
Department of Cinema and Comparative Literature
425 English-Philosophy Building
Iowa City, IA 52242
http://www.uiowa.edu/~cc/

MARYLAND

Goucher College
Communication and Media Studies Department
1021 Dulaney Valley Road
Baltimore, MD 21204-2794
http://www.goucher.edu

MASSACHUSETTS

Boston University
College of Communication
Department of Film and Television
640 Commonwealth Avenue
Boston, MA 02215
http://www.bu.edu/com/filmtv

Clark University
Visual and Performing Arts Department
Screen Studies
950 Main Street
Worcester, MA 01610
http://www.clarku.edu

Emerson College
School of the Arts
The Department of Visual and Media Arts
120 Boylston Street
Boston, MA 02116–4624
http://www.emerson.edu

Hampshire College
School of Humanities, Arts and Cultural Studies
Film, Photo & Video Production
Emily Dickinson Hall
Amherst, MA 01002
http://www.hampshire.edu

Northeastern University
Theatre
150 Richards Hall
Boston, MA 02115
http://www.neu.edu

MICHIGAN

Central Michigan University
College of Communication and Fine Arts
Broadcast and Cinematic Arts
Mount Pleasant, MI 48858
http://www.cmich.edu

NEW YORK

The City College of New York
The Media & Communication Arts Department
Film and Video Production
138th Street & Convent Avenue
New York, NY 10031
http://www.ccny.cuny.edu

Columbia University
Columbia College
School of General Studies
Film Studies
513 Dodge
New York, NY 10027
http://www.columbia.edu
Offers a major in film studies through the School of General Studies. See the listing for the MFA in Film program under graduate programs, Appendix II.

Fordham University
Department of Communication and Media Studies
Rose Hill Campus
Bronx, NY 10458
http://www.fordham.edu

Hofstra University
School of Communication, Department of Audio/Video/Film
College of Liberal Arts and Sciences
Humanities Department, Department of Drama and Dance
Hempstead, NY 11549-1000
http://www.hofstra.edu

Ithaca College
Department of Cinema, Photography, and Media Arts
School of Communication
953 Danby Road
Ithaca, NY 14850-7250
http://www.ithaca.edu

New York University
Tisch School of the Arts
Undergraduate Department of Drama (Institute of Performing Arts)
Department of Design for Stage and Film
Maurice Kanbar Institute of Film and Television
Skirball Center for New Media and Film: Department of Cinema Studies
721 Broadway, 8th floor
New York, NY 10003
http://www.tisch.nyu.edu

Sarah Lawrence College
Theatre Program (Acting)
Visual Arts Program (Film
    History)
One Mead Way
Bronxville, New York 10708–5999
http://www.slc.edu

Syracuse University
College of Visual and Performing
    Arts (VPA)
200 Crouse College
Syracuse, NY 13244
http://www.vpa.syr.edu

S.I. Newhouse School of Public
    Communications
215 University Place
Syracuse, NY 13244
http://www.newhouse.syr.edu

NORTH CAROLINA

**North Carolina School of the
    Arts**
School of Filmmaking
1533 South Main Street
Winston-Salem, NC 27127–2188
http://www.ncarts.edu/filmmaking

OHIO

Oberlin College
Theatre and Dance
Cinema Studies Program
30 North Professor Street
Oberlin, OH 44074
http://www.oberlin.edu/fsc

PENNSYLVANIA

Carnegie Mellon University
School of Drama
Purnell Center for the Arts #218
4908 Forbes Avenue
Pittsburgh, PA 15213
http://www.cmu.edu

University of Pennsylvania
Theatre Arts Program
Philadelphia, PA 19104
http://www.upenn.edu

TEXAS

University of Texas at Austin
College of Communication
The Department of Radio/
    Television/Film
University Station A 0800

Austin, TX 78712–0108
http://www.rtf.utexas.edu

VERMONT

Bennington College
One College Drive
Bennington, VT 05201
http://www.bennington.edu
Offers an interdisciplinary
    curriculum, including directing,
    acting, technical aspects of
    theater, film, and video.

Middlebury College
Theatre & Dance
Film & Media Culture
Wright Theatre
Middlebury, VT 05753
http://www.middlebury.edu

APPENDIX II
COLLEGES, UNIVERSITIES, AND SCHOOLS WITH RELEVANT GRADUATE DEGREE PROGRAMS—MA (MASTER OF ARTS) OR MFA (MASTER OF FINE ARTS)

A. MA OR MFA IN ACTING

CALIFORNIA

University of California at Irvine
Department of Drama
249 Drama
Irvine, CA 92697-2775
http://www.uci.edu

University of California at Los Angeles
School of Theater, Film and Television
Department of Film, Television, and Digital Media
102 East Melnitz Hall
Box 951622
Los Angeles, CA 90095–1622
http://www.tft.ucla.edu

CONNECTICUT

Yale School of Drama
Yale University
P.O. Box 208235
New Haven, CT 06520
http://yale.edu/drama

NEW YORK

Actors Studio MFA
Pace University
One Pace Plaza
New York, NY 10038
http://www.pace.edu

New York University
Tisch School of the Arts

Graduate Acting Program
721 Broadway
New York, NY 1003
http://www.tisch.nyu.edu

PENNSYLVANIA

Temple University
Theatre/Acting, MFA
Tomlinson Theater
1301 West Norris Street
Philadelphia, PA 19122-6075
http://www.temple.edu/theater

B. MA OR MFA IN FILM (ALSO KNOWN AS "FILM SCHOOL")

CALIFORNIA

American Film Institute (AFI)
AFI Conservatory
2021 North Western Avenue
Los Angeles, CA 90027
http://www.afi.com
MFA (Master of Fine Arts) degrees are awarded in these six areas: cinematography, directing, editing, producing, production design, and screenwriting.

University of California at Los Angeles
Department of Film, Television and Digital Media

MFA Programs in Film and Television
P.O. Box 951622
Los Angeles, CA 90095–1622
http://www.tft.ucla.edu
MFA degrees are offered in four specializations: animation, production/directing, screenwriting, and producers.

University of Southern California (USC)
School of Cinema-Television
University Park Campus
3450 Watt Way
Los Angeles, CA 90089–2211
http://www.cntv.usc.edu

MA or MFA degree specializations include film production (Peter Stark Program), writing for screen and television, film and television production, interactive media, or animation and digital arts.

FLORIDA

Florida State University Film School
Masters of University Center 3100A
P.O. Box 3062350
Tallahassee, FL 32306-2350
http://film.fsu.edu/

Offers MFA degree in writing for the stage and screen and an MFA in production.

MASSACHUSETTS

Boston University
Department of Film and Television
College of Communication
Graduate Film Program
640 Commonwealth Avenue
Boston, MA 02215
http://www.bu.edu

Columbia University
School of the Arts
Graduate Film Division
513 Dodge Hall
New York, NY 10027
http://www.columbia.edu
MFA degrees in film and an MA in film studies.

New York University
The Maurice Kanbar Institute of Film and Television
Tisch School of the Arts
Graduate Department of Film and Television
721 Broadway, 10th floor
New York, NY 10003
http://www.tisch.nyu.edu

APPENDIX III
SELECTED NONDEGREE ACTING, DIRECTING, AND FILM COURSES AND PROGRAMS

CALIFORNIA

American Film Institute (AFI)
2021 North Western Avenue
Los Angeles, CA 90027–1657
http://www.afi.com
Check with AFI to see what courses they are currently offering.

Avid Education Seminars
Avid Technology, Inc.
Avid Technology Park
One Park West
Tewksbury, MA 01876
http://www.avid.com/training
Courses in digital video production and editing, including working with 2D and 3D effects based on Avid editing systems.

Cinema Training Center
11335 Magnolia Boulevard, Suite 1C
North Hollywood, CA 91601
http://www.cinematrainingcenter.com
Nondegree courses in filmmaking.

Directing Workshop for Women
American Film Institute
2021 North Western Avenue
Los Angeles, CA 90027–1657
http://www.afi.com/education//dww
Three-week intensive training program in directing, started in 1974, open to women who already have experience in the film industry but want to gain directing training. The actual length of the program, including the projected time to edit the film project that is developed, is eight months, although only three weeks are spent in classes, from eight to 10 hours daily. Visit the Web site for further details, including a list of alumnae, the deadline for the next workshop, as well as an application.

Directors Guild of America
Assistant Directors Training Program
15335 Morrison Street, #225
Sherman Oaks, CA 91403
http://www.trainingplan.org (LA program)
http://www.dgatrainingprogram.org (NY program)
Each year, approximately 20 trainees are accepted out of approximately 1,000 applicants into the DGA's Assistant Directors Training Program, with programs in both Los Angeles and New York City. The program trains second assistant directors for the film industry. Assistant Directors Training Program is intended to train second assistant directors with a typical career ladder of second assistant director, first assistant director, and unit production manager, rather than director.
Applicants must be at least 21 years of age and have a college degree or two years of paid employment that may be considered equal to a BA degree. There is an application and fee that has to be submitted by mid-November; a written test is administered in January; in May, interviews are held for selected candidates accepted into the program. Four hundred days of on-the-job training are required of trainees accepted into the program as well as attending seminars.

Final Cut Pro
http://www.apple.com/training
Training is available online as well as through local training centers (see listings at the Web site) for learning how to use Apple's software, Final Cut Pro, to edit video for filmmaking.

The Hollywood Film Institute
P.O. Box 481252
Los Angeles, CA 90048
http://www.webfilmschool.com
Courses in producing, directing, and writing. Created by Dov S-S Simens, his two-day Film School is offered in major cities throughout the country. Check the Web site

for upcoming schedules for cities outside of Los Angeles. Related online courses are also now offered.

Hollywood Networking Breakfast

P.O. Box 2688
Hollywood, CA 90078
http://www.changingimagesinamerica.org

Monthly event to meet other attendees as well as the guest speakers. It was started in 1993 on the Paramount Studios lot by Sandra Lord, who is also founder of the nonprofit organization Changing Images in America (CHIA). It is now located at the Beverly Hills Country Club. Attendance is open to working professionals in the entertainment industry; some aspiring talent may attend.

The Los Angeles Film School

6363 Sunset Boulevard, #400
Hollywood, CA 90028
http://www.lafilm.com

Nondegree courses in filmmaking.

University of California at Los Angeles

Extension Writers' Program and Film Studies Division
10995 Le Conte Avenue
Los Angeles, CA 90095
http://www.uclaextension.org

Offers dozens of courses each quarter related to film (technique, production, studies, directing, producing, and the business aspects of filmmaking).

UCLA Professional Programs

Professional Program in Producing
Professional Program in Screenwriting
Room 102 East Melnitz Hall
Los Angeles, CA 90095-1622
http://www.filmprograms.ucla.edu

Offers a nondegree screenwriting program in a traditional campus setting as well as an online version; also offers an on-campus nondegree, certificate program in producing.

MICHIGAN

The Motion Picture Institute of Michigan

295 Elm, Suite 4
Birmingham, MI 48009
http://www.mpifilm.com

Founded in 1993, offers courses in filmmaking.

NEW YORK

Inside the Actors Studio

Pace University
One Pace Plaza
New York, NY 10038
http://www.pace.edu

Interviews hosted by James Lipton, with celebrities, before acting students in the MFA program and the general public. Contact Pace University for fees and schedules.

The New School

Communication & Film Studies
Adult Education Courses
66 West 12th Street
New York, NY 10011
http://www.newschool.edu

Noncredit courses in screenwriting, filmmaking, the film business, and acting.

New York Film Academy

100 East 17th Street
New York, NY 10003
http://www.nyfa.com

Offers four-week, six-week, and eight-week intensive filmmaking workshops, as well a more intensive one-year program. High school summer courses are held in several locations throughout the United States and foreign countries. There is also an acting for film workshop.

New York University

School of Continuing & Professional Studies
145 4th Avenue, Room 201
New York, NY 10003
http://www.scps.nyu.edu

Extensive noncredit courses, including an Intensive Workshop, video, broadcast and producing programs.

UTAH

Sundance Institute

Utah office
1825 Three Kings Dr.
Park City, UT 84060
California office
8530 Wilshire Blvd
3rd floor
Beverly Hills, CA 90211
http://www.sundance.org

Founded by actor Robert Redford, Sundance Institute brings screenwriters and feature film directors to Sundance, Utah, to work on their craft. One of the highlights of the year is the acclaimed annual Sundance Film Festival, held in the winter, which showcases new independent films. There is also an annual three-day independent producers' conference, which offers its participants an opportunity to focus on the business of filmmaking, including film financing, production, marketing, and distribution. Applications for the Feature Film Program, which includes the January Screenwriters Lab, the June Filmmakers Lab, and the June Screenwriters Lab, are available online and need to be submitted along with specific accompanying materials and a nonrefundable processing fee during the stipulated application period.

APPENDIX IV
PROFESSIONAL UNIONS AND ASSOCIATIONS

UNIONS

Actors' Equity Association (AEA)
165 West 46th Street
New York, NY 10036
http://ww.actorsequity.org
Labor union founded in 1913 for stage (theatrical) actors and stage managers. For screen actors, see the listing below for Screen Actors Guild.

American Federation of Television & Radio Artists (AFTRA)
260 Madison Avenue
New York, NY 10016
http://www.aftra.org
A national labor union affiliated with the AFL-CIO, with more than 70,000 members and 36 local offices throughout the country. AFTRA members are represented in four areas: 1) news and broadcasting; 2) entertainment programming; 3) the recording business; and 4) commercials and nonbroadcast, industrial, educational media. Film industry professionals may also be members of AFTRA if they work in any of the above areas. Contact AFTRA for details about membership requirements and benefits.

The Animation Guild and Affiliated Optical Electronic and Graphic Arts
Local 839, IATSE
4729 Lankershim Boulevard
North Hollywood, CA 91602-1864
http://www.animationguild.org
A local IATSE union formed between 1947 and 1952 that now represents more than 3,000 animators and graphic artists in the film industry. In 1980, the union founded the American Animation Institute to further the preservation of animated film art as well as public awareness of its history and development in the film industry.

Art Directors Guild & Scenic, Title, and Graphic Artists (ADG)
Local 800, IATSE
11969 Ventura Boulevard
Suite 200
Studio City, CA 91604
http://www.artdirectors.org
A local IATSE union for "the creative talents that conceive and manage the background and setting for most films and television projects" that merged with the Scenic, Title, and Graphic Artists local. Now includes illustrators and matte artists (formerly IATSE Local 790) and set designers and model makers (fomerly IATSE Local 847).

Costume Designers Guild (CDG)
(affiliated with the International Alliance of Theatrical Stage Employees, IATSE)
Local 892
11969 Ventura Boulevard
1st floor
Studio City, CA 91604
http://www.costumedesignersguild.com
Founded in 1953 by 30 film costume designers and now counting more than 575 members, it affiliated in 1976 with IATSE (Local 892). Requirements are a minimum of three screen credits, a presentation before the membership committee, and a completion of a sample project design and budget. Publications include the annual directory and monthly newsletter.

Directors Guild of America
7920 Sunset Boulevard
Los Angeles, CA 90046
http://www.dga.org
The Directors Guild has more than 12,000 members who have met the specific requirements for the following job categories in the film industry: director, second assistant director (2nd AD), first assistant director (1st AD), and unit production manager (UPM). Members of the DGA are required to be employed by companies that are signatories, a company that has signed a collective bargaining agreement with the DGA that they will abide by the guild's basic agreement.

At the DGA's extensive Web site, there is a membership directory where you can search for a DGA member by name or by credit. The online and print versions of the directory are updated yearly. Agents for directors are also listed, along with information about basic agreements and low budget agreements. A list of Web sites of members is also posted at the DGA site.

Directors Guild of America (DGA-NY)
New York/Eastern Region Headquarters Building
110 West 57th Street
New York, NY 10019
http://www.dga.org
    See above description of DGA.

Electricians
Local 40, IBEW, AFL-CIO
http://www.ibewlocal40.com
    The local union of the International Brotherhood of Electrical Workers, started in 1923, that represents a range of works in the film and entertainment industry, including electronics, production, telecommunications, sound, air conditioning, special effects, stage managers, and set lighting.

Film Technicians
Local 683, IATSE
9795 Cabrini Drive
Suite 204
Burbank, CA 91504–7429
Local683@mindspring.com
http://www.ialocal683.com
    Local union of IATSE representing approximately 1,400 film technicians nationally. Contact the local for information on requirements for joining.

The International Alliance of Theatrical Stage Employees, Moving Picture Technicians, Artists and Allied Crafts of the United States and Canada (IATSE)
1430 Broadway, 20th floor
New York, NY 10018
http://www.iatse-intl.org
    This labor union, affiliated with the AFL-CIO, represents technicians, artisans, and craftspersons in the entertainment industry, including film and television production, live theater, and trade shows. Dating back to 1893, when 1,500 stage workers organized, the crafts of the IATSE include stage technology (carpentry and rigging, electronics, sound, and props); cinematographers; costume design; set design; wardrobe art; hair and makeup design; and animation. A directory of the more than 550 local unions of the IATSE is available at the online site.

International Cinematographers Guild
Local 600, IATSE
National Office/Western Region
7755 Sunset Boulevard
Hollywood, CA 90046
http://www.cameraguild.com

A union local with roots that go back more than 75 years to seven cameramen working in New York City that was formed in 1996 by merging Local 644 (New York City), Local 659 (Hollywood), and Local 666 (in Chicago). Local 600 has more than 5,000 members who are directors of photography, camera operators, assistants, still photographers, and visual effects, animation, and video specialists.

Makeup Artists and Hairstylists Guild
Local 706 (MPMO, Motion Picture Machine Operators), IATSE
15503 Ventura Boulevard
Encino, CA 91436
http://www.local706.org
    A local IATSE and MPMO union for makeup artists and hairstylists chartered in 1937. Check their Web site or contact the union for guidelines for applying to join Local 706.

Motion Picture Editors Guild (MPEG)
Local 776, IATSE
West Coast office
7715 Sunset Boulevard
Suite 200
Hollywood, CA 90046
http://www.editorsguild.com
    A local union of IATSE for motion picture editors with more than 6,000 members.

Publicists Guild of America
Local 600 (formerly Local 818), IATSE
7715 Sunset Boulevard
Suite 300
Los Angeles, CA 90046
A local IATSE union for publicists in the film industry. Merged in 2002 with the International Cinematographers Guild, Local 600.

Scenic, Title, and Graphic Artists
Local 800 (formerly Local 816), IATSE, AFL-CIO
http://www.artdirectors.org
    A local union chartered in 1949 for scenic, title, and graphic artists. Merged with the former Local 876 (Art Directors Guild) and is now Local 800. See listing for Art Directors Guild and Scenic, Title, and Graphic Artists, Local 800.

Script Supervisors/Continuity and Allied Production Specialists Guild
Local 871, IATSE
11519 Chandler Boulevard

North Hollywood, CA 91601
http://www.ialocal871.org

A local union of IATSE for script supervisors and those concerned with the continuity of a film script and film.

Studio Electrical Lighting Technicians Local 728, IATSE

International Alliance of Theatrical Stage Employees
14629 Nordhoff Street
Panorama City, CA 91402
http://www.iatse728.org

A local union of IATSE for electrical lighting technicians working in the film industry.

The Studio Teachers Local 884, IATSE

P.O. Box 461467
Los Angeles, CA 90046
http://www.studioteachers.com

A union representing teachers who educate child performers in traditional academic subjects. Founded in 1926.

Screen Actors Guild (SAG Headquarters)

5757 Wilshire Boulevard
Los Angeles, CA 90036
http://www.sag.org

A union founded in 1933 by 15 actors, including Boris Karloff, Lucille Gleason, and James Gleason, it was recognized by the AFL-CIO as an affiliate in 1935. To qualify for membership in SAG you must meet certain eligibility requirements, both requiring proof of SAG employment, one for a principal performer and another for background players employment. (For more information, go to the new membership page at the Web site: http://www.sag.com/newmembers.html.) In addition to semiannual basic dues paid twice a year (May 1 and November 1), there is an initiation fee of $2,211 plus the first basic dues for six months. SAG dues are computed on all earnings under SAG contracts in the previous calendar year. There are 20 branches throughout the United States.

Screen Actors Guild (SAG-NY)

360 Madison Avenue, 12th floor
New York, NY 10017
http://www.sag.org/new-york-division
See above description of SAG.

Writers Guild of America East (WGAE)

555 West 57th Street
Suite 1230
New York, NY 10019
http://www.wgaeast.org

The Mississippi River serves as the line that determines if a qualified writer will be a member of WGA in the East or WGA in the West (see listing that follows). Membership for both WGAE and WGAW totals approximately 11,000. At the Web site, there is information for new screenwriters. WGAE also holds an annual awards dinner in Manhattan in early spring.

Writers Guild of America West (WGAW)

7000 West Third Street
Los Angeles, CA 90048-4329
http://www.wga.org

Union of screenwriters who meet minimum requirements, pay an initiation fee, and annual dues in quarterly installments (a minimum amount plus a percentage of earnings). WGA represents writers so that they are guaranteed a basic minimum for their writings in these industries: film, broadcast, cable, and new media. WGA also provides a popular script registration service for members and nonmembers, registering more than 30,000 literary works, including treatments, screenplays, synopses, outlines, novels, manuscripts, and plays. (Fees are $10 for members and $20 for nonmembers.) For more information or an application form, contact WGA headquarters or go to the Web site. Materials are registered for five years and are renewable for another five. (Note: Registering with the WGA does not replace or substitute for applying for a copyright through the Library of Congress.) WGA West also publishes a monthly magazine, Written By.

ASSOCIATIONS

Academy of Motion Picture Arts & Sciences (AMPAS)

8949 Wilshire Boulevard
Beverly Hills, CA 90211-1972
http://www.oscars.org

This is the association responsible for coordinating the annual competition for excellence in the motion picture industry as symbolized by the awarding of Academy Awards and the prestigious Oscar statue annually in March. (See also the separate Web site for the Academy Awards: http://www.oscar.com.) Other components include the Margaret Herrick Library, with more than 6,000 screenplays of produced films, the Academy Foundation, and the Academy Film Archive.

The Academy of Science Fiction, Fantasy & Horror Films

334 West 54th Street
Los Angeles, CA 90037-3806
http://www.saturnawards.org

A nonprofit membership association, founded in 1972, dedicated to commemorating films and TV in this genre, such as *Frankenstein*, *The Wizard of Oz*, and *Harry Potter and the Sorcerer's Stone*. Screens movies in Southern California; bestows an annual Saturn Award for the best entertainment in these genres.

Alliance of Motion Picture & Television Producers (AMPTP)

15503 Ventura Boulevard
Encino, CA 91436
http://www.amptp.org

Trade association founded in 1982 concerned with labor issues in the film and television industries.

American Cinema Editors, Inc. (ACE)

100 Universal City Plaza
Rose Hunter Building B, suite 202
Universal City, CA 91608
http://www.ace-filmeditors.org

An honorary society for editors, founded in 1950. Membership requirements include at least 60 months of features or television editing experience, sponsorship by at least two active members, approval by the board of directors, and acceptance by the general membership. Publishes the magazine *Cinema Editor*.

American Federation of Film Producers (AFFP)

http://www.filmfederation.net

Membership association of filmmakers who have successfully completed at least one film that was commercially distributed.

American Film Institute (AFI)

2021 North Western Avenue
Los Angeles, CA 90027
http://www.afi.com

A nonprofit organization established in 1967 by the National Endowment for the Arts to foster new talent, ensure the preservation of film and video, and promote the appreciation of film as an art form. (See also listings for the AFI masters of fine arts (MFA) degree and certificate programs in six film disciplines listed in Appendixes II and III.)

American Screenwriters Association (ASA)

269 S. Beverly Drive
Suite 2600
Beverly Hills, CA 90212-3807
http://www.goasa.com

International membership association for more than 1,300 screenwriters in 36 countries. There is a free newsletter that may also be accessed by nonmembers; a members-only section requires a password, which you assign yourself upon joining the association.

American Society of Cinematographers (ASC)

1782 North Orange Drive
Hollywood, CA 90028
http://www.theasc.com

Founded in 1919, this association of directors of photography is open by invitation only. Publishes *American Cinematographer* magazine. Provides educational and professional activities as well as sponsoring awards.

American Society of Composers, Authors & Publishers

ASCAP Building
One Lincoln Plaza
New York, NY 10023
http://www.ascap.com

A membership association of music composers, songwriters, and publishers in the United States and worldwide. ASCAP was created by and is currently run by composers, songwriters, and music publishers; the board of directors is elected by and from the membership. ASCAP protects the rights of its members by licensing and distributing royalties for the nondramatic public performances of their copyrighted works.

Association of Film Commissioners International (AFCI)

See listing in Appendix VII, Film Commissions.

Association of Talent Agents (ATA)

9255 Sunset Boulevard
Suite 930
Los Angeles, CA 90069
http://www.agentassociation.com

Nonprofit trade association of 100 talent agencies started in 1937. Member agencies represent a range of talent in the film industry, from actors, directors, and puppeteers to choreographers. You may search for an actor or actress at the site by putting the name of the person into the search engine, which will get you to the name of his or her talent agent, if the person has one. More than 40,000 actors and actresses are listed.

Broadcast Film Critics Association (BFCA)

9220 Sunset Boulevard
Los Angeles, CA 90069
http://www.bfca.org

Founded in 1995, this association has 199 members who are television, radio, and online film critics from the United States and Canada.

Casting Society of America (CSA)

606 North Larchmont Blvd
Suite 4B
Los Angeles, CA 90004-1309
http://www.castingsociety.com

Membership in CSA, an association with more than 350 members, is open to casting directors who have at least two years' credit as a casting director and are sponsored by two current CSA members. At their Web site, there are several helpful tips on how to become a casting director, how to become an actor, and how to get an agent.

Filmmakers Alliance (FA)

1030 West Hillcrest Boulevard
Inglewood, CA 90301
http://www.filmmakersalliance.com

Founded in 1993, this is a membership organization for networking; offers educational activities for filmmakers as well as offering help in getting independent movies made, screened at film festivals, and distributed.

The Hollywood Foreign Press Association (HFPA)

646 North Robertson Boulevard
West Hollywood, CA 90069
http://www.hfpa.org

Nonprofit organization of journalists from around the world who write about the movie industry and television. It is known internationally because of the Golden Globe Awards, held at the end of January each year, recognizing the best acting, directing, and producing, among other categories, for the previous year's films and TV programs.

Independent Feature Project Headquarters

104 West 29th Street, 12th floor
New York, NY 10001
http://www.ifp.org

A national not-for-profit membership association of filmmakers with five chapters (Chicago, New York, Minnesota, Seattle, and Phoenix). In addition to providing networking opportunities and membership discounts, it holds annual film festivals that offer screening opportunities of new features to independent filmmakers and directors, as well as give exposure to completed but unproduced screenplays. Publishes the quarterly magazine *Filmmaker*.

IFP/Chicago sponsors the annual screening and educational festival in Chicago. The New York branch of IFP sponsors an annual September screening and educational program known as the Independent Feature Film Market (IFFM).

Independent Film & Television Alliance (IFTA)

10850 Wilshire Boulevard, 9th floor
Los Angeles, CA 90024-4321
http://www.ifta.org

A trade association of companies joined to promote the distribution of American films. It sponsors the annual American Film Market (AFM) held in Santa Monica, California, each November, attended by hundreds of companies from the film and television industries who show and sell their new products for local and foreign distribution. The AFM Finance Conference of seminars and Pitch Me! Event precedes the film market.

Los Angeles Film Critics Association (LAFCA)

http://www.lafca.net

Founded in 1975, a membership association of L.A.–based film critics who write for publications or electronic media. There is an annual awards ceremony each January honoring screen excellence. Members are listed by name on the Web site, without contact details.

Motion Picture Association of America (MPAA)

15301 Ventura Boulevard
Sherman Oaks, CA 91403
(http://www.mpaa.org)

The trade association of the film industry founded in 1922, MPAA plays an advocacy role throughout the United States and internationally for the American motion picture industry. The chairperson and president of the seven largest movie production companies—Walt Disney Company, Sony Pictures Entertainment, Inc., Metro-Goldwyn-Mayer, Inc., Paramount Pictures Corporation, Twentieth Century Fox Film Corporation, Universal Studios, Inc., and Warner Bros.—are on its board of directors.

National Academy of Recording Arts & Sciences

3402 Pico Boulevard
Santa Monica, CA 90405

Founded in 1957, this group of music professionals and recording industry executives celebrates achievements annually with a variety of awards, including the Grammy Awards (http://www.grammy.com). Also known as the Recording Academy, it is an advocacy group that promotes the value of music education and takes stands on a variety of critical issues affecting the musical community, such as record piracy and censorship.

The National Academy of Television Arts and Sciences (NATAS)

111 West 57th Street, Suite 600
New York, NY 10019
http://www.emmyonline.org

Founded in 1957, this national association recognizes excellence in television through the prestigious annual Emmy Award. There are 18 chapters throughout the United States, including Seattle, Boston, Atlanta, Cleveland, Colorado, and Texas. (See the Web site for a list of local chapters with contact information.) Membership is open to professionals working in television, for at least one year or who have been approved by the Membership Committee. Members work in a wide range of jobs in television, from executives, producers, newscasters, and performers to writers, directors, designers, entertainment attorneys, academics, camera operators, and others. The NATAS has a free job bank for its members and also publishes *Television Quarterly.*

National Association of Latino Independent Producers (NALIP)

P.O. Box 1247
Santa Monica, CA 90406
http://www.nalip.org

A membership association, offering educational workshops, networking, advocacy, and mentoring. There is also an East Coast office in New York City.

National Association of Theatre Owners (NATO)

750 First Street NE
Suite 1130
Washington, DC 20002
http://www.natoonline.org

Trade association representing almost 38,800 movie screens throughout the United States and additional screens internationally. Sponsors trade shows and gathers and publishes statistics about the film industry, including box office revenue.

New York Film Critics Circle

http://www.nyfcc.com

Founded in 1935, this is an association of film critics who write for New York–based publications, such as *People, Entertainment Weekly,* and the *Wall Street Journal,* with membership over the years varying from 11 to 31 members. Current members are listed at the site, with their photograph, professional affiliation, and a bio.

New York Women in Film and Television (NYWIFT)

6 East 39th Street, Suite 1200
New York, NY 10016-0112
http://www.nywift.org

This professional membership association, founded in 1978, is part of the Women in Film network of chapters, with approximately 1,200 members, each with a minimum of four years of professional experience in film or television, above entry level. Offers educational opportunities including screenwriting readings, film screenings, and an annual holiday luncheon that recognizes women who have been role models for those in the industry. In addition to dues, new members need to be sponsored by two current members and pay a onetime initiation fee. Maintains a directory, updated annually, for networking with other members, and also coordinates the Revlon Intern/Mentor Program (see listing in Appendix V).

Online Film Critics Association (OFCS)

http://ofcs.rottentomatoes.com

Founded in 1997, this is an international membership association of Internet-based film critics and writers. Member profiles at the association's Web site include the writer's photograph, a bio, and his or her e-mail address.

Organization of Black Screenwriters (OBS)

1968 West Adams Boulevard
Los Angeles, CA 90018
http://www.obswriter.com

Founded in 1988, this international membership association assists screenwriters who are creating works for film and television, through educational programs, workshops, networking, and job openings posted and updated at the Web site.

Producers Guild of America, Inc. (PGA)

8530 Wilshire Boulevard, Suite 450
Beverly Hills, CA 90211
http://www.producersguild.org

An association of more than 3,500 members with strict membership criteria for those who are part of a film's production team, including executive producers, producers, line producers, associate producers, postproduction supervisors, and managers, among others. PGA's mission statement at their Web site: "The New PGA represents, protects, and promotes the interests of all members of the producing team."

Recording Musicians Association (RMA)

817 Vine Street
Suite 209
Hollywood, CA 90038-3716
http://www.rmala.org

Membership association of American film musicians offering educational events, advocacy work, networking opportunities, and a directory of members.

Set Decorators Society of America (SDSA)

1646 North Cherokee Avenue
Hollywood, CA 90038
http://www.setdecorators.org

Founded in 1993, it is a nonprofit membership organization for set decorating professionals in film and TV.

Society of Motion Picture and Television Engineers (SMPTE)

3 Barker Avenue
White Plains, New York 10601
http://www.smpte.org

Founded in 1916, the members of this society for the technical aspects of the motion picture and TV industries include engineers, technical directors, camerapersons, editors, technicians, manufacturers, educators, and consultants.

Women in Film (WIF) (Los Angeles)

8857 West Olympic Boulevard, Suite 201
Beverly Hills, CA 90211
http://www.wif.org

Professional membership association founded in 1973 dedicated to providing networking and educational opportunities for women in film. It publishes a monthly newsletter, as well as holds workshops and seminars throughout the year. Women in Film (LA) has more than 2,400 women and male members and is part of a network of 40 Women in Film associations with more than 10,000 members worldwide, including chapters in Africa, Europe, Canada, Mexico, the Caribbean, Australia, New Zealand, and 11 cities and regions in the United States, including New England, Seattle, New York (see separate listing above for New York Women in Film and Television), Atlanta, Arizona, Dallas, Florida, Houston, Maryland, and Washington, D.C.

Women in Film and Television International (WIFTI)

c/o New York Women in Film and Television
6 East 39th Street, Suite 1200
New York, NY 10016-0112
http://www.wifti.org

International membership association coordinating information on the activities of the local chapters of Women in Film throughout the United States and worldwide. At the Web site there is contact information on Women in Film associations worldwide as well as on the next international summit, held every two years. (See also the listings for New York Women in Film and Television and Women in Film [Los Angeles].)

Women Make Movies (WMM)

462 Broadway, Suite 500WS
New York, NY 10013
http://www.wmm.com

Membership association founded in 1972 to help support the production, promotion, distribution, and exhibition of independent films by and about women. From the Web site: "The organization provides services to both users and makers of film and video programs, with a special emphasis on supporting work by women of color." Media workshops throughout the year offer opportunities for women to learn more about financing a film. A production assistance program provides fiscal sponsorship, which enables women filmmakers to complete their films. There is also the Women Make Movies' Distribution Service.

Women's Media Group (WMG)

P.O. Box 2119
Grand Central Station
New York, NY 10163-2119
http://www.womensmediagroup.org

Membership networking association for women working in the media, including publishing, journalism, film, television, and online media. Information about membership procedures as well as the internship program it sponsors each summer is available at its Web site. Monthly luncheons.

APPENDIX V
COMPETITIONS, FELLOWSHIPS, AND INTERNSHIPS

There are hundreds of competitions for almost every aspect of filmmaking, from screenwriting and directing to cinematography and costume design. The list that follows is a very small sample of the available competitions, fellowships, and internships. Other sources of information for competitions, fellowships, and internships include the unions and associations listed in Appendix IV. Contact the union or association related to the area of film that you wish to explore, such as makeup, acting, or screenwriting, and see if they have information posted on their Web site or available through the mail on competitions, fellowships, or internships. Film industry information Web sites may also provide information; for example, at http://www.moviebytes.com there are listings of hundreds of contests for screenwriters along with links to more information on each award, entry fees, and deadlines. (For additional film industry information Web sites, go to "Web Site Resources," page 258.)

Another way to get on-the-job experience and networking opportunities in the film industry is to volunteer to help at any of the hundreds of film festivals each year. Many festivals, including Sundance, are dependent upon volunteers to help out during the week or 10 days of screenings, seminars, and parties. Some festivals, like the Chicago International Film Festival, offer unpaid internships in a variety of areas, including film programming, marketing, and graphic design. Volunteers may get tickets to screenings or invitations to seminars or parties, space permitting, in exchange for performing various functions at the festival. Although the cost of getting to an out-of-town film festival is usually picked up by the volunteer, admission fees to events are usually waived in exchange for volunteer service. (See Appendix VI: Film Festivals, for listings for possible volunteer or internship opportunities. Check the festival's Web site for information, including application procedures or deadlines.)

Academy of Motion Pictures Arts & Sciences (AMPAS)
8949 Wilshire Boulevard
Beverly Hills, CA 90211-1972
http://www.oscars.org
The Academy's annual grant activities extend support to film festivals and college film departments with internship programs. Grants are not usually awarded to individuals.

BlueCat Screenplay Competition
P.O. Box 2630
Hollywood, CA 90028
http://www.bluecatscreenplay.com
Established in 1998, the grand prize winner of this competition wins $10,000, and the four finalists win $1,500. There is an entry fee of $50 and a March deadline; each entrant is sent a written script analysis.

Don and Gee Nicholl Fellowships in Screenwriting
Academy of Motion Pictures Arts &
Sciences Academy Foundation

1313 North Vine Street
Beverly Hills, CA 90028
http://www.oscars.org/nicholl
Annual international screenwriting fellowship, started in 1986, open to screenwriters who have not earned more than $5,000 writing for film or television. Each year, up to five $30,000 fellowships are awarded. May 1 is the final submission deadline. See the Web site for submissions, guidelines, and application.

The 48 Hour Film Project, Inc.
PO Box 40008
Washington, DC 20016
http://www.48hourfilm.com
Started in 2001, a team on Friday night gets a character, a prop, a line of dialogue, and a genre to be part of the movie and then creates a film from scratch—between Friday at 7 P.M. until Sunday at 7 P.M. The movie is usually screened locally the following week. Films are also entered in a competition, and winners are announced later. The length of the finished film is allowed to range from four minutes to a maximum of seven minutes. In 2007, more than 30,000 filmmakers

participated in cities throughout the United States and internationally. There is a fee to enter the competition and very specific rules to be followed. The number of people on a team has ranged from as few as one to as many as 103. For more information, including dates for participating cities, visit the project's Web site.

Guy A. Hanks & Marvin Miller Screenwriting Program

USC School of Cinema-Television
850 West 34th Street, GT 132
Los Angeles, CA 90089-2211
http://www.usc.edu

A 15-week intensive writing program established by Drs. Bill and Camille Cosby in 1993, named in honor of Camille's father, Guy Alexander Hanks, and Bill's producer, Marvin Miller. The Web site lists two purposes for the program: "to assist writers in the completion of a film or television script" and "to deepen the participants' appreciation for and comprehension of African-American history and culture." Applications and submissions must be postmarked between August 15 and October 15 of the current year; recipients are notified in December.

Hollywood Discovery Awards

Hollywood Film Festival
433 North Camden Drive
Suite 600
Beverly Hills, CA 90210
http://www.hollywoodawards.com

Formerly known as the "Hollywood Columbus Screenplay Discovery Awards," this award was created by authors and producers Carlos de Abreu and Janice Pennington de Abreu to encourage new screenwriters. There is an application and processing fee for each submission; check the Web site for fees, deadlines, and application procedures.

The Julliard School

Professional Intern Program
Technical Theater and Arts Administration
Attention: Program Director
60 Lincoln Center Plaza
New York, NY 10023
http://www.julliard.edu/about/internprogram.html

Started in 1977, this nondegree program offers full-time internships from September through May. A weekly stipend of $295 is provided. Filing deadline for the following year is June 1. Technical theater internships are offered in costumes, wigs and makeup, electronics, props, scene painting, stage management, and production assistance.

New York Women in Film and Television (NYWIFT)

Intern/Mentor
6 East 39th Street, Suite 1200
New York, NY 10016-0112
http://www.nywift.org

Provides professionals in the film industry who are mentors to NYWIFT interns.

APPENDIX VI
FILM FESTIVALS

As Adam Langer notes in his comprehensive *The Film Festival Guide,* there are over 500 film festivals held annually worldwide. Fifteen of the more prominent film festivals are included in this Appendix. For listings in addition to Langer's book, here is a Web site that offers up-to-date information on film festivals throughout the world: http://www.filmfestivals.com.

Austin Film Festival (AFF)
http://www.austinfilmfestival.com
Started in 1994, the Austin Film Festival (AFF) is held annually in October, with an emphasis on the role of the writer in filmmaking. Events include screenings of winners of the screenplay, teleplay, and film competitions, as well as a conference and other events, such as a Writers Ranch, which was held in 2007.

Berlin International Film Festival
Potsdamer Strasse 5
D-10785 Berlin
Germany
http://www.berlinale.de
Established in 1951, held annually in February, it has an entry deadline in November.

Cannes Film Festival
3, rue Amelie
75007 Paris
France
http://www.festival-cannes.fr
The most well-known of the international film festivals, dating back more than 50 years, and held annually in May in Cannes, France.

Chicago International Film Festival
32 West Randolph Street
Chicago, IL 60601
http://www.chicagofilmfestival.org
Founded in 1967, the festival is held for two weeks in October. There is an August deadline for entries.

Montreal World Film Festival
1432 de Bleury Street
Montreal, Quebec H3A 2J1
http://ww.ffm-montreal.org
Established in 1977, this is one of the premier film festivals, held in late August through early September. July is the deadline for entries.

New York Film Festival
The Film Society of Lincoln Center
70 Lincoln Center Plaza
New York, NY 10023–6595
http://www.filminc.com/nyff/nyff.htm
Founded in 1963, this prestigious festival screens about 50 films for two weeks in late September and early October. Entry deadline is July.

San Sebastián International Film Festival
P.O. Box 397
20080 San Sebastián Donostia
Spain
http://www.sansebastianfestival.com
Established more than 50 years ago, this international film festival is held every September. Deadline for entries is late July.

Seattle International Film Festival
400 9th Avenue North
Seattle, WA 98109
http://www.seattlefilm.com
Held for three weeks in late May to early June, this festival screens more than 400 features and shorts. Entry deadline is March.

Slamdance Film Festival
Slamdance, Inc.
5634 Melrose Ave.
Los Angeles, California 90038
http://www.slamdance.com
Started in 1995 by a group of writers, directors, and producers, Slamdance is a film festival held in Park City, Utah, timed to run at the same time as the Sundance Film Festival. Go to the festival's Web site for information on how to submit a film for consideration. This festival premieres independent features by first-time directors working with limited budgets.

Sundance Film Festival

Sundance Institute
1825 Three Kings Drive
Park City, UT 84060
http://www.sundance.org

Annual prestigious competition for independently made feature films and documentaries. Held in Park City, Utah, each January, it is part of an initiative to develop and foster new screenwriters and directors and was founded in 1981 by actor Robert Redford. Approximately 125 feature films are selected to be shown out of more than 3,000 submissions. Having a film accepted by the Sundance Film Festival, and winning an award, can launch a new film and its director, screenwriter, or actors, as major studios and film distributors attend the festival looking for features to pick up for release during the upcoming season. Also sponsors the Sundance Online Film Festival, focused on films created for the Internet.

Tokyo International Film Festival (TIFF)

http://www.tiff-jp.net

Started in 1985, this annual film festival is usually held in October. In 2007, it included a film critics project that selected the best critiques of films that were viewed in the competitive part of the festival. Entries had to be between 800 and 1,500 Japanese characters per piece.

Toronto International Film Festival

2 Carlton Street, 16th floor
Toronto, ON M5B 1J3
Canada
http://www.tiffg.ca

One of the premier international film festivals, it is held for 10 days in September in Toronto, Canada, each year. Founded in 1976, more than 300 films are screened each year. The entry deadline is June.

Tribeca Film Festival

Tribeca Entertainment
375 Greenwich Street
New York, NY 10013
http://www.tribecafilmfestival.org

Started in 2002 by actor Robert De Niro, producer Jane Rosenthal, and Tribeca Entertainment, takes place in May.

Venice Film Festival

Palazzo Giustinian Lolin, San Vidal
San Marco 2893
30124 Venice
Italy
http://www.labiennale.org/en/cinema

Started in 1932, this major film festival is held at the end of August to early September. There is a June deadline for submissions.

WorldFest Houston International Film Festival

WorldFest-Houston
P.O. Box 56566
Houston, TX 77256
http://www.worldfest.org

This annual film festival is an outgrowth of the International Film Society, founded in 1961 by Hunter Todd. The festival has 12 competitions in more than 200 subcategories.

APPENDIX VII
FILM COMMISSIONS

Association of Film Commissioners International (AFCI)
109 East 17th Street
Cheyenne, WY 82001
http://www.afci.org
　　Membership association of more than 300 local film commissions worldwide, although each film commission operates under the authority of its local government. In additional to a mentor program and a publication entitled *Locations,* AFCI has a Web site and headquarters, which provides updated information on member film commissions, searchable by name or by region. The AFCI Locations Trade Show is held annually in California and provides information related to local locations for shooting films. Offers an online course on how to run a film commission entitled, "Film Commission Fundamentals Online," which is available to AFCI members for $150 and to nonmembers for $250.

Film Commission HQ
http://www.FilmCommissionHQ.com
　　Membership site for location experts as well as those seeking out locations, ranging from free to $85 per year, depending on the features you select, for film commissioners and vendors who wish to be in the online directory or get the FCHQ newsletter.

ALABAMA

Alabama Film Office
401 Adams Avenue
Montgomery, AL 36104
http://www.alabamafilm.org

ALASKA

Alaska Film Program
550 West 7th Avenue
Suite 1770
Anchorage, AK 99501
http://www.alaskafilm.org

ARIZONA

Arizona Film Commission
3800 North Central Avenue
Bldg. D
Phoenix, AZ 85012
http://www.azcommerce.com

ARKANSAS

Arkansas Economic Development Commission Film Unit
1 Capitol Mall
Room 4B-505
Little Rock, AR 72201
http://www.arkansasedc.com

CALIFORNIA

California Film Commission
7080 Hollywood Boulevard
Suite 900
Hollywood, CA 90028
http://www.film.ca.gov

COLORADO

Colorado Film Commission
1625 Broadway
Suite #1700
Denver, CO 80202-4729
http://ww.coloradofilm.org

CONNECTICUT

Connecticut Commission on Culture & Tourism
Film Division
One Constitution Plaza
2nd floor
Hartford, CT 06103
http://www.ctfilm.com

DELAWARE

Delaware Film Office
99 Kings Highway
Dover, DE 19901
http://www.state.de.us

DISTRICT OF COLUMBIA

Washington, D.C., Office of Motion Picture & TV Development
http://www.film.dc.gov

FLORIDA

Florida Film Commission
Executive Office of the Governor
Bloxham Bldg.
Suite G-14
Tallahassee, FL 32399-0001
http://www.filminflorida.com

Metro Orlando Film & Television Commission
301 East Pine Street
Suite 900
Orlando, FL 32801-2705
http://www.filmorlando.com

GEORGIA

Georgia Film & Videotape Office
285 Peachtree Center Avenue
Suite 1000
Atlanta, GA 30303
http://www.georgia.org

HAWAII

Hawaii Film Office
P.O. Box 2359

Honolulu, HI 96804
http://www.hawaiifilmoffice.com

IDAHO

Idaho Film Bureau
700 West State Street, Box 83720
Boise, ID 83720-0093
http://www.filmidaho.com

ILLINOIS

Illinois Film Office
100 West Randolph, 3rd floor
Chicago, IL 60601
http://www.commerce.state.il/us/
  dceo/Bureaus/Film

INDIANA

Indiana Film Commission
1 North Capitol, #700
Indianapolis, IN 46204-2288
http://www.state.in.us/film

IOWA

**Iowa Department of Economic
  Development**
Iowa Film Office
200 East Grand Avenue
Des Moines, IA 50309
http://www.traveliowa.com/film

KANSAS

Kansas Film Commission
700 Southwest Harrison Street
Suite 1300
Topeka, KS 66603-3712
http://www.kansascommerce.com

KENTUCKY

Kentucky Film Commission
500 Mero Street
220 Capitol Plaza Tower
Frankfort, KY 40601
http://www.kyfilmoffice.com

LOUISIANA

Louisiana Film Commission
343 Third Street

Suite 400
Baton Rouge, LS 70801
http://www.lafilm.org

MAINE

Maine Film Office
59 State House Station
Augusta, ME 04333-0059
http://www.filminmaine.com

MARYLAND

Maryland Film Office
217 East Redwood Street, 9th floor
Baltimore, MD 21202
http://www.marylandfilm.org

MASSACHUSETTS

Massachusetts Film Bureau
198 Tremont Street
PMB 135
Boston, MA 02116
http://www.massfilmbureau.org

MICHIGAN

Michigan Film Office
P.O. Box 30739
Lansing, MI 48915
http://www.michigan.gov/filmoffice

MINNESOTA

Minnesota Film & TV Board
2446 University Avenue West
Saint Paul, MN 55114
http://www.mnfilmtv.org

MISSISSIPPI

Mississippi Film Office
P.O. Box 849
Jackson, MS 390205
http://www.mississippi.org

MISSOURI

Missouri Film Commission
301 West High Street, #620
P.O. Box 118
Jefferson City, MO 65102
http://www.showmemissouri.org/film

MONTANA

Montana Film Office
1424 9th Avenue
Helena, MT 59620
http://www.montanafilm.com

NEBRASKA

Nebraska Film Office
Department of Economic
  Development
301 Centennial Mall, 4th floor
Lincoln, NE 69509–4666
http://www.filmnebraska.org

NEVADA

**Nevada Film Office—
  Las Vegas**
555 East Washington
Suite 5400
Las Vegas, NV 89101–1078
http://www.nevadafilm.com

NEW HAMPSHIRE

**New Hampshire Film & TV
  Office**
20 Park Street
Concord, NH 03301
http://www.nh.gov/film

NEW JERSEY

**New Jersey Motion Picture and
  Television Commission**
153 Halsey Street
P.O. Box 47023
Newark, NJ 07101
http://www.njfilm.org

NEW MEXICO

New Mexico Film Office
P.O. Box 20003
Santa Fe, NM 87504-5003
http://www.nmfilm.com

NEW YORK

**New York State Governor's
  Office for Motion Picture &
  TV Development**
633 Third Avenue, 33rd floor

New York, NY 10017
http://www.nylovesfilm.com

The City of New York Mayor's Office of Film, Theatre & Broadcasting
1697 Broadway, #602
New York, NY 10019
http://www.nyc.gov/film

NORTH CAROLINA

North Carolina Film Commission
4317 Mail Service Center
Raleigh, NC 27699-4317
http://www.ncfilm.com

NORTH DAKOTA

North Dakota Film Commission
604 East Boulevard, 2nd floor
Bismarck, ND 58505
http://www.ndtourism.com

OHIO

Ohio Film Office
77 South High Street, 29th floor
P.O. Box 1001
Columbus, OH 43216-5156
http://www.discoverohiofilm.com

OKLAHOMA

Oklahoma Film Commission
15 North Robinson, #802
Oklahoma City, OK 73102
http://www.oklahomafilm.org

OREGON

Oregon Film & Video Office
121 Southwest Salmon Street
Suite 1205
Portland, OR 97204
http://www.oregonfilm.org

PENNSYLVANIA

Greater Philadelphia Film Office
100 South Broad Street

Suite 600
Philadelphia, PA 19110
http://www.film.org

Pennsylvania Film Office
400 North Street, 4th floor
Commonwealth Keyston Building
Harrisburg, PA 17120
http://www.filminpa.com

RHODE ISLAND

Rhode Island Film & Television Office
One Capitol Hill
Providence, RI 02908
http://www.film.ri.gov

SOUTH CAROLINA

South Carolina Film Office
1210 Main Street
Suite 2010
Columbia, SC 29201
http://www.scfilmoffice.com

SOUTH DAKOTA

South Dakota Film Commission
711 East Wells Avenue
Sierre, SD 57501-3369
http://www.state.sd.us

TENNESSEE

Tennessee Film, Entertainment & Music Commission
312 8th Avenue North, 9th floor
Nashville, TN 37243
http://www.state.tn.us/film

TEXAS

Texas Film Commission
P.O. Box 13246
Austin, TX 78711
http://www.governor.state.tx.us/film

UTAH

Utah Film Commission
American Plaza III
47 West 200 South

Suite 600
Salt Lake City, UT 84101
http://www.film.utah.org

VERMONT

Vermont Film Commission
10 Baldwin Street, Drawer 33
Montpelier, VT 05633-2001
http://www.vermontfilm.com

VIRGINIA

Virginia Film Office
901 East Byrd Street
Richmond, VA 23219-4048
http://www.film.virginia.org

WASHINGTON

Washington State Film Office
2001 6th Avenue
Suite 2600
Seattle, WA 98121
http://www.wafilm.wa.gov

WEST VIRGINIA

West Virginia Film Office
90 MacCorkle Avenue SW
South Charleston, WV 25303
http://www.wvfilm.com

WISCONSIN

Wisconsin Film Office
648 North Plankinton Avenue
Suite 425
Milwaukee, WI 53203
http://www.filmwisconsin.net

WYOMING

Wyoming Business Council
214 West 15th Street
Cheyenne, WY 82002
http://www.wyomingfilm.org

APPENDIX VIII
SELECTED AGENCIES, FILM STUDIOS AND COMPANIES, AND LIBRARIES AND MUSEUMS

SELECTED AGENCIES

Note: These agencies will not consider unsolicited screenplays. Do not send materials directly; instead, go through a literary or talent agent or entertainment attorney. Lists of possible literary agents for screenwriters can be found in directories noted in the Bibliography and at the Web site of the Writers Guild of America, http://www.wga.org.

Agency for the Performing Arts (APA)

405 South Beverly Drive
Beverly Hills, CA 90212
Nashville office:
3017 Poston Avenue
Nashville, TN 37203
New York office:
250 West 57th Street, #1701
New York, NY 10107
http://www.apa-agency.com
Represents directors, songwriters, screenwriters, producers, and talent.

Creative Artists Agency (CAA)

2000 Avenue of the Stars
Los Angeles, CA 90067
http://www.caa.com
Represents actors, directors, producers, and screenwriters. Offices in eight cities.

Endeavor Agency

9601 Wilshire Boulevard, 3rd floor
Beverly Hills, CA 90212
New York office:
23 Watts Street, 6th floor
New York, NY 10013

The Gersh Agency (TGA)

232 North Canon Drive
Suite 201
Beverly Hills, CA 90210
New York office:
41 Madison Avenue, 33rd floor
New York, NY 10010
http://www.gershagency.com

International Creative Management (ICM)

8942 Wilshire Boulevard
Beverly Hills, CA 90211
New York office:
40 West 57th Street
New York, NY 10019
http://www.icmtalent.com
Represents actors, directors, producers, and writers.

William Morris Agency

One William Morris Place
Beverly Hills, CA 90212
New York office:
1325 Avenue of the Americas
New York, NY 10019
http://www.wma.com
Represents actors, directors, producers, and screenwriters.

Writers & Artists Agency

360 North Crescent Drive
Building N
Beverly Hills, CA 90210-6820
New York office:
19 West 14th Street
New York, NY 10011
Represents actors, directors, producers, and screenwriters.

CASTING DIRECTORS

For a list of members of the Casting Society of America (CSA), go to:
http://www.castingsociety.com/members

TALENT AGENTS OR MANAGERS

For a list of members of the Association of Talent Agents (ATA), go to:
http://www.agentassociation.com/frontdoor/membership_directory.cfm

FILM STUDIOS AND COMPANIES

ABC Entertainment Television Group

500 South Buena Vista Street
Burbank, CA 91521-4551
http://www.abc.com

Baltimore Pictures, Inc.

3335 North Maple Drive
Suite 205
Beverly Hills, CA 90210
http://www.levinson.com

CBS Entertainment

7800 Beverly Boulevard
Los Angeles, CA 90023
http://www.cbs.com

Columbia Pictures

10202 West Washington Boulevard
Culver City, CA 90232
See listing for Sony Pictures.

Dreamworks SKG
100 Universal Plaza
Building 10
Universal City, CA 91608-1085
http://www.dreamworks.com

Fine Line Features
116 North Roberston Boulevard
Los Angeles, CA 90048
http://www.finelinefeatures.com

HBO Films
2049 Century Park East
Suite #3600
Los Angeles, CA 90067-3215
http://www.hbo.com/films

Miramax Films
375 Greenwich Street
New York, NY 10013-2338
http://www.miramax.com

NBC Entertainment
3000 West Alameda Avenue
Burbank, CA 91523-40001
http://www.nbc.com

New Line Cinema Corporation
888 7th Avenue
19th Floor
New York, NY 10106
http://www.newline.com

Paramount Pictures
5555 Melrose Avenue
Los Angeles, CA 90038-3197
http://www.paramount.com

Showtime Networks, Inc.
1633 Broadway
New York, NY 10019
http://www.sho.com

Sony Pictures Entertainment
10202 West Washington Boulevard
Culver City, CA 90232-3195
http://www.sonypictures.com

Tribeca Productions
375 Greenwich Street
New York, NY 10013
http://www.tribecafilm.com

Twentieth Century Fox
10201 West Pico Boulevard
Los Angeles, CA 90035
http://www.foxmovies.com

United Artists (UA)
http://www.unitedartists.com

Universal Studios
100 Universal City Plaza
Universal City, CA 91608-1085
http://www.universalstudios.com

**Walt Disney Pictures/
Touchstone Pictures**
500 South Buena Vista Street
Burbank, CA 91521
http://www.disney.go.com/
disneypictures

Warner Brothers Pictures
4000 Warner Boulevard
Burbank CA 91522
http://www.warnerbros.com

LIBRARIES AND MUSEUMS

**American Museum of the
Moving Image**
35 Avenue at 36th Street
Astoria, NY 11106
http://www.ammi.org

Margaret Herrick Library
Fairbanks Center for Motion
Picture Study
Academy of Motion Picture Arts &
Sciences
333 South LaCienega Boulevard
Beverly Hills, CA 90211
http://www.oscars.org

**New York Public Library for
the Performing Arts**
40 Lincoln Center Plaza
New York, NY 10023-7498
http://www.nypl.org/research/lpa/
lpa.html

**The Paley Center for Media
(formerly Museum of
Television and Radio)**
25 West 52nd Street
New York, NY 10019
http://www.mtr.org

Shavelson-Webb Library
Writers Guild Foundation
7000 West Third Street
Los Angeles, CA 90048-4329
http://www.wga.org

GLOSSARY

above-the-line Costs related to producing a film that occur before a production begins; usually includes salaries for the film's producer, director, actors, and screenwriter (including rights to a property if the screenplay is based on a novel or play, or buying the rights to someone's life story).

action Said by the director to indicate that the scene is to begin.

actors Men and women trained to perform in feature films by taking on whatever role they are assigned to portray. They may change their appearance through makeup, hairstyles, costumes, or dialects, or they may appear in contemporary dress, conveying their specific character in more subtle but significant gestures, nuances, and mannerisms.

AFI American Film Institute, a national nonprofit association dedicated to preserving film and to training the future generations of filmmakers.

art director Works with the production designer to create drawings and produce ideas about how a film should look, including sets and costumes.

assistant director (AD) See First assistant director or Second assistant director.

audition The trial performance requested of an actor. Auditions may include reading the actual screenplay being cast or performing a favorite scene or song.

below-the-line Costs related to producing a film excluding above-the-line costs; includes all other salaries, equipment purchases or rentals, and materials.

best boy Second electrician, responsible for maintaining and ordering electrical equipment; assistant to the chief electrician or head gaffer. The best boy is usually the person who actually gives the orders to the rest of the crew for setting up the lights, laying cables, moving cranes, installing generators, and moving equipment.

blue screen A blue backdrop that is digitally replaced by some other background footage, which will be seen in the film.

boom A long pole to which a microphone is attached.

breakdown A screenplay or script divided into detailed sections to explain and provide descriptions of every single role in the movie; used as a tool in casting the film.

casting director The individual responsible for a film's casting or for suggesting actors to a film's producer or director. He or she may be required to do a breakdown of the script for the purpose of casting.

CGI Computer-generated imagery or images.

cinematographer Director of photography.

completion bond An insurance policy from a bonding company that guarantees that the company will provide any money needed to finish or complete the picture if it goes over budget. A completion bond usually costs 3 percent of the film's budget.

coverage Written synopsis of a screenplay, including a script reader's decision about whether the material is to be recommended, considered, or passed on as a possible movie project for development.

craft services The group responsible for providing the cast and crew all meals and snacks on location and on the studio set.

dailies A day's footage, usually screened at the end of the day for the producer, director, editor or studio executives. Sometimes, principal actors are invited to attend as well.

dolly A platform on wheels upon which a camera is mounted so that it can move smoothly.

dolly grip The person who operates the dolly upon which a camera is mounted.

editor Person who assembles the shots and scenes to reflect the director's vision.

exhibitor Person who owns a theater in which movies are shown to the public.

extras People who appear in a film's background.

filmography Term sometimes used in reference to the biography of someone in the film industry, such as an actor or director.

first assistant director The director's chief assistant during preproduction and production.

foley artist In a foley sound studio, the person responsible for adding specific sounds to a film, such as breaking glass, rain, or footsteps.

FX Special effects.

FX artist See Special effects makeup artist.

gaffer Chief electrician in charge of the electrical and lighting crew on the film set.

greenlight The formal approval to move a screenplay or project forward into production. The term usually applies to the go-ahead given to a project by one of the major studios.

grip Person who moves materials and helps set up equipment required on a set or location, including the camera dollies.

HD High definition

independent A director or producer who is not employed by a major studio but instead obtains initial funding for a film project from private sources, such as banks, wealthy investors, or friends and family members.

key grip The supervisor responsible to the director of photography and the gaffer.

line producer Person responsible for all the details of moving a movie along, on schedule and on budget. This job contrasts with that of the producer, who usually puts the project together but then turns over the day-to-day concerns to a line producer.

literary material A screenplay or any book, play, article, or movie from which a screenplay is derived.

makeup artist Person responsible for the makeup of the actors in a movie, from the principal actors to the extras. The makeup may be contemporary or might include making someone up to portray a character from history, aging a contemporary character, or producing special effects. See also Special effects makeup artist.

negative costs The cost of a film, including above-the-line and below-the-line costs, but excluding costs related to marketing and distributing the film.

option A payment made by a director, producer, or studio for a screenplay or literary material for the right to find independent funding sources or a studio to finance making the movie. If the funding sources are not available, or if the talent that the producer hoped to obtain cannot commit to the project, the option may expire, and there are no further financial or creative obligations to the writer. Options are usually for anywhere from six to 18 months; some options have provisions for an additional payment if the option is renewed. The option may be part of an agreement that also covers the payment and terms of sale for the screenplay or property if a movie does commence production, or the option can be a completely separate agreement with another agreement drawn up once the project is greenlighted or definitely moving forward.

pitch A succinct verbal synopsis of the key concept, plot, and characters behind a screenplay or film project that a screenwriter or literary agent gives to a director or producer, in person or over the phone, with the hope that he or she will want to read the screenplay, purchase the property, and make the movie.

postproduction The phase that begins once principal photography is finished. The film is edited. A final print is then copied and distributed to audiences.

preproduction The first of the three phases of creating a film (the other two phases are production and postproduction). During preproduction, financing will be raised; the cast will be chosen; the script will be purchased and written or rewritten; the film crew for production will be hired; and the location or locations where the film will be shot will be scouted.

producer Brings together all the elements needed to make the movie. Often, movies begin with a producer finding literary material he or she wants to see developed into a screenplay, hiring a screenwriter to write an original screenplay, or purchasing a completed screenplay (known as a spec screenplay).

production The actual shooting of a film; also referred to as the commencing of principal photography.

rough cut An early assembly of the scenes, often lacking final music and looping dialogue, color correction, and some scenes that may require special effects.

screenplay Term used for the script that serves as the basis of a movie. Screenplays adhere to certain conventions in terms of technical specifications for presentation, such as the margins and font to be used and how dialogue or directions are presented, and based on the projected length of the final movie. For example, the standard is one page of a screenplay for approximately one minute of a movie.

screenwriter One who writes feature films, which follow a strict format in terms of writing style, look, and length. Unlike writing a novel or a play, writing feature films is usually a collaborative effort. Rarely will the final film be exactly the way the screenwriter first wrote it, or shot without the benefit of one or more rewrites by the original screenwriter, other screenwriters, and, in some instances, by the director or producer.

scrim A type of screen used to diffuse the light on a set in order to eliminate or at least soften the shadows. It also reduces glare.

script reader Reader of screenplays who summarizes the work and issues a written report to a studio or film company; this report notes which of these actions the studio or company should take regarding the script: recommend, consider, or pass.

script supervisor Keeps track of the different takes while the movie is being shot, times the takes, and makes notes for the director as a way of maintaining continuity when the director edits the film.

second assistant director Works for the first assistant director (the director's chief assistant); prepares and distributes daily paperwork, such as shooting schedules, cast and crew calls, and the production report.

signatory A company agreeing to comply with minimum wage requirements and other conditions of employment, such as the rules set forth by the Writers Guild of America (WGA) for production companies who employ screenwriters.

spec screenplay A complete screenplay written without any commitment from a producer that the movie will get made.

special effects makeup artist Through the use of makeup as well as prosthetics, the special effects makeup artist can transform principal actors or extras into imaginary creatures and animals.

story editor Looks for material that a company might want to develop into a movie, whether it is in the form of an original screenplay, a book, a play, or a true life story written up in a newspaper or magazine article.

swing gang Part of the set dressing crew, this group actual moves the furniture and other parts of a set.

talent This term refers to an actor, director, or writer.

trades Magazines that cover the film industry, such as the *Hollywood Reporter* and *Variety*.

treatment A short narrative version of the screenplay, often longer than a synopsis, that includes the story line, characters, and a fairly accurate representation of what the script will contain.

turnaround When a studio does not move a project into production, it becomes available to the owner, often for a price, to take it elsewhere.

writer See Screenwriter.

SELECTED BIBLIOGRAPHY

A. BOOKS

ACTORS, ACTING, AND CASTING DIRECTORS

Adler, Stella. *The Art of Acting.* New York: Applause Theatre Book Publishers, 2000.

Caine, Michael. *Acting in Film: An Actor's Take on Moviemaking.* Rev. ed. New York: Applause Theatre Book Publishers, 1997.

Chekov, Michael. *On the Technique of Acting: The First Complete Edition of Chekov's Classic to the Actor.* New York: HarperCollins, 1993.

Hagen, Uta, with Haskel Frankel. *Respect for Acting.* New York: Wiley, 1973.

Henry, Mari Lyn, and Lynne Rogers. *How to Be a Working Actor: The Insider's Guide to Finding Jobs in Theater, Film, and Television.* 4th ed. New York: Watson-Guptill, 2000.

Hollywood Creative Directory. *Film Actors.* 6th edition. Los Angeles, Calif.: Hollywood Creative Directory, 2003.

Joseph, Erik. *Glam Scam: Successfully Avoiding the Casting Couch, and Other Talent and Modeling Scams.* Los Angeles, Calif.: Lone Eagle Publishing, 1994.

Kanner, Ellie, and Paul F. Bens, Jr. *Next! An Actor's Guide to Auditioning.* Los Angeles, Calif.: Lone Eagle Publishing, 1996.

Kondazian, Karen, and Eddie Shapiro. *The Actor's Encyclopedia of Casting Directors: Conversations with over 100 Casting Directors on How to Get the Job.* Los Angeles, Calif.: Lone Eagle Publishing, 2000.

Lewis, M. K., and Rosemary R. Lewis. *Your Film Acting Career: How to Break into the Movies & TV & Survive in Hollywood.* 4th ed. Santa Monica, Calif.: Gorham House Publishers, 1997.

Meisner, Sanford. *Meisner on Acting.* New York: Vintage, 1987.

Nicholas, Michael S. *An Actor's Guide: Your First Year in Hollywood.* New York: Allworth Press, 2000.

Shurtleff, Michael. *Audition: Everything an Actor Needs to Know to Get the Part.* Studio City, Calif.: Players Press, 1984.

Stanislavski, Constantin. *An Actor Prepares.* Translated by Elizabeth Reynolds Hapgood. Philadelphia, Penn.: Taylor & Francis, 1989.

AGENTS

Hollywood Creative Directory. *Hollywood Representation Directory Agents & Managers.* 62nd edition. Los Angeles, Calif.: Hollywood Creative Directory, 2008.

Rainford, Nancy. *How to Agent Your Agent.* Los Angeles, Calif.: Lone Eagle Publishing, 2002.

DIRECTORS AND DIRECTING

Bare, Richard. *The Film Director.* New York: Collier Books, 1971.

Katz, Steven D. *Cinematic Motion: A Workshop for Staging Scenes.* Studio City, Calif.: Michael Wiese Productions, 1992.

———. *Shot by Shot: Film Directing, Visualizing from Concept to Screen.* Studio City, Calif.: Michael Wiese Productions, 1991.

Landau, Camille, and Tiare White. *What They Don't Teach You at Film School: 161 Strategies for Making Your Own Movie No Matter What.* New York: Hyperion, 2000.

Lone Eagle Publishing. *Film Directors.* 16th edition. Los Angeles, Calif.: Lone Eagle Publishing, 2002.

Lowenstein, Stephen, ed. *My First Movie: Twenty Celebrated Directors Talk about Their First Film.* New York: Penguin, 2002.

Rodriguez, Robert. *Rebel Without a Crew: Or How a 23-Year-Old Filmmaker with $7,000 Became a Hollywood Player.* New York: Plume, 1996.

Singer, Michael. *A Cut Above: 50 Directors Talk about Their Craft.* Los Angeles, Calif.: Lone Eagle Publishing, 1998.

Tibbetts, John C., and James M. Welsh. *The Encyclopedia of Filmmakers.* 2 vols. New York: Facts On File, 2002.

FILM FESTIVALS

Gore, Chris. *The Ultimate Film Festival Survival Guide.* 2d edition. Los Angeles, Calif.: Lone Eagle Publishing, 2001.

Langer, Adam. *The Film Festival Guide.* 2d ed. Chicago: Chicago Review Press, 2000.

FILM INDUSTRY (GENERAL)

Anonymous. *The Hollywood Rules.* Beverly Hills, Calif: The Writers Network, 2000.

Brouwer, Alexandra, and Thomas Lee Wright. *Working in Hollywood: 64 Film Professionals Talk about Moviemaking.* New York: Crown Publishers, 1990.

Epstein, Edward Jay. *The Big Picture: The New Logic of Money and Power in Hollywood.* New York: Random House, 2006.

Greenspon, Jaq. *Careers for Film Buffs & Other Hollywood Types.* 2d edition. New York: McGraw-Hill, 2003.

Harris, Mark. *Pictures at a Revolution: Five Movies and the Birth of the New Hollywood.* New York: Penguin Group, 2008.

Levy, Frederick. *Hollywood 101: The Film Industry.* Los Angeles, Calif: Renaissance Books, 2000.

Lumme, Helena. *Great Women of Film.* Photographs by Mika Manninen and Helena Lumme. New York: Watson-Guptill, 2002.

Rensin, David. *The Mailroom: Hollywood History from the Bottom Up.* New York: Ballantine Books, 2003.

PRODUCERS AND PRODUCING

Baumgarten, Paul A., Donald C. Farber, and Mark Fleischer. *Producing, Financing and Distributing Film.* 2d ed. New York: Limelight Editions, 1992.

Brown, David. *Let Me Entertain You.* New York: William Morrow, 1990.

Buzzell, Linda. *How to Make It in Hollywood: All the Right Moves.* New York: HarperPerennial, 1992.

Evans, Robert. *The Kid Stays in the Picture.* Beverly Hills, Calif.: New Millennium, 2002.

Guber, Peter, and Peter Bart. *Shoot Out: Surviving Fame and (Mis)fortune in Hollywood.* New York: Penguin, 2002.

Hollywood Creative Directory. *Hollywood Creative Directory.* Vol. 47. Los Angeles, Calif.: Hollywood Creative Directory, 2003.

Lazarus, Paul N., III. *The Film Producer: A Handbook for Producing.* New York: St. Martin's Press, 1992.

Levison, Louise, *Filmmakers and Financing: Business Plans for Independents.* Boston: Focal Press, 1994.

Medavoy, Mike. *You're Only as Good as Your Next One.* New York: Simon & Schuster, 2003.

Obst, Lynda. *Hello, He Lied, and Other Truths from the Hollywood Trenches.* Boston: Little, Brown, 1996.

Vachon, Christine, with David Edelstein. *Shooting to Kill: How an Independent Producer Blasts Through the Barriers to Make Movies That Matter.* New York: Avon, 1998.

SCREENWRITING

Abreu, Carlos de, and Howard Jay Smith. *Opening the Doors to Hollywood: How to Sell Your Idea, Story, Screenplay, Manuscript.* New York: Three Rivers Press, 1995.

Atchity, Kenneth, and Chi-Li Wong. *Writing Treatments That Sell.* New York: Holt, 1997.

Dunne, John Gregory. *Monster: Living off the Big Screen.* New York: Random House, 1997.

Field, Syd. *Selling a Screenplay: The Screenwriter's Guide to Hollywood.* Garden City, N.Y.: Dell, 1989.

Goldman, William. *Adventures in the Screen Trade.* New York: Warner, 1983.

———. *Which Lie Did I Tell?* New York: Pantheon, 2000.

Hollywood Creative Directory. *Film Writers.* 10th edition. Santa Monica, Calif.: Hollywood Creative Directory, 2003.

King, Viki. *How to Write a Movie in 21 Days.* New York: Harper & Row, 1988.

Koch, Jonathan, Robert Kosberg, and Tanya Meurer Norman. *Pitching Hollywood.* Sanger, Calif.: Quill Driver Books, 2004.

Lerch, Jennifer. *500 Ways to Beat the Hollywood Script Reader: Writing the Screenplay the Reader Will Recommend.* New York: Simon & Schuster, 1999.

McKee, Robert. *Story: Substance, Structure, Style, and the Principles of Screenwriting.* New York: HarperCollins, 1997.

Seger, Linda. *Creating Unforgettable Characters.* New York: Holt, 1990.

———. *Making a Good Script Great.* 2d ed. Hollywood, Calif.: Samuel French, 1994.

Straczynski, J. Michael. *The Complete Book of Scriptwriting.* Rev. ed. Cincinnati, Ohio: Writer's Digest Books, 1996.

Tibbetts, John C., and James M. Welsh. *The Encyclopedia of Novels into Film.* New York: Facts On File, 1998.

TECHNICAL

Fraioli, James O. *Storyboarding 101: A Crash Course in Professional Storyboarding.* Studio City, Calif.: Michael Wiese Productions, 2000.

Malkiewicz, Kris. *Film Lighting: Talks with Hollywood's Cinematographers and Gaffers.* New York: Simon & Schuster, 1992.

B. INDUSTRY PUBLICATIONS

American Cinematographer
P.O. Box 2230
Hollywood, CA 90078
http://www.theasc.com

Creative Screenwriting
6404 Hollywood Boulevard
Suite 415
Los Angeles, CA 90028
http://www.creativescreenwriting.com

Fade In
289 South Robertson Boulevard
Suite 467
Beverly Hills, CA 90211
http://www.fadeinmagazine.com

Film and Video
P.O. Box 3229
Northbrook, IL 60065-3229
http://www.filmandvideomagazine.com

Filmmaker: The Magazine of Independent Film
501 Fifth Avenue
Suite 1714
New York, NY 10017
http://www.filmmakermagazine.com

Hollywood Reporter
5055 Wilshire Boulevard
Los Angeles, CA 90036-4396
http://www.hollywoodreporter.com

Hollywood Scriptwriter
P.O. Box 10277
Burbank, CA 91510
http://www.hollywoodscriptwriter.com

IATSE Official Bulletin
International Alliance of Theatrical Stage Employees
1430 Broadway, 20th floor
New York, NY 10018
http://www.iatse.lm.com

New York Screenwriter
655 Fulton Street, #276
Brooklyn, NY 11217
http://www.nyscreenwriter.com

Screen Magazine
222 West Ontario Street, Suite 500
Chicago, IL 60610
http://www.screenmag.com

StudentFilmmakers
1133 Broadway, Suite 1503
New York, NY 10010
http://www.studentfilmmakers.com

Variety
5700 Wilshire Boulevard
Suite 120
Los Angeles, CA 90036
http://www.variety.com

C. WEB SITE RESOURCES

http://www.dga.org
The Web site for the Directors Guild of America has an extensive links page with links in the categories of DGA member sites, film festivals, film commissions, film schools, studios and distributors, production and post-production sites, and more.

http://www.filmfinders.com
Started in 1989 as a consulting company for the acquisition of feature films. Offers numerous web-based products on a subscription basis. Although producers may list their projects for free, a required questionnaire may be requested for consideration.

http://www.hollywood.com
Information on movies, including new releases.

http://www.hollywoodlitsales.com
Updates on sales of screenplays.

http://www.hollywoodreporter.com
Information about the film industry at this online version of the *Hollywood Reporter*. Includes a section called "The Box Office," with daily and weekly grosses for the top ten movies.

http://www.iatse.lm.com/crafts.html
The crafts of the union IATSE (International Alliance of Technical Stage Employees, Moving Picture Techni-

cians, Artists and Allied Crafts of the United States and Canada), with information about stage technicians, film and television production, camera, wardrobe, hair and makeup, animation, costume design, set design, publicists, and more.

http://www.ifilm.com
See also the companion site:http://www.ifilmpro.com Started in 1999, provides information for film fans, filmmakers, and industry professionals. Operated by the company that also publishes the Hollywood Creative Directory and maintains the site related to their directories of producers, agents, managers, distributors, and film writers, as well as books about the industry (http://ww.hcdonline.com).

http://www.imdb.com
Database about movies, including who made them, with biographies of actors and directors.

http://www.industrycentral.net
Discussion boards, motion picture and television industry news, and links.

http://www.lindaseger.com
Site of script consultant Linda Seger, with information on her seven published books.

http://www.moviebytes.com
Lists agents, screenplay contests, and some markets for screenplays.

http://www.movieweb.com
Extensive listings of movies, including production notes and detailed biographical information on the key actors and production team behind major movies.

http://www.scriptsales.com
This site, entitled "Done Deal," highlights recent screenplay sales. There are also reviews of books on screenwriting, as well as a list of agents and managers.

http://www.scriptwritersnetwork.com
Requires membership to access (annual fee plus onetime application fee).

http://www.variety.com
Online version of the print publication *Variety,* with industry statistics and articles.

http://www.wga.org
Web site of the Writers Guild of America, with research links "specifically to help writers research their scripts," including sites related to science, law and crime, news sources, film and television, and history. Agents are also listed, by state, including whether or not they will consider new writers or unsolicited material.

D. JOB SEARCH SITES

http://www.actorsaccess.com
A way to manage photos or videos for review by casting directors who search the database for talent. Two photos are posted for free with registration; for a fee, additional photos may be posted. Run by Breakdown Services (see listing below).

http://www.breakdownservices.com
Established in 1971, Breakdown Services, as stated at its Web site, is a "means to reach talent agents as well as actors when casting a project." The company has offices in Los Angeles, New York, and Vancouver and maintains relationships with companies in Toronto, London, and Sydney.

http://corporate.disney.go.com/careers
Home page for the Careers section of The Walt Disney Company including a discussion of the company, student programs, and job openings.

http://entertainmentcareers.net
Listings for jobs (acting, crews, postproduction, marketing, advertising, literary and talent agencies, assistant and entry-level, film festivals, theatrical exhibition) and internships in the entertainment industry, arranged by job category and state, with most listings in southern California. Posted positions are at production companies and studios. You may search for all job openings, which includes everywhere, especially Los Angeles/Hollywood, or you can go to the regional listings and just search through those listings including New York (tristate), northern California, or Chicago. Although the site is free, you may become a member by paying monthly ($4.95 for the first month, $9.95 thereafter) or at a discounted three-, six-, or 12-month rate. Check the Web site for a discussion of the benefits of membership to see if you want to join.

http://www.entertainmentjobs.com

Listings for jobs in the entertainment industry, with a sample posted for free at the site. For more extensive listings, there is a membership fee beginning with a minimum $39 three-month subscription.

http://www/facebook.com

Social networking site that facilitates professional networking.

http://hcdonline.com

Site to purchase the premiere industry directory, the Hollywood Creative Directory, the print or online versions, but you will also find a free job board there of openings in a range of film industry jobs, paid and unpaid, from crew, administrative, and writing, to postproduction, casting, and distribution.

http://www.infolist.com

A free listing of available jobs and upcoming educational events as well as screenings and parties for the film industry. Developed in 2000 by Jeffrey R. Gund to help out some friends who were looking for a job or actors seeking a part, the list kept growing into its current extensive version.

http://www.inktip.com

A subscription-based newsletter that sends out weekly leads for producers, production companies, or directors who are looking for screenplays. In 2007, according to the Web site, through InkTip's Preferred Newsletter, 40 features were optioned, 15 writers were hired, and 4 writers gained representation. Offers a number of other services to agents and managers, producers, directors, and talent as well as screenwriters and authors. The fee for the preferred newsletter is $50 for a four-month subscription. Check out the Web site for other services that are offered as well as the cost and benefits.

http://www.insidehollywood.info

Site developed and maintained by film industry Alicia Hirsch, who began her career as a tour guide at Universal Studios in Hollywood and went on to working on TV shows and movies-of-the-week. Lots of contact information related to finding a job in film especially in Hollywood.

http://www.linkedin.com

Web site that facilitates professional networking among members.

http://www.mandy.com

International film and television directory including current vacancies organized by location. Covers job openings that are fully paid plus low- or no-pay in all aspects of film and TV production including openings for the crew, screenwriters, postproduction, sales and marketing, and new media. There are also casting calls for actors as well as a film market where films are listed that are for sale and seeking distribution. A yellow pages with thousands of listings for producers, technicians, and facilities is at this site as well as classified ads section for buying or selling equipment.

http://www.mediabistro.com

A free site with a job listings section that, although geared to jobs in the publishing industry, occasionally include listings for film or broadcasting jobs, particularly for writers. There is a job alert option that will automatically e-mail you when a new job posting in the categories that you list becomes available. Also offers online or in-person courses related to job seeking at its New York headquarters as well as other cities throughout the United States and internationally. Check the Web site for upcoming events.

http://www.monster.com

Although a general free job search site, there are still some jobs in the film, video, or TV industries. Searches are by keyword for all locations as well as by city or state.

http://www.nywift.org

The members-only section for NYWIFT (New York Women in Film and Television) has listings for fully paid as well as low- or no-pay jobs.

http://www.showbizjobs.com

California-based job site founded in 1996 that enables you to search for jobs for free. Check out the site for a discussion of what you get for free versus what additional services are available for the $35 membership to decide about membership.

http://www.twitter.com

Free social messaging utility that allows communicating in real time.

http://wbjobs.com

Career site for Warner Bros. Entertainment including intern and trainee programs and employment openings by clicking on the "job search" link on the page.

INDEX

Page numbers in **boldface** indicate main articles.

hairstylist **145–146**
Hampshire College 230
Hanks, Tom 24, 60
Harris, Ed 10
Harry Potter 15
Harry Potter and the Sorcerer's Stone
195
Hawaii Film Office 248–249
HBO/Cinemax 74, 215
HBO Films 252
Head, Edith 136
head animal trainer 39, 44
head designer 136
head of acting school 217
head of production **48–50**, 51, 54,
59, 192
head of studio 48, 72
Henson, Jim 130
Herskovitz, Marshal 56
Hester, Laurel 215
Heston, Charlton 201
HFPA. *See* Hollywood Foreign Press
Association
Hirshenson, Janet 20
Hofstra University 230
Hogan, Hulk 24
Hollywood Creative Dictionary 12
Hollywood Discovery Awards 245
Hollywood Film Institute 234–
235
Hollywood Foreign Press
Association (HFPA) 4, 196, 205,
209–210, 241
Hollywood Makeup Artist and
Hair Stylist Guild 142
Hollywood Networking Breakfast
235
Hollywood Operating Systems 27
Hollywood Reporter (magazine)
best boy 112
film instructor 215
line producer 64
mailroom clerk 31
principal actor 25
theater owner 198
Homeward Bound 39
Honess, Peter 171
Hornaday, Jeffrey 37
horse rider 44
The Horse Whisperer 42, 44
Howard University 229
How the West Was Won 44

I

IATSE. *See* International Alliance of
Theatrical Stage Employees
ICG. *See* International
Cinematographers Guild
ICM (International Creative
Management) 251
Idaho Film Bureau 249
IFP. *See* Independent Feature Project
IFTA (Independent Film &
Television Alliance) 241
Illinois Film Office 249
Image Permanence Institute (IPI) 225
Independent Feature Project (IFP) 7,
95, 212, 223, 241
Independent Film & Television
Alliance (IFTA) 241
Indiana Film Commission 249
Indiana Jones (series of films) 15
*Indiana Jones and the Temple of
Doom* 44
Indiana University 230
Industrial Light and Magic 122
In Focus (publication) 198
Inside the Actors Studio 235
intern 94
International Alliance of Theatrical
Stage Employees (IATSE) 238.
See also specific IATSE guilds, e.g.:
Motion Picture Editors Guild
art director 116
best boy 111
camera operator 104
first assistant cameraperson
105
gaffer 109
hairstylist 146
key grip 107, 108
production coordinator 68
production designer 115
property master 133
script supervisor 81
set decorator 126, 127
set designer 125
sound designer 149
sound mixer 151
storyboard artist 120
International Association of Audio/
Video Communicators 151
International Cinematographers
Guild (ICG) (Local 600, IATSE)
104, 105, 238

International Creative Management
(ICM) 251
International Makeup Artist Trade
Show 142
In the Bedroom 193
In the Eyes of a Stranger 60
Into the Blue 49
Iowa Department of Economic
Development 249
IPI (Image Permanence Institute)
225
Ithaca College 230

J

Jack, Andrew 219
Jein, Greg 128
Jenkins, Jane 20
Jesse James 41
Johnston, Susan 61
journalist 208
The Juilliard School 245
Jurassic Park 143, 148

K

Kansas Film Commission 249
Katz, Steven 73
Keaton, Buster 33
Kelly, Gene 37
Kentucky Film Commission 249
Kerrigan, Nancy 201
key costumer 136, **138–139**
key grip **107–108**
King Kong (1975) 130
Kirschenbaum, Gayle 73
Kodak Fellowship 225
Kozler, Maxine 156–157

L

lab worker 224
LAFCA (Los Angeles Film Critics
Association) 241
lamp operator 109, 111
Lane, Stewart F. 52
Lassie 208
The Last Innocent Man 10
Law & Order: Criminal Intent (TV
Series) 94
Lawler, Terry 94, 221
lawyer 88

ABOUT THE AUTHORS

Fred Yager, who received a certificate in film production from New York University, was a reporter for the Associated Press for 13 years, including four years as an entertainment writer and movie critic. During that time, he screened and reviewed hundreds of films each year, as well as interviewed more than 200 film industry professionals, including such industry notables as Steven Spielberg, the late James Cagney, Jane Fonda, Harrison Ford, Francis Ford Coppola, Sylvester Stallone, Jonathan Demme, and Paul Newman. A member of the Writers Guild of America, East, since 1983, he has had several of his screenplays optioned, including one to Walter Hill, the director of *48 Hours,* and another to Aaron Russo, the producer of *Trading Places.* After two years as a full-time screenwriter, Fred worked as a writer for *CBS Morning News* and, for a year, as the editor of *Fox Evening News.* He worked at Merrill Lynch for 14 years, the last seven years working as a producer of television business news and director of broadcast services.

Jan Yager, the former J.L. (Janet) Barkas, studied acting at the American Academy of Dramatic Arts, the State University of New York at Buffalo, and the Gene Frankel Theatre Workshop; she also studied mime with Paul Curtis. A former theater critic for *Back Stage* newspaper for seven years and a member of the Dramatists Guild, she has written full-length plays and has cowritten several screenplays with her husband Fred Yager, including a romantic comedy, *No Time for Love,* which was optioned. In addition to writing, producing, and directing several short films, Jan attended Dov S-S Simens' weekend Hollywood Film Institute and a one-week intensive producing class at New York University. A member of New York Women in Film and Television (NYWIFT), Women in Film, and Womens Media Group, she is the author of numerous nonfiction books including *When Friendship Hurts, Work Less, Do More, Victims, Effective Business and Nonfiction Writing,* and *Meatless Cooking: Celebrity Style,* for which she conducted interviews in East Hampton, Manhattan, and Hollywood with such film celebrities as Cliff Robertson, Dina Merrill, Paula Prentiss, Richard Benjamin, Rip Torn, and Paul Winfield.

The Yagers, who live in Fairfield County, Connecticut, have a film company with several projects in development.

Fred and Jan Yager have cowritten two suspense screenplays and novels: *Untimely Death* and *Just Your Everyday People.* Fred is the author of the screenplay and novel *Rex* and the sci-fi thriller *Cybersona.*

For more information on the Yagers, go to: www. fredandjanyager.com or www.janyager.com/writing, contact the Yagers by e-mail: yagerinquiries2@aol.com, by mail: Fred and Jan Yager, P.O. Box 8038, Stamford, CT 06905-8038, or call (212) 560-5638 (the authors' 24-hour voice mail).